A Postcolonial Relationship

A
Postcolonial
Relationship

Challenges of Asian Immigrants as the Third Other

Choi Hee An

SUNY
PRESS

Published by State University of New York Press, Albany

© 2022 State University of New York Press

Library of Congress Cataloging-in-Publication Data

Names: Choi, Hee An, author.
Title: A postcolonial relationship : challenges of Asian immigrants as the third other / Choi Hee An.
Description: Albany : State University of New York Press, [2022] | Includes bibliographical references and index.
Identifiers: LCCN 2021008190 | ISBN 9781438486574 (hardcover) | ISBN 9781438486567 (paperback) | ISBN 9781438486581 (ebook)
Subjects: LCSH: Asian Americans—Social conditions. | Immigrants—United States—Social conditions. | Postcolonialism. | United States—Ethnic relations. | United States—Race relations. | United States—Emigration and immigration. | Asia—Emigration and immigration.
Classification: LCC E184.A75 C496 2021 | DDC 305.895/073—dc23
LC record available at https://lccn.loc.gov/2021008190

10 9 8 7 6 5 4 3 2 1

For My Sisters,
Choi Jae Yeon (최재연) *and Choi Kyoung Hwa* (최경화)

Contents

Acknowledgments

Relationship has been the most important core value that I cherish and care for in my life even though I get hurt and feel the pain quite often. As I run toward relationship, sometimes it hurts. As I run away from it, it always hurts more. At the same time, as I cherish it, I find happiness often. As I care for it, I find joy more often than not. I notice that forgiveness, reconciliation, and/or hospitality are required if relationships are to form and trust is to be built. As I go through the process of forgiveness and reconciliation inside and outside of me, I can see hope in people. As I receive and/or act upon hospitality, I feel God.

I want to thank my mother and father, who gave me the foundation of relationship, love, and trust. I want to thank my sisters, who showed me how the fragile and vulnerable could be the powerful by building solidarity and support. I want to thank my aunt, who demonstrated what persistence looked like in difficult relationships through hospitality. I deeply want to thank my late father-in-law and mother-in-law, who manifested the meaning of love in sacrifice and faith in unjust situations.

I want to thank my friends and mentors who listened to my lamentations and gave me great encouragement. I want to thank my colleagues and students at the Boston University School of Theology and the Anna Howard Shaw Center. I especially want to thank my beloved student Shaunesse' Arielle Jacobs, who edited this book with great enthusiasm and support. I also want to thank my editor at the State University of New York Press, James Peltz, who recognized the value of this book with great confidence.

Lastly and mostly, I want to thank my husband, who criticized the first draft of this book mercilessly and inspired me to reinterpret the position of third otherness for Asian immigrants. Without his critical comments and insights and without his warm and kind encouragement, this book would never have come to light.

ACKNOWLEDGMENTS

I want to thank God, who gave me wisdom and passion to reflect and write this book for the people who continuously and persistently care about building good relationships among us.

Introduction

When I talk about ethnic relations, I often hear words similar to these: "We (whites) are privileged, and it's at other people's expense. We especially benefitted from slavery. Black people were forced to be here, unlike other immigrants who came to America voluntarily. For about two hundred years, they were forced to be slaves, brutally abused, and forced to build this country under free labor. Most other groups didn't have it anywhere near as bad," "We (whites) have fought a lot and worked to give up our privilege to bring about justice and equality for everyone. How long do we have to be blamed for injustices? I'm tired of hearing everyone else's complaints. Our situations aren't perfect either," "Don't ask us (blacks) to teach you what to do or how to be better. You need to figure it out for yourself. Study history and culture before you ask us for help. We're so tired of teaching people who don't make any effort to learn themselves," "Now they (whites) always complain about experiencing reverse racism and are tired of hearing our complaints. I laugh. They have no idea what we (blacks) go through every single day," "In this country everything is black and white. There is no room for us (Latinx). We're invisible. And if we aren't invisible, we're just illegal immigrants to them (whites). They ask us to work for next to nothing, then tell us to leave because we're taking their jobs," "Even though many of us (Asians) are here escaping colonial and postcolonial war and white imperialism, they say that we are here voluntarily and need to go back to our homelands. We aren't allowed to stay. They always treat us as foreigners in this country. They say we don't belong to America, so we don't talk about racism. It's easier to stay out of it."

Although people hear these conversations in private domains within each ethnic group, these conversations are not seriously discussed cross-ethnically in the public domain. Even in private domains, people often feel uncomfortable or fearful of discussing racial relations with other ethnic groups. Some white elite liberal groups confess their colonial history and criticize white racism, whereas some conservative white groups express their feeling of reverse racism and confirm white supremacy. Both elite liberal and conservative white groups are concerned about their relationships with black groups, but in different manners. Some black groups try to teach the problems of white racism, whereas other black groups express their exhaustion from teaching others about white racism when there is no effort made by white groups. Both black groups give more attention to white domination and supremacy than other racial relations. Some Latinx groups observe that racism is not about racial discrimination against all racial minorities, but only white/black relations. Other Latinx groups are much more into immigration issues than racism issues. Some Asian groups want to stay out of racism issues because they believe they are white/black issues, whereas other Asian groups stay out of racism discussions because they feel ignored by both black and white groups. Both Latinx and Asian groups often feel that racism in U.S. society focuses on black/white relations only. They claim that black and white racism dominates all ethnic relations, and their voices are not heard.

Each ethnic group points to different standpoints when observing ethnic relations. However, their different standpoints are not acknowledged equally. The current construction of racial/ethnic relations is heavily built on the foundation of a black/white binary relationship. Various other racial relations are discussed selectively with different weight, with or without intentionality. This black/white relationship is often thrown into the talk of white/black racism, which is treated as a completely separate issue from Asian and Latinx racial issues. In fact, Asian and Latinx racial issues are often misunderstood as problems of immigration, not racism. The discussion of their issues in conversations around racism is not appreciated. In fact, they are not allowed to engage in black/white racism conversations. Rather, talking about racism among other racial groups is often misunderstood as a tool to dismiss the importance of black/white racism, especially as a tool to weaken the importance of African Americans' suffering. Adding more racial problems that various groups bring to the table is seen as an act of jeopardizing and distracting from the weight of black/white racial conversations.

Although many uncomfortable and uneasy relations among and between Asian, Latinx, and black groups exist, it is taboo to talk about these complicated, conflictive relations collectively. These groups are urged to suppress their differences and merge them into one similar narrative from a unidirectional approach. Their focus of conversation is quickly moved to either dismantling white privilege and criticizing white power only or developing multicultural and intercultural diversities generally that are more socially and politically correct in this society. Understanding socioeconomic political power relations among various racial groups in this country usually starts from and ends with black/white binary racial relations without critical investigation to understand these uncomfortable and uneasy relations among nonwhite and nonblack groups. Even when discussing the dismantling of white privilege in various contexts, the focus is exclusively on the discussion of a black/white relation within the black/white binary divide in the U.S. context. It disregards any attention to where all racial ethnic groups stand domestically and transnationally, how they relate with each other, and what it takes to recover the broken relationships among these groups.

In a similar manner, when people talk about immigrant issues, they are mainly focused on the discussion of Latinx aliens and white natives. "Colonial" and "postcolonial" power, and its relationship among various ethnic groups, hardly enters into the discussion of immigrant issues. Dismantling white privilege in terms of natives' rights and security is not even considered as an agenda on the table of native/alien divides, especially from a non-Latinx immigrant perspective. Even though awkward relationships among different ethnic groups exist inside and outside of U.S. borders, these relationships are simply recognized as foreigners' problems, not as racial relations of natives. Perceiving immigrant issues as either a competition or a survival necessity among undeveloped and/or developing countries' citizens, the native/alien divide easily erases the presence of each ethnic group in the United States and dismisses their different ways of experiencing suffering as an unfortunate alien incident that is a separate, independent issue from that of natives.

The main goal of this book is neither simply dismantling white privilege from a point of black/white relations nor understanding other racial relations from a point of native/alien relations. The main focus of this book is to dismantle binary relational divides that support white privilege and colonial and postcolonial domination and to provide a deeper understanding of Asian racial relations. Examining interactions and intersections of black/white, native/alien, and host/guest binary divides, it addresses the current structures of sociohistorical paradigms, investigates the unique challenges of Asian racial positions, analyzes the position of their *third otherness*, and explores the possibilities of transforming binary relationships into postcolonial Asian racial relationships based on ethical and theological religious traditions and practices.

This book has three parts. The first part of this book analyzes two sociopolitical cultural binary paradigms: the black/white binary divide and the native/alien binary divide. The black/white binary divide is one of the most powerful paradigms that U.S. society has traditionally practiced. It dominates and changes the dynamics of ethnic relations among various ethnic groups. By analyzing the black/white binary paradigm, this part shows how Asian immigrants are used to support white people and alienate black people. The native/alien binary divide is another paradigm that dominates ethnic relations. Asian immigrants are forever called foreigners and aliens. This binary divide locates Asian immigrants in between natives (white) and aliens (Latinx). The current immigration issues and discussions are heavily focused on Latinx groups regardless of their nationalities. Asian immigrants are seen neither as complete aliens nor as complete natives. Rather, they are treated as visitors, foreigners, and temporary workers. In between black/white binary and native/alien binary paradigms, Asian immigrants occupy the positions of double in-betweenness. Exploring the function of the black/white binary as a paradigm to dismiss racial discrimination against nonblack and nonwhite racial minority groups and analyzing the function of the native/alien binary as a paradigm to dismiss voices of various racial immigrants, the first portion of the book shows how Asian immigrants are doubly ignored and marginalized at the intersections of these two paradigms.

The second part of this book addresses the unique challenges that Asian immigrants experience. Examining the dynamics of racial triangulation, anti-Asian sentiment, minority/nonminority issues, and in-group struggles, this part demonstrates the uniqueness of Asian immigrant struggles and explores how Asian immigrants are blamed and excluded by various racial groups in these complicated issues. In the beginning of U.S. immigrant history, Asian immigrants were compared with black people, including black immigrant communities and African Americans. This comparison eventually resulted in racial triangulation. Embedded in white racial racism, racial triangulation has since been used not only by white privileged groups but also by various Asian immigrant groups. This triangulation has caused severe problems and violence between Asian, black, and white people. As Asian immigrants accept and exercise white racism against blacks on the side of whites, blacks and whites practice anti-Asian sentiment under the influence of white colonial and postcolonial power. From this binary relationship, anti-Asian sentiment is cultivated and exercised institutionally and individually. Minority/nonminority issues are another challenge that only Asian immigrants experience. This chapter shows how they are concomitantly treated as both a minority and a nonminority depending on the needs of black/white and native/alien divides. Examining these dilemmas of Asian immigrants' in-betweenness illustrates how they navigate these double barriers. This part also reinterprets the strength Asian immigrant groups possess to transform their lives in the face of their unique challenges and barriers.

The last part of this book shows how these binary divides and the unique challenges of Asian immigrants place them in a position as *the third other*. This part introduces the meaning of the third otherness and demonstrates how Asian immigrants are used and played as the third other in the interactions and intersections of black/white and native/alien binary paradigms by examining three different practices. The first practice shows the conflictive message of assimilation to locate Asian immigrants in the position of third other, and the second practice addresses the complications of coalition work that made Asian immigrants the third other. These practices invent the position of Asian immigrants as the third other institutionally and sociopolitically. The third practice explores how these institutional practices impact Asian immigrants psychologically and emotionally as the third other.

Analyzing black/white, native/alien, and host/guest binary divides from an Asian immigrant perspective, this book critically examines the problems of current U.S. racial relations and provides a new understanding of the complications that Asian immigrants uniquely experience. These findings can open a new understanding of race relations and introduce a better way to understand Asian immigrants in relation to other racial groups beyond the current binary structures. This book can contribute not only to reevaluating and reinterpreting the current racial theories but also to widening the horizons of creating new racial theories in relation to Asian religious practices.

Before I move to the chapter 1, there are two definitions that I need to address in this book: Asian immigrants and colonial/colonialism/postcolonial/postcolonialism. Because the main discourses of this book are deeply engaged with these concepts, it is important to clarify them at this point. First, who are Asian immigrants? The definition of "Asian immigrants" in this book follows the definition that I described in my previous work, *A Postcolonial Leadership: Asian Immigrant Christian Leadership and Its Challenges*.

> Asian immigrants are not one fixed group. They are not exactly identified as Asian Americans only. They include Asian Americans, but go beyond Asian American groups. In fact, US society creates various categories to define Asian immigrants such as immigrant generations, sociopolitical status, nationalities, and other characteristics. In terms of immigrant generations, Asian immigrants can be the people who both migrated from Asian countries and are born in the United States. First-generation immigrants are defined as people who migrate to this country when they are adults. Second-generation immigrants are people who are born in this country with Asian ancestry. 1.5 generation immigrants are the people who migrate to this country before adulthood. In terms of visa statuses and citizenship, Asian immigrants can include people who permanently live in the United States and people who temporarily stay in the United States with the intention to go back to their mother countries such as students and temporary workers. In terms of nationality, they can be both Asians from Asia and US Asian Americans who stay in the US. It includes transnational Asian groups. In terms of Asian ancestry, Asian immigrants can include both Asians from non-interracial marriages and Asians from interracial marriages.

> In terms of legal status, Asian immigrants can include both docu-
> mented and undocumented populations of Asians and people with
> Asian ancestry. Even though these binary distinctions exist in the US
> social system, in reality, Asian immigrants do not hold fixed statuses
> or clear boundaries. Especially in terms of economic status, they are
> all over the spectrum from the upper class to the lower class. Most
> of them do not or cannot stay in fixed positions. Rather, their social,
> political and economic positions are always in flux. The boundaries
> are not static but are permeable and open. . . . Asian immigrants
> can be defined as the people who belong to these various categories
> and go beyond and in-between colonial and postcolonial immigrant
> spaces simultaneously.[1]

I am aware that my attempt to define Asian immigrants in this book is not
sufficient to show the complete picture of who Asian immigrants are because
Asian immigrants are hybridizing, growing, and extending as they keep interacting with others and among themselves. However, in order to understand
the relationships of Asian immigrants and analyze their positionality in the
current postcolonial U.S. context, this definition can provide some critical
parts of what it means to be Asian immigrants. Instead of using the Asian
Americans/immigrant binary concept, the term "Asian immigrants" will be
used throughout this book to encompass all of the above variations.

Second, what are the meanings of colonial/colonialism/postcolonial/
postcolonialism? As I defined in my previous work, *A Postcolonial Self:
Korean Immigrant Theology and Church*, "Colonialism is a physical, psychological, and even spiritual exercise of a nation's sovereign power beyond
its borders, involving physical, geographical dominion; psychological
oppression; spiritual manipulation."[2] Based on this definition, the definition
of "colonial" in this book indicates the various texts and contexts of colonial
discourses that include the Western and Eastern colonial history, culture,
and characteristics of colonialism. The "colonial" can refer to the colonial
past/present, its sociopolitical economic oppressive constructions, and its
religious and cultural interactions.

What about "postcolonial" then? Even though the common assumptions
of "postcolonial" are often understood as the remnants of (neo)colonialism,
"postcolonial" in this book is neither a simple notion of "after" or "neo"colonialism, nor just a resurgence of colonialism.

> Although many former colonies have now achieved national inde-
> pendence and tend to believe that they are free from colonialism,
> world power dynamics have not changed. With or without geo-
> graphical dominance, the same colonial and imperial policies and

INTRODUCTION   7

rules dominate formerly colonized countries culturally, socially, and politically. Even though physical domination is limited because of the newly won independence of formerly colonized countries, the descendants of colonizers create persistent sociocultural, religious, and even linguistic structures to portray the formerly colonized as inferiors. Many colonial rules and cultures are still influential and dominant in the formerly colonized world. It is a new form of colonialism: postcolonialism.

The power of postcolonialism *within power structures and institutional ideologies* reaches far beyond any territories or borders. Its methods involve geographical visibility/invisibility, psychological control/manipulation, religious distortion, and more. . . . However, unlike the power of postcolonialism *within power structures and institutional ideologies*, there is the power of postcolonialism *within people*, which is not just a resurgence of colonialism. . . . The power of postcolonialism that people exercise is the power of resistance and challenge. It resists the colonial and postcolonial power structures and challenges their impacts on toxic postcolonial, sociocultural, and political manipulations and institutional ideologies. It is the power to resist postcolonial domination.[3]

"Postcolonial" includes discourses of colonialism, neocolonialism, anticolonialism, and postcolonialism as it analyzes both the liberative and the hierarchical/imperial paradigms of these discourses. I agree with Kwok Pui-lan that "postcolonial" indicates not only "merely a temporal period or a political transition of power but also a reading strategy and discursive practice that seek to unmask colonial epistemological frameworks, unravel Eurocentric logics, and interrogate stereotypical cultural representations."[4] I use the term to reveal how Western colonial domination is constructed and to examine how the colonizers and the colonized interact and interrelate. Critically examining colonial and postcolonial power structures and institutional ideologies, using the term "postcolonial" shows how new forms of colonial and imperial power reproduce colonial paradigms and regenerate its colonial practices in the current economy, politics, history, and culture.

At the same time, "postcolonial" also denotes the movements of people's resistance and challenges. It explores how people resist the colonial and postcolonial dominations and challenge the power structures and institutional ideologies. It reveals how they hybridize and negotiate the colonial and postcolonial reality in their daily life. Therefore, "postcolonial" refers to the simultaneous process of deconstructing the current dominant discourses and structures of colonial/neocolonial and postcolonial constructions and reconstructing/reimagining the past, present, and future with the power of people's resistance and challenges. It is a create-*ing* space to understand and analyze multilayers of dynamics between institutionally represented colonialism and people's actual resistance and challenge to create hope. Therefore, the definition of postcolonialism in this book includes not only deconstructing and challenging discourses and practices of colonialism, neo-colonialism, anticolonialism, and postcolonialism but also reinterpreting the movements of people and their power to negotiate, hybridize, and transform these colonial/postcolonial realities into hope for justice and freedom. It is not an ideology that merely condemns colonialism, but a reimagining process that demands a subversive paradigm shift. Intentionally focusing on recon-structing the values of difference and otherness, this book introduces a new postcolonial paradigm that goes beyond the binary notions of I/the other, center/margin, black/white, native/alien, host/guest, and so forth.

CHAPTER 1

Sociopolitical Postcolonial Relations of Asian Immigrants

Struggle between Black/White Racial Binary and Native/Alien Binary

The United States has historically been fertile ground for the man-
ufacture of pan-ethnic identities, and the lumping of very different
ethnic groups under a single pan-ethnic label. Race is a social con-
struct with no scientific basis and, to that extent, it would matter
little whether distinctions were made between Chinese, Indians,
Japanese, or Malays as opposed to the simple-minded amalgamation of all Asian nationalities into a single category. It mattered a lot,
however to the immigrants who found themselves suddenly identified with very different national groups with whom they had little in
common and which may even be historic enemies. It also makes it
difficult to disentangle the historical facts, including those pertain-
ing to the relationships between African Americans and persons of
Asian origin.

What is of special interest here is the "racial" basis of such
forced amalgamation. The dichotomous American racial tradition
led to classifying groups in terms of an imaginary "blood quantum,"
a false hematogenesis by which "Asians" came to be considered
as a "race." The administrative category of "Asian" (Cf. the U.S.
Office of Management and Budget's Directive 15) does not exist
either in the Asian countries themselves or in any other country of
immigration.[1]

Asian immigrants are often perceived as the other through various images. These include perpetual others as foreigners, racial others as Orientals, unassimilable others as Mongolians, religious others as non-Christians, invisible others as second- and/or third-class citizens, and so forth. These images of otherness are the distinctive images of Asian immigrants that the current dominant society has created, inherited, and re-created. As whiteness became the norm, their Asian "flat noses," "yellow skin color," and accents were designated something abnormal, strange, and uncivil. As "white noses" and "double eyelids" became standard, "Asians' flat noses" and "single eyelids" became funny. As white skin color became the normal skin color, Asians' "yellow skin color" was comparably too yellow and strange. As European heights and body shapes were pursued, Asians' short heights and skinny body shapes were disdained. Whereas European English accents were respected, Asian accents were heard as frivolous and cheap. As European culture and religions were recognized as something advanced and civilized, Asian cultures and religions were perceived as something exotic, shamanistic, and uncivilized. Because of this perceived otherness, Asian immigrants were and still are the target of hidden discrimination.

In terms of race relations, this perceived otherness leads Asian immigrants into a deeper problem. As soon as Asian immigrants enter U.S. territory, they are classified as Asian, one race. As the position of Asian immigrants is commonly perceived as noncitizens, foreigners, and visitors in the U.S. context, even if they are citizens, they have not been recognized as citizens, but homogenously as foreign immigrants. The problem with this classification is that their different nationalities do not count. Their national differences are not recognized as races, but as one race (Orientals and/or Mongolians) or no race.[2]

Asians in Asian countries do not perceive themselves as Asians. Their perception of themselves is contingent upon their nationalities. However, the United States manufactures Asians as one category. It forces various Asian national identities into a single panethnic identity. As one race or no race, Asian immigrants of different national backgrounds are classified and amalgamated. From the beginning of U.S. history, this category was not invented to designate Asian immigrants as Asian Americans. Rather, it ordered Asian immigrants as the "Yellow Peril" that threatens "both 'American' culture and white racial purity."[3] As the Yellow Peril, they are treated as permanent outsiders who need to leave. Therefore, discussions of their race are frequently located outside of the dominant discussion of race, which is often occupied by only black and white groups. This means their experience of racial discrimination is not perceived as racism, unlike a black/white racial problem. Their racial discourse is repeatedly treated as an immigrant problem, which is not a problem to solve within, but a problem to fight against. An understanding of

Asian immigrants as racial others who do not belong to this country implies that their struggles with racial discrimination do not belong to this country either. As a consequence, their struggles against racial discrimination are not counted as racial discrimination. They are counted as problems of foreigners, visitors, and uninvited guests who are not the residents of this country. Their problems are preserved as problems of outsiders. However, the problem is that they are not outsiders. They are insiders who live in this country. They are citizens, permanent and temporary residents, legal and illegal residents, invited and uninvited guests, visitors, tourists, and so forth. They are insiders in actuality, but they are outsiders in prominent public relational discourses such as black/white relations and native/alien relations.

Given the colonial history of and slavery in the U.S., the concept of a black/white binary is established as the main instrument to talk about racial relations in past and current U.S. contexts. Current prominent racial discussions mostly, and often exclusively, occur within the framework between and around black/white relations. Because black/white relations have been established as the main racial discussion, relations of other racial groups, including Asian immigrants, are categorized as nonracial discussions. When black/white relations are exaggerated and emphasized, other relations and problems are dismissed and disappear. In many cases, the black/white binary concept has become the paradigm to push Asian immigrants out from any engagement with racial relations. At the same time in this process, their racial discussion is assigned to the native/alien binary divide, with the assumption that they are aliens. However, even in the native/alien binary divide, the presence of Asian immigrants is ambiguous. Their relationship with other groups is questioned and even suspected.

Understanding the black/white racial divide and native/alien divide is one of the most important paradigms for defining the current position of Asian immigrants in the U.S. context. What is the black/white racial binary divide? What is the native/alien binary divide? What are the goals of these divides? How does the black/white binary divide impact Asian immigrants? How does the native/alien binary locate them? How do these binary divides collide to marginalize Asian immigrants in white society? How do they struggle between these binaries? How do the problems of Asian immigrants need to be addressed?

Black/White Racial Binary

Of all the major racial groups in the United States, only African Americans have historically experienced the ravages of slavery on a consistent basis. It can be plausibly argued that, with the exception

of Native Americans, no racial group in the United States has historically suffered the amount of racial oppression that African Americans
have faced. However, unlike Native Americans, African Americans
still have sufficient numbers to create the visibility necessary to
produce aversive reactions from majority group members. This is
important since there is evidence that the number of minorities present in a given area is correlated to the level of racial hostility a group
receives (Olzak, Shanahan, and West 1994; Giles and Hertz 1994;
Taylor 1998). Given this social history and constant threat some perceive from the African American community, it can be hypothesized
that blacks will face more racial animosity than other racial groups.[4]

Some observers argue that there is a special history of blacks and
whites, which makes this relationship more important than other
racial combinations. They believe that there are characteristics of
this special relationship—the degree of oppression faced by African Americans, their population size, and their long history in the
United States—that can justify a special focus on the racial differences between blacks and majority group members, and that the
darker skin color of African Americans may bring about a distinctiveness that attracts more hostility from European Americans than
from other racial groups. Given the unique history of slavery, it is
reasonable to argue that it is more important to understand white/
black differences than those between other racial groups, as white/
black relations represent American race relations at their fullest,
and often at their worst.[5]

The black/white binary divide is often claimed to be important because of
the special relations between white masters and black slaves in U.S. history.
Because of the intensity of blacks' suffering and oppression, and the privileges of whites' power and control, this binary divide is commonly accepted
and legitimated. From the early immigrant history of the United States, the
black/white binary racial concept has been politically constructed under
European colonial hegemony. It was constructed to support white colonial
power because this white/black binary divide was useful for whites to legitimate their colonial violence in the name of civilization. After its invention,
this divide continued to be accepted for the use of dismantling white privilege from both white and black groups. As white power and privilege are
claimed to be dismantled, black suffering and oppression are lifted up for
recognition and affirmation.

Black people have long lived under restricted colonial, sociopolitical,
economic, and structural constraints such as slavery, the rules of Jim Crow,

and institutional and systematic discrimination in the job market, educational opportunities, and residential housing. Their economic and sociopolitical conditions constantly thwart and threaten their black lives. It is clear that emancipation did not bring them complete freedom. Some white Christian groups, like the American Colonization Society, saw black people as the group who could never assimilate into American society. Removing free blacks from America, known as the black colonization movement, was cast as a solution to end slavery.[6] Many others still treated black people as servants and saw them as cheap labor to abuse. White "power is expressed either by preventing people from moving or by making them move against their will."[7] Black groups' mobility was limited and restricted, and their freedom still has not been completely granted. Black people's suffering has continued. "The violence and oppression of white supremacy took different forms and employed different means to achieve the same end: the subjugation of black people."[8] James H. Cone claims that the subjugation of black people was and is the goal of white domination. Specifically, black women's bodies have been most severely targeted for black subjugation.

> The great majority of black women became "strange and bitter crop" because they courageously challenged white supremacy, refusing to stay in any place that denied their dignity. Although women constitute only 2 percent of blacks actually killed by lynching, it would be a mistake to assume that violence against women was not widespread and brutal. Black women were neither incidental objects of white vigilante violence nor marginal participants in the black resistance against it. Like black men, they were tortured, beaten and scarred, mutilated and hanged, burned and shot, tarred and feathered, stabbed and dragged, whipped and raped by angry white mobs. They fought back any way they could—individually and collectively, with black men and by themselves—refusing to submit to white supremacy. Black women suffered when black men suffered and when black men did not. In the physical and spiritual struggle for survival and dignity, some atrocities were "more bitter than death," and many women, like Addie Hunton of the National Association of Colored Women (NACW), placed rape in that category—especially sexual violation in one's home by white Christian men who regarded black women as whores incapable of being violated.[9]

Black women have lived in unimaginable suffering. From rape to lynching in the Jim Crow era, and from continued sexual violence to domestic labor abuse in the postcolonial era, black women have been constantly abused and tortured under white domination and patriarchy. However, even though they suffered severely, including from sexual abuse and physical torture, their suffering was not recognized in public. Rather, their abused bodies were exhibited as dirty and contaminated. White Christian men regarded them as whores and treated them as nonhumans who had no rights of any kind. In relation to white women, their surrogate roles have remained unchanged. Before emancipation, black women were slaves, often serving as nannies in domestic settings and fieldworkers. After emancipation, they were hired as domestic workers and laborers and received one of the lowest wages among all ethnic groups in modern slavery. In the case of black men, a similar pattern is shown. Before emancipation, black men were slaves, serving as laborers who were the subject of physical brutality from white masters. Since emancipation, they have been the target of physical brutality from white police and white institutions. Black men have been perceived as the most dangerous group, one that needed to be incarcerated. They have been physically, psychologically, and spiritually tortured and targeted for killing. This suffering has continued without much improvement.

Under these disimproved life conditions, both black women and black men have severely suffered with identity and self-worth issues. Numerous black scholars named these issues as the main challenges of black issues. Lee H. Butler understands identity as the most serious black issue that many black people suffer from. He denounces the challenges of African Americans' distorted identity and finds a way to develop self-worth for black people under racism, sexism, and other discriminations.[10] He argues that as African Americans are "'trained' to be slaves by the forces of racism, sexism, classism, and heterosexism," it is important to "educate" them to know who they are and where they have come from.[11] Instead of asking, "Who am I?" he reshapes the identity question as "Who are we?" and requests the rediscovery of the development of African American identity.

Cornel West also sees identity and self-worth issues as the most difficult to restore among black lives. Defining nihilism as "the lived experience of coping with a life of horrifying meaninglessness, hopelessness, and (most important) lovelessness,"[12] he claims that "the major enemy of black survival in America has been and is, neither oppression nor exploitation, but rather the nihilistic threat—that is, loss of hope and absence of meaning."[13] The unbearable suffering under unchangeable situations leads blacks to accept meaninglessness, hopelessness, and lovelessness as their reality and even their future. West believes that there are two main reasons to cause this suffering, "the saturation of market forces and market moralities in black life and the present crisis in black leadership."[14] He feels that a free individual market mentality and consumerism lead the majority of citizens into individual privatization and ignore the collective destiny of community. This individualism and capitalism has deteriorated black communal mentality and identity. Furthermore, lack of black leadership contributes to black reality being at its worst. Many black leaders themselves are influenced by nihilistic senses of meaninglessness, hopelessness, and lovelessness. Specifically, many elite middle-class black groups collide with a white colonial mentality of capitalism and individualism and are afraid of sharing their middle-class privileges. They forget black collective traditions and abandon the communal responsibilities that sustained their lives from generation to generation.

Dale P. Andrews claims that American individualism and racism are the main barriers to the enhancement of black lives. He observes how this free individual market mentality merges into individual privatization, not only in sociopolitical lives but also in spiritual lives. In his book, *Practical Theology for Black Churches: Bridging Black Theology and African American Folk Religion*, he rightly illustrates how the impacts of American individualism and racism transfer to personal salvation and piety in current African American churches and act against communal advancement, socioeconomically and spiritually.[15] Black identity and self-worth issues are raised and challenged in every dimension of their physical, socioeconomic, psychological, and spiritual lives.

Under these heavy influences of individual market mentality, capitalism, and individual privatization, many U.S. citizens, including blacks, tend to choose "sour cynicism, political apathy, and cultural escapism."[16] As they choose and practice cynicism, apathy, and escapism based on their individual rights to be cynical and their freedom to be indifferent, they not only ignore the life of community but also hurt their individual lives. This modern capitalistic, imperialistic mentality has created an invasive movement to destroy communal mentality and collective responsibility by exhibiting individualistic egocentrism, a calculated free market mentality, and selective group selfishness in terms of sociopolitical and economic statuses. Under these circumstances, black lives face constant struggles without hope, meaning, or love.

Many black scholars suggest that the black prophetic Christian tradition is the critical essence for the enhancement and survival of black lives. West puts "a love ethic at the center of a politics of conversation"[17] and encourages black people to challenge and overcome poverty, fear, depression, and disbelief. Pulling on the two opposite tendencies of imperialism and democratization within U.S. democracy, he asserts the black prophetic Christian tradition's ability to revitalize democracy and envision universal moral vision.[18] Analyzing their exclusive relations, he sees race relations between blacks and whites as the most explosive issue in U.S. life.[19] Andrews also includes the black prophetic Christian tradition and the black folk religious tradition for the betterment of black lives. He believes that the black church is the most important institution for changing the black community. Both West and Andrews see the Christian faith as the main resource for changing and enhancing black lives. Butler also agrees that the Christian tradition is the best resource for advancing black lives. By reinterpreting rage/creativity as the transformative energy to change black minds and hearts, he introduces the African American Communal Identity Formation Process as a development theory to show how the interaction between the historical African self and African spirituality can improve and develop black lives and change lived conditions.[20] In order to restore the values of black lives, many black scholars and leaders analyze the problems of black/white relations and rightly emphasize the prophetic black religious traditions and cultures as the most important resources for reinstating black lives.

As black people fight against racial injustice, some white groups also want to work together to address antiracism. Some call these white groups white liberals who are often part of so-called white middle-class groups and believe themselves to be antiracists. Shannon Sullivan refers to them as "good white people."[21]

> These are the white liberals of which Lerone Bennett speaks, the "good" white people whose goodness is marked by their difference from the "bad" white people who are considered responsible for any lingering racism in a progressive, liberal society. . . . What is particularly interesting and frightening about white liberals is that, unlike white supremacists, they usually think they know what white people can do to fight white racism. . . . For white liberals, knowing and acting according to these answers ensures that a sharp, bright line is drawn between good anti-racist white people and bad white supremacists. But white liberals and white supremacists are not as different as white liberals would like to believe and would like others to believe. They grow from the same tree of white domination, as Bennett suggests, and this means that many of the "anti-racist" habits, practices, and beliefs of the white liberal also are rooted in and help nourish white racism.[22]

Many white liberals believe that they understand racial justice and want to fight against white domination of black people. They condemn white colonial history, confess their ancestors' wrongdoings, and fight against white supremacists. They claim that even though they did not commit this racial injustice, out of their own "production and display of white middle-class moral goodness,"[23] they feel obligated to work for *all* people. They believe doing racial justice work *for* black people proves that they are morally superior to others and deserve "being worthy of praise."[24] They feel proud that they do good and constantly try to justify that they are good.

Moral sanctimoniousness is a crucial process for this justification.[25] This belief is the main drive for white elite liberal groups to work toward antiracism. As they believe they are morally good, they interpret that their moral sanctimonious acts are their actions of justice. Their moral sanctimoniousness stems from their self-righteousness to claim their innocence from sin. This act is deeply related to Christian beliefs. In their Christian belief system, goodness should originate from the absence of sin. Goodness itself has to be pure and clean. It should not be associated with sin by any means. In order to dissociate from sin, they must disconnect themselves from this sin.

There are two ways to approach the disconnection from sin. The first is to see that disconnection from sin means to allow forgiveness. It assumes that people already committed sin but want to be cleansed of it. They have sinned but sought absolution. Disconnection from sin requires forgiveness from others and taking responsibility for what they have done to others. The subjectivity of forgiveness does not belong to the people who committed sin. Forgiveness belongs to those who suffered because of the sinner. For the groups who committed sin, it requires passivity and losing control. When white elite privileged Christian groups are condemned by the formerly colonized others to confess their sin and seek for forgiveness, they fear. They recognize that forgiveness is something that they cannot control. Rather, it requires complete passivity and letting go of control. As they feel uncomfortable accepting this passivity and letting go of control, they do not see forgiveness as their option for disconnection from sin. Even though forgiveness is believed to be the most important act of disconnection from sin, there is a stronger tendency for the groups and/or persons who commit sin to not seek forgiveness, and they avoid any responsibility. These groups believe that losing control and waiting for others to forgive them does not grant their sanctification. They also recognize that there is a strong possibility that they will never be forgiven completely. When they realize this, their white sanctimonious consciousness becomes vulnerable. It seeks another way to take control back.

In order to take control, disconnection from sin requires not having sinned from the beginning. If they can prove that they have not sinned from the beginning, they do not need to be concerned with any forgiveness or responsibility. This is the second way to approach disconnection from sin. It requires original innocence and purity. It means that sin should not be their own. It should be someone else's. In order for them to affirm their goodness in public, they need to create "the other" who does not work the same way that they do. When white middle-class groups see white slaveowners, whom they find morally bad, they identify these groups with "being worthy of blame."[26] Supporting multicultural events and celebrations, they distinguish themselves from their ancestors who owned slaves. Inventing others (their slave-owning ancestors) as sinners or demons, they desire to remain morally sanctioned and clean. They believe that sin belongs to their white ancestors, not to them. They claim that sin is not inheritable, even though they have received these inherited privileged political positions and socioeconomic benefits from the history of slavery. Instead of recognizing these inherited privileges and benefits, they deny these privileges and try to disconnect themselves from their ancestors. *Unconsciously and consciously* they do not want to recognize these privileges. White middle-class liberals tend to choose disconnecting from their roots and demonizing their white ancestors as sinners. Instead of confessing their own participation in privilege, they believe total disconnection from white slave-owning ancestors can bring complete sanctification from sin. They claim that they are innocent from this sin because they did not participate in this sin from the beginning. It is not their sin; it is not their injustice. This total disconnection makes them innocent and clean from their colonial past. It resolves the problem of their own sin. They are sanctified. Thus, they can justify their goodness. Even though they did not commit this sin, they still work very hard to bring about justice because they have goodness in their heart. Their work for justice is the evidence of proving their goodness, and proving their goodness is the evidence of confirming white moral superiority.

However, sin is not inheritable as long as privileges are not inherited. If privileges are continuously inherited by means of others' suffering, sin is inherited through privilege. Privileges are the actuality of sin in U.S. racial relations. However, in the mind of white moral sanctimoniousness, sin is not associated with privileges. Sin remains with white slave owners only. There is no communal responsibility for this sin. Sin is treated as individuals' responsibility to confess. By this logic, whoever associates with sin is a sinner, and a sinner remains a sinner forever. It implies that there is no pardon. It means that there is no room for forgiveness. Even if God forgives the sinner, there is no possibility of the sinner becoming good in this belief. Their white goodness has to be perfectly clean from the beginning. Forgiveness and absolution cannot clean sin, but only original innocence and purity can protect their goodness. In this logic of belief, white goodness means untouched white cleanliness from beginning to end. There is no chance that a sinner can be transformed by taking responsibility and dismantling privileges. In order to perfectly protect white good morality, white middle-class groups deny their past.[27]

The process of otherness starts from this disconnection process of the past and continues to the present by isolating other white groups, such as the white poor/working class and white supremacists. When white middle-class liberal groups disconnect their past from their ancestors, they still find the problem of sin against racial justice in the present context. Even though the problem of racial injustice originated from their ancestors and was passed down to them through inherited privileges, they do not find these privileges to be the cause of this injustice. They instead find another group to blame for the cause of injustice. Sullivan argues that they dump this sin on "poor white people—so called white trash, rednecks, and hillbillies—[who] often are automatically assumed to be white racists."[28] Disguising class hierarchy, they blame the white lower-class and working-class people for racist practices. Sullivan describes the threefold way poor white people, often described as white trash, are seen in this society.

> First, white trash allegedly are uneducated and stupid. . . . Second, the bodies of the white trash are problematic. They yell and shout, talking too loudly and coarsely. . . . And they are sluggish and lazy which is why they are poor. . . . Finally—and intimately related to the first two "failures"—white trash share too many similarities of speech, behavior, diet, and lifestyle with black people. White trash are uncomfortably close to those whom they are supposed to be radically different from. Whether willfully or ignorantly, white trash fail to speak, eat, dress, and otherwise behave as proper (middle-class) white people are supposed to do, and their breach of white social etiquette threatens the boundary between white and non-white (especially black) people.[29]

Trash is something that is unclean, used up, dirty, necessary to get rid of, contaminated, leading to illness, and threatening to the well-being of society. Using trash as a symbol of uncleanness, "white trash" signifies the contamination of whiteness. The image of white trash implies not having certain features, such as obtaining higher education, demonstrating proper high-society bodily mannerisms and white social etiquette, and distancing from black groups. In order to be genuinely white, they need to demonstrate these features. When white poor/working-class people cannot deliver these features, they are not recognized as real white people. Even though they are white, they are not the same white as white middle-class groups. They are seen as the group who fails to keep white standards of living and good white morality. White middle-class groups see white poor/working-class people as the groups that pollute good white middle-class morality and contaminate clean and pure whiteness. White poor/working-class groups are treated as unclean and dirty, like trash.[30]

This uncleanness leads them to the image of sinners who do not know what they do. Failing to deliver on their manner and social etiquette and to obtain higher education is perceived as an act of not knowing what they do. It is the sin of ignorance. Therefore, their ignorance becomes their sin. Being ignorant and not meeting white standards are reasons to be considered white trash. White liberal middle-class groups dump white colonial sinfulness on white poor/working-class groups. They make these poor/working-class groups out to be ignorant, dirty, unclean, and contaminated sinners. These poor/working-class groups become a threat to whiteness. In order to protect good whiteness, they require the other, white poor/working-class groups to be sinners again. By designating white poor/working-class people as white trash, their good whiteness is protected.

Trash is the remnant of a product. It is the evidence of existence of an original product, showing some connection with the original product. However, because of its contamination and pollution, it needs to perish completely. The existence of trash is dangerous. It threatens society and its well-being. White poor/working-class groups show some connection with white middle-class liberal groups in terms of skin color. In the eyes of white liberal middle-class groups, the existence of white poor/working-class people threatens their good white morality because their existence mirrors the remnant of colonial sinful whiteness. Unlike white ancestors, who are in the past of white middle-class groups, white poor/working class groups exist in their present. Total disconnection from poor white people seems impossible in public because of whiteness. In order to intensify visibility of this disconnection, white middle-class liberals invented "white trash" as the symbol of contaminated whiteness. White people are originally good, but they are contaminated by this white trash. White trash taints their original whiteness, their white good morality. White middle-class liberals divide their white groups into two different groups and see white middle-class groups as good and clean and white poor groups as bad and unclean. They push this binary approach to insinuate which groups are morally good and bad. Inventing poor white groups as trash, white middle-class liberals blame poor white people and white supremacists of being the main cause of racism in society.[31]

Even though, originally, the discourse of moral goodness was not entirely the product of colonial Christianity, it has been predominantly developed and misinterpreted under the influences of colonial/postcolonial Christianity. How is "morally good" understood in Christianity? Why is this concept important to white middle-class liberals? There are many different explanations to answer these questions, but here is one example to think about when searching for answers. Richard Swinburne introduces three different accounts of defining "morally good" in the Christian tradition.

> One account presents the moral as the overall, the important and the overriding. If an action is morally good, then, even if there are bad aspects to it, it is overall good. It is important, it matters that it should be done. And it is better, it matters more that it be done than that any action that is not morally good be done; moral goodness, that is, is overriding goodness. To believe that an action is morally good is to believe that it is of overriding importance (in comparison

with actions which are not believed to be morally good) that it should be done. . . . The second account of the moral adds to the previous account in terms of the overall, the important, and the overriding, that the goodness of the action proceed from its possession of universal properties. Moral beliefs are "universalizable" beliefs. . . . This account does, of course allow it as a moral view that certain individuals—for example, the king, parliament, or pope—are entitled to special treatment; so long as that view holds that the special treatment is due to the individual because of universal properties which he or it has—"having been elected by democratic suffrage" or "being Head of the Universal Church." . . . The third account of moral goodness analyses an action being morally good in terms of it forwarding or exemplifying goodness of a certain kind. Moral goodness is a species of goodness, it need not be important or overriding, but it does arise from the possession of universal properties. There can be different versions of this account, according to the kind of goodness picked out; but the most common version of this view . . . claims that moral goodness is the goodness of general human well-being. A belief that an action is morally good is a belief that it forwards general human well-being.[32]

In this understanding, as long as the moral brings overall good, it does not matter that some bad things occur on the way. As long as the moral demonstrates the good intention to contribute to others and to protect universal properties, it is allowed to give certain groups special power. Because the action of the morally good is assumed to bring the advancement of others and to care for universal properties, it is not just allowed but encouraged for some designated groups to have certain powers and control as a necessary discourse. It means in order to forward the goodness of general human well-being, it is necessary to exemplify goodness of a certain manner, behavior, and action. It is the logic of colonialism. White colonizers claim that their colonial invasion is from the good moral intention bringing economic advancement, civilization, and enlightenment to all people. The action of white colonial invasion becomes the authentication of their moral goodness that leads to all people's well-being. This validation often requires religious affirmation. Religions, especially Christianity, play an important role in affirming that their goodness is from God's goodness and their action is God's request. White colonizers try to legitimate colonial violence as the act of God's calling on behalf of all people and claim racial injustice as an unavoidable and inevitable action for the betterment of general human well-being.

Unconsciously and consciously, this colonial Christian narrative has been embedded in the process of forming white morality. White liberals, especially white middle-class Christians, uphold the statutes of the morally good as their superior nature and identify their goodness with God. Because they believe that they are morally and spiritually good, they claim that God chooses them to be God's agents to better all people's lives. Their privileges and power are sanctified by God to fulfill their calling to bring about general human well-being. In this narrative, their action of vilifying white poor classes, black groups, and other ethnic groups is validated as long as they can protect and/or enhance universal properties for the well-being of all humanity. They firmly believe that as long as their goodness is granted, their goodness validates their privileges.

This manipulative Christian belief causes a psychological and spiritual moral dilemma. On the one hand, they try to rationalize their colonial violence as an act for the better management of universal properties and well-being of all people. They claim that their action is for saving all people. It was necessary to have that *temporary* violence to set up the better management system to keep universal properties secure. Because it leads to overall good, this violence should be sanctioned. On the other hand, they consciously recognize they cannot justify their sinful colonial and postcolonial violence against other groups, as others call out their violence as sin. They know that this doubtful justification would not be easily accepted in public. They seek scapegoats to take the blame. Because of the need of this scapegoating, white middle-class elite groups must locate a certain group who looks like them but has a different social makeup to take responsibility for their sinful acts. Casting white poor/working-class groups as white trash, white middle-class liberals pass the violence on to poor/working white class groups and save their white good morality from sin. This morality is affirmed by this colonial religious belief.

As white middle-class Christians believe they are cleansed from sin by their faith, their white good morality is restored. They believe God knows their good hearts. Their good hearts are from God. They claim that God calls them to lead the world because God knows who they are and how good they are. Whatever they do, it is from God for the world. Their Christian belief says that God's way is their way and their way is God's way. They try to set up the world under their control. This setup is called "a global norm that is invisible, working in the background as a standard, not of one particular way of being in the world, but as normalcy, as universalizability, of just being 'the way things are.'"[33] In this global norm, their privileges are not privileges but are accepted as the norm. It is simply seen as "the way things are." They "constitute ways of 'bodying,'" "ways of thinking," and ways of believing.[34] By declaring that God gives them these blessings and asks them to lead the world for the sake of general human well-being and universal properties, these privileges became not only their unconscious habits but also conscious spiritual beliefs. White middle-class groups do not see their privileges as privileges, but the way things are and the way they live. They interpret these privileges as the result of God's affirmation for what they did and do. They unconsciously want to believe and consciously want to claim that God protects their privileges as compensation for their hard work.

This belief is the colonial and postcolonial sociopsychological and spiritual defense to legitimate their past and present. Elite white liberals in leadership try to run away from their past, not only because they finally recognize their ancestors' wrongdoings but also because other racial/ethnic domestic and global groups criticize what has happened in the past and the present. They realize that running away from the past does not solve these conflicts. Rather, they recognize that they need to defend themselves from their past and present. If they want to keep their privileges and control the world, they need to legitimate their acts and validate their privileges in public. Legitimation and validation of white colonial history is a very important part of this defense. As discussed above, the main purpose of defending themselves from the past and present is to show who they are and to prove how good they are. The axiom of this defense is that who they are equalizes who they ought to be. Who they ought to be has to be identical to who they are. The process of this defense is to get rid of the gap between who they ought to be and who they are. When white middle-class liberals discover how they were evaluated in the past, they recognize how far they are from who they ought to be. Their moral goodness is a good example that has played a significant role in explaining who they ought to be. There are many scholars who try to explain the process and dilemma of this defense. Some scholars, such as Samantha Vice and Daniel Haggerty, explain this defense as white guilt and white shame, while other scholars, such as Shannon Sullivan, Robin DiAngelo, and Marzia Milazzo, call it white good morality, white habits, white fragility, white ignorance, and other things.

Samantha Vice uses moral damage as one of white people's defenses to explain who they are. She claims that under colonial conditions, both black groups and white groups are morally damaged.[35] As white groups are born and raised in an already racialized society, what they see and experience is the way things have been in their lives. Under this privileged habitual living, white groups are raised as racists. Then some consciousness arises. Vice calls it "white shame." Reflecting on her white South African experience and struggle, she analyzes shame as the starting point to explain who white people ought to be in relation to white privilege.

> Shame seems an appropriate response to the recognition of one's unavoidable privilege. For white privilege does not attach merely to what one does or how one benefits, but, more fundamentally, to

who one is. And one does not wish to be a person whose welfare
is dependent upon harm to others. One does not wish to be a person with vicious traits that are helping, however passively, to sustain
privilege and oppression. . . . That is one aspect of shame: we are
not as we ought to be. But on the other hand, having a desire to
respond appropriately to the world is one mark of a morally con-
scientious person. If we are as bad as the thesis of white privilege
suggests, then any white person should feel shame, and our obeying
this imperative means we are responding as we should, fulfilling at
least a moral emotional duty. It is morally appropriate to accept and
live with shame, aware of oneself always as privileged and existing
in a world that accommodates one at the expense of others. It would
be morally worse if one did not feel and know these things.[36]

In Vice's understanding, white shame comes from the recognition of one's
unavoidable privilege. As white people realize how much privilege they have,
they feel shame. She believes that they would recognize the shame of privileges by themselves. She presumes two things. First, white people have the
ability to know who people ought to be through recognizing privileges. They
do not wish to be people who harm others. They would feel shame when they
recognize the suffering of other people. Second, if white people feel shame,
it proves that they are morally good in their hearts. Without their goodness,
shame does not exist. Existence of shame is proof of white moral goodness.
Vice argues that shame is a necessary feeling that many white people carry.
Because of this shame, they work for racial justice. She sees this white shame
as white people's duty to know how they should feel. Her personal struggle to
be white in a racially unjust prefixed social caste system leads her to understand shame as that which white people must feel. She fills the gap between
who whites are and who they ought to be with shame. Shame makes white
people react against racial injustice. In this understanding, shame substitutes
for white people's responsibility. Instead of taking economic political responsibility for reparations to other groups, shame can compensate white privileges easily. By equalizing who whites are and who they ought to be, shame
saves them from culpability. As long as they feel shame, it proves that they
are good people. It restores white good morality without actual reparations.

    Vice understands white shame from her emotional individual struggles,
whereas Haggerty claims white shame and guilt are a part of the "moral psychology of whiteness that is socially constructed."[37] He sees shame and guilt
differently depending on experiences of the other. Shame experiences the
other as a watcher or witness who personally judges them, while guilt experiences the other as a victim or enforcer who institutionally demands reparation.[38] When people overemphasize shame, they fear losing personal respect

and honor but do not recognize the importance of justice and individual rights. When they overemphasize guilt, they fear institutional punishment but lose the sense of character and community.[39] Haggerty sees guilt two different ways, as institutional white guilt and as liberal white guilt. Institutional white guilt is not about individual feelings but about limited political and institutional response owing to fear of black power and the influence of civil rights. This guilt has nothing to do with taking the responsibility to apologize for racial injustices. Rather, it is a defense to protect white institutions from any accusations of racism.[40] Liberal white guilt is about individual and personal moral guilt. It emphasizes individual personal responsibility. It means that if individuals do not do any harm or wrongdoing directly, they are not responsible. Even if they inherit all privileges and benefits, these privileges and benefits do not count toward their responsibility. They believe that they are only responsible for what they individually and personally have done to others in current situations. They take privileges and benefits without guilt as they dismiss individual personal responsibility.[41] Haggerty believes that contemporary U.S. society emphasizes guilt more than shame. Using white resistance against white supremacy as an example, he emphasizes the power of white shame as the grounds to form responsibility. Because this shame is not just individual feeling but socially constructed emotions, he believes that white people will work hard until they change social and cultural environments.

In his conclusion, Haggerty uses "taint" as an essential concept of defending white good morality. His defense is that white people are tainted by the things for which they are not individually responsible; but as a part of white groups, they need to take collective responsibility. Even though he emphasizes the collective responsibility of all white groups, he leaves white good morality for only certain white groups. He blames groups such as white supremacists, who taint good white morality, and encourages good white groups to take responsibility for getting rid of that taint. Sullivan's criticism is that white supremacists (white slave-owning ancestors and white trash) are cast to take the fall for tainting good white morality. And shame is used repeatedly to restore white integrity and to prove the existence of good morality for only white middle-class liberals. Many white middle-class liberals, including scholars and activists, try to avoid any taint or sins themselves. They say that they feel responsible because they are good, but they are not responsible technically because they are not the ones who caused the harm. They feel responsible collectively when they feel shame and guilt but are not responsible individually when they need to take responsibility. They transfer their individual responsibility to institutional collective responsibility. Their individual responsibility rides on collective responsibility. Then it is vaporized into collective responsibility. However, when collective responsibility is requested, it disperses into individual responsibility. Collective responsibility becomes no one's responsibility. Their individual and collective responsibilities disappear in the midst of this vicious chase. No one is responsible. In the end, only shame is left.

If white shame and guilt are somewhat active defenses to protect whiteness, there is a passive defense. Most white people, including both white middle-class and poor/working-class groups, insulate themselves from any uncomfortable situations consciously and unconsciously. Robin DiAngelo calls this tendency "white fragility."[42] White groups are privileged to avoid racial issues and environments, whereas other racial groups do not have any choice but to encounter these issues on a daily basis. Because of these privileges, white groups do not want to tolerate any uncomfortable situations. DiAngelo introduces segregation as one good example to describe how white groups avoid uncomfortable situations in reality and develop white fragility, psychologically and geographically. She identifies universalism and individualism, entitlement to racial comfort, racial arrogance, racial belonging, and psychic freedom as the fostering factors to white fragility.

> Further, white people are taught not to feel any loss over the absence of people of color in their lives and in fact, this absence is what defines their schools and neighborhoods as "good"; whites come to understand that a "good school" or "good neighborhood" is coded language for "white." The quality of white space being in large part measured via the absence of people of color (and Blacks in particular) is a profound message indeed, one that is deeply internalized and reinforced daily through normalized discourses about good schools and neighborhoods. This dynamic of gain rather than loss via racial segregation may be the most profound aspect of white racial socialization of all. Yet, while discourses about what makes a space good are tacitly understood as racially coded, this coding is explicitly denied by whites.[43]

As white groups try to avoid dealing with any racial issues, they lock themselves into their own world. Segregation is not just mental psychological avoidance but physical disconnection from other groups. They equate white with good and get rid of the presence of other groups in their sights geographically, physically, and psychologically. Fostering white-only environments, they feel safe. They develop intolerance for other groups. When they encounter nonwhite environments, they feel uncomfortable. They become fragile. When they see the presence of other racial groups, they become fearful and are easily stressed out. If they are exposed in these circumstances, they even show anger and violence. In order not to be exposed in these circumstances, they guide their territory and segregate themselves from others. White fragility creates segregation, universalism, individualism, and other discriminations to protect fragile white ego, morality, and consciousness, among other things. Like white shame and guilt, white fragility is another defense for protecting whiteness. Protecting whiteness is the most important subject for white groups to work on.

Marzia Milazzo interprets this kind of defense, especially Vice's work on white shame, as "rescuing whiteness."[44] She argues that Vice describes white privilege as something inherited simply from ancestors and does not consider the suffering of black people under postcolonial/neocolonial conditions. Even though white domination is still active and oppressive, and the majority of white people actively participate in economic and political exploitation of black people, Vice does not indicate the problem of current white domination directly. Instead, she implies that white privilege is passive and that white people have no control over it. Milazzo calls the concept of shame that Vice constructed "*the* privileged emotion."[45] This privileged emotion does not require any responsibility but demonstrates white people's goodness in their hearts. By using shame, Milazzo critiques Vice's removal of white people's active participation in racial injustice situations. Shame plays a role in establishing white people as victims of racism. It reinforces the preservation of white privileges. It also reconfirms the goodness of whiteness. Many white people feel shame because they are good people. Because they have good morality, despite their privileges, they do not simply accept these privileges. They struggle. They struggle emotionally and psychologically. This proves that white people's morality exhibits their high standard of maturity and integrity. Their moral goodness is carefully presented and praised. In Milazzo's evaluation, Vice rescues whiteness, misconceptualizes racial dynamics, and restores white pride. Milazzo concludes that approaches from emotions such as shame, guilt, and morality make people "forget that desegregating neighborhoods, schools, and workplaces are crucial steps in the fight against white supremacy and that de-racialisation must have a financial cost for white people."[46]

In summary, some scholars, such as Vice, Haggerty, Lawrence Blum, and John Rawls, insist that even though white people try to hide or legitimate what they did in colonial history, their morality, faith, and/or consciousness cannot let them hide their wrongdoings. Illustrating the formation of white shame and guilt, these scholars want to demonstrate how good white individuals struggle and fight against racial injustice for other groups. They try to explain their reason for this defense by offering several concepts, such as white good morality, white shame, white guilt, white ignorance, white habits, and other concepts. White groups try to minimize their colonial history and inherited privileges and claim these as the way things are instead of recognizing them and taking responsibility collectively and individually. Taking responsibility for white groups causes great fear and fosters white fragility. As they recognize that it demands personal and institutional reparation, they fear losing privileges and control. Fear of taking responsibility prevents them from getting out of their own comfortable spaces. It is possible that the individual psychological and spiritual white consciousness tries to stop white violence and shows their wrongdoings in the forms of morality, goodness, and spiritual faith. Some individual and personal struggles in white groups are real and deserve recognition.

However, their individual struggles cannot simply give white groups sanction for their racial colonial history and violence. Their fragility and shame should not be used as a defense to legitimate their privileges. Scholars such as Milazzo, DiAngelo, and Tommie Shelby critique white people's use of moral or psychological approaches as a way of hiding colonial violence and establishing their white goodness. These scholars want to point out that these moral and psychological approaches are used as a tool to dismiss white people's communal responsibilities in terms of socioeconomic and political reparation for others. They choose these approaches, not to recognize the suffering of others but to legitimate their course of actions. Instead of defending their good whiteness, they need to take the first step of taking responsibility for socioeconomic and political reparations. The reality that other groups encounter daily is not their choice but their given conditions to deal with. It is an absolutely unavoidable reality that they live in. However, white groups, especially white upper/middle-class groups, have the privilege of avoiding and/or abandoning racial struggles, whereas other groups have to face these struggles with their lives and deaths. When white privileged groups try to legitimate their wrongdoings in defense mode—such as extolling the value of civilization, enlightenment, and globalization—other racial/ethnic groups try to undo white groups' wrongdoings in survival mode—such as by condemning anticolonialism, antiracism, and localization. When white groups try to avoid their individual and communal responsibility from their colonial past, other racial/ethnic groups suffer in white privileged colonial and postcolonial reality. This gap between white groups and other racial/ethnic groups becomes deeper and wider. White groups and other racial/ethnic groups occupy opposite positions in this gap. As other racial/ethnic groups and global society demand reparations from white colonial and postcolonial past and present, white domination and its system invent another defense to protect their privileges and benefits. That is the black/white racial binary divide.

Problems in the Black/White Racial Binary Divide

The black/white racial binary divide is very important, not only to the communal psychological defense of whites but also as a powerful sociopolitical paradigm to protect whiteness. As other racial/ethnic groups demand socioeconomic restoration, white colonial and postcolonial sociopolitical system functions to minimize responsibility. In order to minimize responsibility, it focuses on only one ethnic group, blacks. Struggling to protect whiteness, the black/white racial binary divide is often sugarcoated as either supporting black people's rights or demonstrating white people's admirable efforts in support of black people's movements. White colonial and postcolonial social construction invents the black/white binary divide approach to frame these discussions only within black/white relations. By forming these discussions as *the* race problem, black/white relations are presented as relations of all races. These relations precede and dominate all relations and minimize other racial relations. The discussions between black and white people are often overemphasized and greatly misused in the dominant white discourses to dismiss people of other races within the logic of the black/white racial binary divide.[47] This black/white binary divide assumes that as long as white people confess and reconcile what they have done to black people, all of their violent acts will be excused by people of all races. Black/white binary logic falsely generates pernicious permission for white colonial and postcolonial power to perform an action of apology without recognizing all the consequences of violence and discrimination against all people. As white intellectual sociopolitical discourses generate a course of action to confess inventing colonial laws to control black slaves only, they hid postcolonial rules casting black and other racial/ethnic groups as modern slaves.

Recognizing the importance of black/white relations and analyzing the danger of the black/white binary divide approach, many scholars debate this binary approach with different viewpoints. Katerina Deliovsky and Tamari Kitossa understand the black/white binary racial concept as Manicheanism, which is deeply associated with good (whiteness) and evil (darkness) in Eurocentric culture.[48] Borrowing the concept of paradigm from Thomas Kuhn, Juan F. Perea called this concept the black/white binary paradigm that "race in America consists, either exclusively or primarily, of only two constituent racial groups, the Black and the White."[49] Placing white on the top and black on the bottom, the black/white binary paradigm and/or black/white Manicheanism creates a white/black binary hierarchical order that is dangerously, but legitimately, established and practiced in the current U.S. immigrant context.[50]

As Deliovsky and Kitossa indicate, the black/white binary concept is often used in good and evil dualistic Eurocentric approaches for the purpose of producing antiblackness.[51] White is associated with the positive perceptions of innocence, purity, and justice, whereas black is associated with the negative perceptions of impurity, danger, and guilt. Placing these two in opposing positions, black is contrasted with white in a relegated manner. Scholars such as Deliovsky and Kitossa understand this binary concept as the main concept to deconstruct the binary system and reveal the problem of antiblack racism.[52] Instead of moving beyond a black/white binary framework, they use this black/white binary concept as a starting point to reveal antiblack racism. As they lay out antiblackness, they focus exclusively on white/black relations only. They do not give much attention to the problems that cause discrimination and injustice to other racial ethnic groups. As they utilize the black/white binary divide as a useful tool to dismantle black/white relations, they unconsciously dismiss other racial ethnic relations from the public square. Only black/white relations are spotlighted on the stage.

This black/white binary concept is often exchanged with a black/non-black binary concept. Many scholars, like Deliovsky and Kitossa, George Yancey, Philip Kretsedemas, and Claire Jean Kim, indicate that the black/white binary becomes the black/nonblack binary. It is not about how to be white but about how to not be black. "In other words, to be white is to not be black."[53] They identify whiteness as nonblackness. By way of not associating with blackness, other racial ethnic groups learn how to live and act differently from black groups. As the black/white binary locates black at the bottom, it cultivates fear for nonwhite racial ethnic groups of associating with blacks. This fear dominates not only white but also nonblack ethnic groups' attitudes toward blacks and creates an irreconcilable distance from blacks. The story of Chinese immigrants in the Mississippi Delta from the 1800s to the 1920s–1930s is a good example of this fear. Chinese immigrants in the Mississippi Delta shifted their status from near black to near white by dissociating themselves from blacks. They prohibited interracial marriage with blacks, punished any interactions with blacks, recommended the use of white names, and encouraged participation in white churches. By claiming themselves as not black, they achieved a higher social status than blacks.[54]

As the story of the Mississippi Chinese immigrants illustrates, marriage laws play a significant role in keeping this clashing, fearful distance between white and nonwhite groups. Miscegenation between white and nonwhite races was prohibited by law until the 1950s. Interracial marriage was one of the biggest fears of white systems, so white systems tried to control it in the name of protecting white purity, especially white womanhood.[55] This fear or hate of miscegenation was coded in laws, customs, culture, and religious practices. It was beyond sociocultural discouragement. It was sociocultural and political systematic discrimination. Interracial marriage was not just prohibited by law but also punished by all dimensions of personal and communal lives. Despite the ruling in 1967 by the U.S. Supreme Court in the case of *Loving v. Virginia* that antimiscegenation laws were unconstitutional, interracial marriage was a social taboo until the twenty-first century in many local and global communities.

As antimiscegenation sets the boundary of social distance from black people, it intensifies the black/nonblack binary. It makes black groups more isolated and discourages any social interaction with other racial groups. Promoting the black/nonblack binary divide to maintain distance from blacks, the black/white binary divide manipulates other racial ethnic groups into believing that they are not black and do not have to live like blacks. The black/nonblack binary divide generates fear to control other racial ethnic groups and alienate blacks. It is believed that because they are different from blacks, their lives should be better than black lives. This manipulation aggravates racial alienation among racial/ethnic groups from blacks and isolates blacks from them. At the same time, it produces racial alienation from each other. It cultivates vicious competitions among nonblack racial/ethnic groups. They compete with each other to secure what they can have from the limited institutional resources rather than collaborate to support each other and share these resources. In this sense, the black/nonblack binary divide can be exchanged with the black/white binary divide.

However, it does not mean the black/nonblack binary divide exactly equates with the black/white binary divide. The axiom "To be white is to not be black" implies that as long as people are not black and as long as they are not associated with blackness, they all belong to white groups and enjoy the benefits that black groups cannot have. It erases the fact that to be white is also not to be Asian or Latinx immigrants in current U.S. society. After all, to be white means to not be nonwhite in reality. However, by emphasizing the presence of blackness, the black/nonblack binary divide equates nonblackness with whiteness. It emphasizes that blacks are the worst victims of the racial hierarchy and turns other nonwhite groups white. It assumes that black people are only black in the black/nonblack category and everyone else belongs to the category of white. The black/nonblack binary divide dismisses the differences of various racial ethnic groups and implants the misbelief of the possibility of becoming white. In other words, even though this binary divide propagates the possibility of becoming white to the people who are not white on the surface, it constructs a clear line not only between white and black but also between white and nonwhite people. As the previous section illustrated, even among white groups, there is a clear line that permits only a certain class of white people to be truly allowed to be white. By emphasizing the victimization of black groups, this black/nonblack binary minimizes the suffering of nonwhite and nonblack groups and condemns their dissociating themselves from blacks as foolish racism, while it conceals the privileges of whites.

The goal of the black/nonblack binary divide is antiblackness, producing fear of being associated with blackness and making blacks more isolated. However, it is not the whole purpose of creating the black/nonblack binary divide. By producing antiblackness, the black/nonblack binary divide seeks to legitimately disregard anti-Asian and anti-Latinx sentiments. As the black/nonblack binary divide emphasizes the distinction from blacks and makes all other groups white, the black/white binary divide emphasizes the comparison between white and black and locates nonwhite and nonblack in the black category. The black/nonblack binary divide has blackness as a starting point for discrimination, whereas the black/white binary presents whiteness as a starting point for assimilation. As both divides emphasize the binary presence of blackness and whiteness, both divides dismiss the presence of nonwhite and nonblack groups. In the intersection between the black/nonblack binary divide and the black/white binary divide, black groups are more isolated and nonblack and nonwhite groups are more invisible, whereas white groups are not white but still remain "normal" people.

This process of forming these binary divides shows how black/white racial relations became one single power paradigm in control. On the one hand, the black/white binary divide promotes being white. It encourages all racial groups, including blacks, to follow and adopt white colonial and postcolonial culture, rules, laws, norms, socioeconomic values, and political history. It intentionally leads all people to admire these white constructions as the goal of their advancement. Even though no groups can be white, the goal of this binary divide makes it clear that every group needs to recognize what it means to be white and what makes whiteness. Assimilation is required. However, the goal of this binary divide is not learning to be white but learning to accept the impossibility of being white. It forces nonwhite groups to accept their current status quo. On the other hand, when this black/white binary divide becomes the black/nonblack binary divide, it insinuates the alienation and negation of black groups. As discussed above, it manipulates all racial groups not to associate with black groups. It shows all racial groups how to not be black. Furthermore, it provokes fear, discouraging them from being in solidarity with black groups. However, learning not to be black does not mean that they can be white. The hidden assumption is this: as long as you are not black, you will not be treated like blacks. And, as long as you are not treated like blacks, you should be grateful. By manipulating antiblackness, the black/nonblack divide drives other groups' attention to accepting the current status quo gracefully. It shows a clear line not to cross.

Both the black/white binary divide and black/nonblack binary divide put all racial ethnic groups in a dilemma between learning about whiteness and blackness with different purposes. These divides make them recognize the strong existence of both whites and blacks only and deny the existence of other racial ethnic groups. Under colonial/postcolonial power and control, the black/white binary paradigm controls not only black groups but all racial groups. Emphasizing the distinctive history and situation of blacks in relation to whites, this paradigm legitimates the black/white binary in the form of legal and socioeconomic constructions and makes it valid not to recognize the presence of other racial ethnic groups. George Yancey argues that underscoring the black experience, this binary paradigm intentionally ignores the social conditions of other racial ethnic groups at the expense of their suffering.[56] The black/white binary divide is another form of *racial discrimination* against other racial groups to dismiss their struggles, including blacks.

As long as society shows efforts to restore black rights and equality, and as long as the top and the bottom are assigned to two specific races, the locations of other racial ethnic groups neither matter nor are noticeable. The black/white binary paradigm demands that other racial ethnic groups stay in intermediary positions. It dismisses equality and creates the specific hierarchical order. In this hierarchical order, the black/white binary divide carefully places other racial ethnic groups in between whites and blacks without visibility. Intentional invisibility of other racial ethnic groups is very important in this concept because the existence of this binary system requires racial ethnic others' invisible presence and muted voices. Invention of the black/white binary paradigm creates the negation of others. It tends to simplify complicated multiplicities of racial relations to the single problem of white/black race relations and racism. Reviewing the legal history of forming the U.S. Constitution and policies on race and justice shows that narratives of civil rights and equality are exclusively focused on the black struggle, and the struggles of other racial ethnic groups are simply not heard.[57] In this black/white binary construction, it is important to present blacks as the most disadvantaged group among others and whites as the most advantaged group who can save all. This binary divide presents the truth of blacks and whites as the whole truth.

In summary, depicting black groups as the problem to fix, this binary concept locates the scope of the problem within only black/white relations. As it misleads people into thinking that black/white inequality is the only problem, it locates problems among other groups in a marginalized space. It assumes that as long as black/white problems are fixed, other problems will naturally disappear. Disadvantages among other groups could easily vanish without serious consideration. It pretends that as long as this paradigm puts blacks at the center of attention and grants their experience as "a paradigm for the experiences of all people of color," the presence of other racial ethnic groups can fade away, and different experiences of other people of color are not issues to consider anymore.[58] The danger of a black/white binary concept of race is that by overemphasizing black/white relations and damages between them, one can easily dismiss other racial relations without any careful consideration. Many racial ethnic groups, including Asian immigrants and Latinx immigrants, can be caught in between these dynamics. Moreover, presenting their struggles can be simply perceived as dismissing or jeopardizing the importance of the black struggle. This paradigm puts other racial ethnic groups in the position of endless pity for and competition with black groups.

This endless competition with black groups becomes a serious problem in relation to Asian immigrant groups especially. Feeding the destructive typical stereotypes between "the 'unreliable, threatening' black customer" and "the 'contemptuous, exploitative' Asian shopkeeper," the black/nonblack binary divide and black/white binary divide evoke conflicts between black and Asian immigrant groups and leads them to miscommunicate their common needs for collaboration.[59] These divides bring a more rigid boundary of ethnic differences and eliminate the room for harmonious efforts between black and Asian immigrant groups. These binary paradigms are a racial classification device to encourage discriminatory practices to protect white supremacy and discourage nonwhite groups to collaborate.[60] Even though leaders of black and Asian immigrant groups try to support each other in their struggle against white domination, their collaboration is often interrupted by these black/nonblack and black/white binary divides when Asian immigrants are seen as white. Even though U.S. society never allowed Asian immigrants to be white, black/nonblack and black/white binary divides profile Asian immigrants as white to confuse both black and nonwhite racial groups into competition. When the white system manipulates the relationship between Asian immigrant groups and black groups, it gives occasional preferential treatment to either black groups or Asian immigrant groups to fight against each other by changing policy that benefits one group over other groups, such as Asian exclusion. While these divides locate black groups as the alienated, unequal members in society, they cast Asian immigrants as the forever aliens outside of U.S. society.[61]

Native/Alien Binary

The black/white binary concept is often used as *the* measure of race and class stratification in the U.S. context to dismiss other racial discussions, including Asian American and Asian immigrant issues. It often accompanies another binary divide, the native/alien paradigm. Like the black/white binary divide, the native/alien binary divide becomes a power paradigm since it has been exclusively built as the U.S. nation-centered paradigm to legitimately exclude other racial ethnic groups, especially immigrants, as outsiders of black/white race relations.[62] Despite the fact that the native/alien paradigm has a long story of colonial/postcolonial oppression in and outside of the U.S. in relation to race, the discrimination caused by this paradigm against other racial ethnic groups, including Asian immigrants, is often trivialized and dismissed as a nonracial discussion. Rather, it is used to support racial violence as a security matter to legitimate discrimination against so-called outsiders, immigrants.

As the black/white binary paradigm is used to dismiss the presence of racial others, the native/alien binary paradigm has been used as another form to disempower the presence of these groups, leaving them seriously damaged. The key concept of this paradigm is based on the concept of nativism. What is nativism? How does it relate to the issues of Asian immigrants?

What Is Nativism?

Nativism is often defined based on the binary concept between immigrants and natives and is associated with a negative sentiment toward immigrants. The 2003 third edition of the *Oxford English Dictionary* defines nativism as "Chiefly U.S. The attitude, practice, or policy of protecting the interests of native-born or existing inhabitants against those of immigrants; *spec.* the ideology of the Native American party (now hist.)."[63] This dictionary definition makes two assumptions. First, protecting the interests of native-born or existing inhabitants is the main ideology of nativism. Policy, practice, and attitude are formed and exercised to protect their interests. Discriminatory immigrant policies toward Asian immigrants, such as the Chinese Exclusion Act of 1882, and hostile attitudes against them are examples of nativist politics. Second, in this definition, native-born/existing inhabitants and immigrants are shown as in oppositional, conflictive positions. In this propositionally opposite position, immigrants are seen as a threat or a problem that shatters the benefits of native-born or existing inhabitants.

Nativism is broadly presumed to be associated with the notion of birthright and existing inhabitants who are *legal* citizens of the country. Even though Native Americans are the only existing inhabitants in the United States, they were never considered native born or existing inhabitants under the power of colonial/postcolonial history and culture. In fact, Native Americans were totally excluded and marginalized in this discussion. They were treated as colonial projects and the target of civilization in colonial era discourse.[64] Because they were considered as lesser humans than the white colonizers/settlers, their native rights were taken away. While their nativity was transferred to inferior nature to justify their training for civilization, white colonial invasion was transformed into superior quality of naturalization and turned into nativity for white U.S. citizenship. White colonizers/settlers turned these identifiers upside-down to redesign nativity from colonial invasion to civilizational restructure. They placed Native Americans outside of the black/white binary framework and kept Native Americans in line with nonwhite racial immigrant groups outside of the legal framework. The nativity of Native Americans was denied, and their rights and benefits of U.S. citizenship were deflated by not granting their full legal status. Their presence is often dismissed in public racial discussions. In the U.S. context, the positions of native-born and/or existing inhabitants have been occupied predominantly by European white colonizers/settlers only.

The current binary oppositional positions of the native/alien paradigm have originated and been controlled by this colonial white hegemony. It identifies white colonizers/settlers as natives, invents the ideology of U.S. American nativity to justify this identification, and demands the protection of their privileges and interests as the natives' rights. They use nativism as the main defense for discrimination against other racial ethnic groups, especially immigrant groups, including Asian immigrant groups. Within this native/alien paradigm, immigrants are impulsively identified as the aliens and have been treated as a commodity to be controlled and exploited for the benefits of natives.[65]

Nativism as Antiforeignness

John Higham, in his book *Strangers in the Land*, defines nativism as "the anti-foreign spirit"[66] and as "intense opposition to an internal minority on the ground of its foreign (i.e., 'un-American') connections."[67] He further says that "nativism as a habit of mind illuminates darkly some of the large contours of the American past; it has mirrored our anxieties and marked out the bounds of our tolerance."[68] He explained how anti-Catholic, anti-radical, and Anglo-Saxon traditions in the late nineteenth and twentieth centuries shaped American nationalism before it formed American nativism.[69] Aristide Zolberg interpreted Higham's conceptualization of nativism as "frustration-aggression" syndrome by which "Americans, frustrated by the disruptions that accompanied industrialization and urbanization, projected their anger upon strangers."[70] Whether nativism is a habit of mind, anxiety, or frustration-aggression syndrome, one of the common grounds to understand nativism is foreignness. It is something from which the white colonizers/settlers try to disassociate. Observing antiforeign attitudes and identifying nativism deeply rooted in nationalism and ethnocentrism, Higham recognized the serious growing danger of nativism against non-European immigrants in terms of racism. As he described, the notion of "un-American" is interpreted as nonwhite non-European connection. As he points out that nativism is involved with nationalism and ethnocentrism of white Anglo-Saxon traditions, the notion of "un-American" draws the clear line between the white Anglo-Saxon race and other races. Whoever presents nonwhite, non-Anglo-Saxon connections are seen as strangers in the land and become the target of discrimination.

In this sense, nativism is not interested in identifying who natives are. It is not about protecting the rights and interests of native-born and existing inhabitants. Rather, it focuses on expressing white settlers' anger against, frustration with, and aggression toward non-white immigrant racial ethnic groups who exhibit different physical appearances, accents, cultural manners, behaviors, and so forth. By expressing this anger, frustration, and aggression, nativism can justify violence and discrimination as a defense mechanism against foreignness. Then, violence and discrimination against immigrants is not understood as violence and discrimination but as a defense of national security and identity. Asian immigrants' connections with Asian heritage and culture have been the target of discrimination. Their Mongolian physical bodies, Asian cultural psychological minds, and Oriental spiritual practices become symbols of un-Americanness. In the nativist approach, this un-Americanness is an object of frustration. It is believed that this un-Americanness brings fear to provoke anger and frustration among natives. To express this anger and frustration, aggression is used as one of the tactics by white settlers against Asian immigrants to dissociate themselves from Asianness. Asianness equates to un-Americanness. It represents foreignness in a perpetual manner. As long as un-Americanness equates Asianness to foreignness, anger, frustration, and aggression against Asian immigrants gain validity to use violence and discrimination against them. Nativism against foreignness is defended in the name of protecting national interests. This interpretation of nativism has continuously cultivated antialien, anti-non-European movement toward immigrants as it intensifies the native/alien paradigm in more of an anti-Asian immigrant mode.

In a similar manner, Robin Dale Jacobson sees "a perceived 'foreignness'" as the cause of nativism.[71] Like Higham, she focuses on nativism as discrimination against foreigners, nonwhite immigrants. Describing Proposition 187, which prohibits undocumented immigrants from using any public support systems, as a renewed nativist movement, Jacobson explains how color-blind conservatism and racial realism worked side by side in coalition to discriminate against immigrants and shape the current economic sociopolitical terrain to refortify the concept of nativism. Separating immigrants from racial categories, "color-blind conservatism argues that race is no longer a relevant category" for immigrants.[72] Putting immigrants outside of racial categories forces them to become invisible within the black/white binary framework. Within the black/white binary paradigm, yellow is not a color. It is neither white nor black. Yellow is not yellow, but no color. This binary paradigm allows selective color-blind spots. Because race is no longer a relevant category for Asian immigrants, they have no right to demand their equality from this country. The rights of race and the notion of race are only applied to the people who are natives. The basic assumption is that "race matters discussions" only belong to white and black relations even though people in the category of immigrants have human rights to participate in that discussion. At the same time, "racial realism suggests that race is a fundamental dividing category in society and that races have singular interests that compete with the interests of other races."[73] Putting immigrants back in racial categories results in immigrants being seen as groups who do not have proper rights but compete for or steal jobs and welfare from white and black groups.

By creating a gap between natives and aliens in the logic of "color-blind conservatism and racial realism" as "two sides of the same coin," Jacobson observed how this white society created and constantly re-creates the images of immigrants as criminalized illegal aliens/races and projects these images with otherness.[74] Using color-blind conservatism and racial realism within the native/alien paradigm, it is much easier for the black/white binary system to exclude nonwhite and nonblack groups from making demands or requests of human rights. In this binary divide, whites and blacks, especially by lifting up white American and African American citizen groups, are treated as native-born or existing inhabitants with full legal status and other racial groups are assumed to be 'illegal' aliens. The black/white binary divide assumes that only whites and blacks have the right to discuss racial issues, while the native/alien binary divide assumes that only the white and black legal citizens have the right to discuss the issues of national security and interests. In order to be politically correct, the native/alien binary divide urges the inclusion of African American groups as natives so that white European immigrant and descendent groups are seen as natives without many explanations. To protect the rights and privileges of white construction, the native/alien binary divide implicates black groups as the only groups who need to be considered more seriously in terms of the rights of natives. As the black/white binary divide politically lifts up African American groups in a public exhibition as natives, it easily dismisses the presence of other racial/ethnic groups. All these nonwhite and nonblack groups are treated as aliens who do not deserve intentional attention. Justice and equality are not subjects of discussion for aliens, but for natives only in this logic. This logic reiterates the fact that by constructing and continuously reframing images of immigrants as dangerous criminal others, nativism meets the current economic sociopolitical terrain to identify the images of immigrants as job stealers and welfare takers in a repeated manner.[75]

Lifting up the hardship of blacks as natives who deserve proper rights, the paradigms coerce other racial ethnic groups to take blame for the suffering of blacks. As it carefully locates blacks in opposition to other racial ethnic groups, it perpetuates a vicious cycle of competition between blacks and other racial ethnic groups. Manipulating the hardships of blacks, this native/alien binary divide intentionally affirms rights of white natives over rights of nonwhite groups. Designating blacks as natives and placing blacks at the center of attention in racial discussions, this native/alien binary divide justifies dismissing the voices of other racial groups. The meaning of nativism is constantly changed and transformed into new meanings to meet the current needs of dominant white privileged groups. The function of nativism is then used by different privileged political parties to legitimately exploit immigrants, especially undocumented immigrants.

Nativism as Nation Building/National Interests

Zolberg understands and interprets immigrant policy as a "major instrument of nation-building."[76] Creating immigrant policy as a way to design the nation, he defines nativism as "representing [the] conservative position on [an] 'identity' continuum which allows for other positions ranging through the acceptance of shifting boundaries as a concomitant of historical change—where I would roughly place myself—all the way to the advocacy of radical transformation."[77] He uses two cross-cutting axes, "the putative or actual effects of immigration on material conditions" and "cultural political conditions,"[78] to explain how immigrant policy is created and re-created in constant changes of transformation. He sees nativism as a form of resistance to protect natives from immigrants who might cause actual or possible changes in economic effects and cultural political conditions. In his interpretation, nativism is not evaluated as a negative power paradigm to protect white privileges necessarily, but one of several forces to control immigrants to make a balanced nation. The nation needs to keep the front door open for immigrants when it needs human capital to raise the economy for natives. At the same time, it closes the front door (but opens a back door) when it needs to control resources and secular benefits for natives. Using nativism as a tool to control the doors, the nation protects its own resources and supports economic growth.

As nation building is claimed to be the main reason for the existence of nativism, nativism is emphasized to establish the singular version of the nation and its identity. As nativism originated from white European colonial history and its domination, it is still under the powerful influence of a colonial and postcolonial vision of building a colonial nation, which emphasizes benefits for whites as natives and legitimates exploitation of aliens. In the colonial era, the colonized in their own lands were exploited for the colonizers who came from other countries. In the postcolonial era, immigrants who moved into the colonizers' lands voluntarily or forcefully became the target of exploitation. When immigrants enter the U.S., they are under the suspicion that they will threaten the singular version of the nation and its identity as the protector of natives' rights and benefits. As many current immigrants, whether they are citizens or not, have kept their strong connections with their home countries and frequently contact the people in their home countries, it is seen as a threat to U.S. national security and its resources. Their loyalty to the United States is questioned. Because they connect and live with both nations, they become *trans*nationalists."[79] Instead of keeping a single national identity, these immigrants bring multiple identities from their motherlands and develop transnational identities in the United States. It is perceived that these transnational immigrants jeopardize a singular vision of the "nation" and circulate multiculturalism/transnationalism, not assimilation.[80] The native/alien paradigm interprets their transnational activities as unstable acts that disturb the nation and its identity. In this paradigm, immigrants, including Asian immigrants, are required to exist for natives' rights and benefits, even though they come to this land for better lives of their own. As natives' rights and benefits are more emphasized and demanded, their transnational identities and multicultural identities become subjects to contest their loyalty to and trust in the nation. The native/alien paradigm locks these immigrants in a box of an unassimilable un-American class.

Brian N. Fry is another scholar to define nativism to show how it functions to discriminate against immigrants in the native/alien paradigm. He defines nativism as "a collective attempt by self-identified natives to secure or retain prior or exclusive rights to valued resources against the challenges reputedly posed by resident or prospective populations on the basis of their perceived foreignness."[81] Putting a restrictionist discourse of immigration as a national question in opposition to an expansionist discourse of immigration as a humanitarian and economic question, he explores two different positions of immigration and nativism. Restrictionists see immigrants as the problem of the nation, adding unnecessary overpopulation in the face of limited resources. In this discourse, immigrants are seen as people who hurt the national economy and steal the nation's resources. Restrictionists see immigrants as criminals or illegal undocumented groups. Expansionists perceive immigrants as human capital. The U.S. economy needs immigrant proficiencies to build a stronger nation as immigrants take advantage of opportunities in the U.S.[82] In this discourse, immigrants are perceived as cheap laborers. They are the subject of exploitation.

Even though it seems that restrictionists and expansionists present an almost opposite view of immigration, they always work side by side to control immigrants. They are two sides of the same coin. Women are especially the main objects of their control. Chinese and Japanese exclusion in the U.S. between 1870 and 1924 is a good example. Chinese and Japanese groups were the first Asian immigrant groups, including Filipinos and Koreans, to arrive at the U.S. shore in the nineteenth century. Under the strong white European colonialism and imperialism, in cooperation with Christian missionaries, their cheap labor was intentionally recruited. It was seen as a very attractive factor to build a new nation quicker and stronger. Expansionists perceived Chinese and Japanese groups as cheap laborers for developing railroads and mines. As they needed strong, physically intense laborers, they targeted Chinese and Japanese men for recruitment but excluded women. They allowed temporary stays for these men to build the nation but expected them to leave. From the fear of permanent settlement of Chinese and Japanese groups, they created the Page Law in 1875 to prohibit the entrance of any Asian women, especially Chinese women.[83] Any family-related immigration was prohibited, and the presence of any Asian women was completely denied. The rationale behind creating this law was to protect their country and preserve their white identity. In order to protect their country and preserve their white identity, the sexuality of Asian women was marked as "lewd and immoral,"[84] and their social appearance was assumed as "prostitutes."[85] These women were perceived as a contaminated group who could spread immorality and disloyalty to the nation. Using the Page Law as the gate keeper, Chinese women's sexuality was used as the key element to control Chinese immigration.

When China became weakened and Japan became stronger, the U.S. changed its political attitudes. A new policy, the Chinese Exclusion Act of 1882, was quickly created. This policy was severely exercised and it discriminated against Chinese groups, giving more favor to Japanese groups. In this period, Japanese groups were differentiated from Chinese groups racially. Ethnic racial differentiation was used as a tactic to justify a preferential treatment for Japanese groups. However, this treatment did not last long. As global relations changed, favor toward Japanese immigrants turned into anti-Japanese attitudes. Another law, the Immigration Act of 1924, was created and Japanese groups were banned from immigration.[86] Ethnic racial differentiation quickly disappeared. Chinese and Japanese groups were treated as the same Asian group. Anti-Chinese and anti-Japanese sentiments were aroused, beginning as anti-Chinese then quickly morphing into anti-Japanese. Later, the sentiments spread as anti-Asian sentiment.

This example illustrates how expansionists recruited Asian immigrants to use their labor and how restrictionists dismissed them to protect the natives' rights and benefits. As expansionists used their colonial power to collect them, restrictionists used their colonial power to expel them whenever they wanted. Both views unveil that immigrants are the subject of control for national interests.[87] Both parties use racial ethnic differentiation as a device to control immigrants. Racial ethnic differentiation appears when nativism needs to provoke competition between two racial ethnic groups to isolate one targeted group for punishment. As it keeps one specific group away from other groups for punishment, other groups usually receive some preferential treatment in order to amplify the nation's purpose. When punishment is performed, preferential treatments disappear. It is quickly stopped because both groups eventually are equally discriminated against and suppressed. As restrictionists create the rules to close the door to the targeted groups, expansionists open the back door to recruit other groups to compensate for the loss.

Whether it is political, economic, and/or cultural, these discourses intend to use immigrants to serve national interests. Controlling immigrants by either reducing or expanding, immigration is a postcolonial apparatus to produce benefits for economic growth and political gain for natives. Migrant Filipina domestic workers are another example. Filipina women were internationally transferred from the Philippines to the U.S. to support white privileged classes and substitute for their domestic labor. They were classified as domestic workers, in between "clean mistresses" and "dirty servants," during the pre-World War II era.[88] The low-wage labor of Asian domestic workers was used for national capitalistic growth. In these view, immigrants were "wanted but not welcome."[89] Both discourses treat immigrants as an economic commodity to only support national advancement. Yet their presence is never welcome. Their expenses, living conditions, advancement, and well-being are not the subject of discussion but an object of unnecessary consideration. They are perceived as movable bodies. Specifically, women's bodies are demanded for cheap domestic labor. They are treated as trivial commodities. "Gender is a structural determinant of migration by showing that the greater demand for low-wage female workers in this particular receiving community initiated the primary migration of women."[90]

In the position of nativism, Filipina women's bodies were brought here for the purpose of providing human capital for natives' advancement, but not for the purpose of their own betterment. In terms of nativism and capitalism, natives do not have any intention to share human rights and advancements/benefits with immigrants. Immigrant rights merely infringe upon the natives' rights and/or, often, bring the fear that sharing and extending certain rights to immigrants "affect the value of the (corresponding or other) rights" and benefits of natives.[91] It is assumed that immigrants need to be treated as less than natives in the narrative of nativism. Immigrants are considered as commodities and bodies to control, and immigrant women are very often seen as troubling bodies to control more than immigrant men. Their sexuality is conceived of as a key to control immigration population. From prostitutes to free riders, they are pictured as a group who does not produce any economic growth but threatens the current economic system and national identity. Because of this distorted image, both expansionists and restrictionists deliberately require complete control over these immigrant women and their sexuality. By controlling immigrants and their sexuality, restrictionists and expansionists alike claim that they are on a mission to support natives' rights and national economic growth and protect national identity.

Who Are Natives? Territorial Controllers

Then, the next main question is who are natives and what makes them natives? Even though natives are generally understood as the people who are native born or existing inhabitants, this definition does not draw the clear boundary between natives and aliens/immigrants. Rather, its boundary is now more indefinable and obscure. It is usually self-identified and self-claimed. Fry explains how self-identified natives define themselves and how they control the gate.

> Self-identified natives define themselves vis-à-vis other populations by using their *perceptions* of foreignness to generate, sustain and legitimate a contrastive identity and set of attendant proprietary claims. Natives know who they are by knowing who they are not, and use this distinction as a basis for controlling access to valued resources. . . . Their efforts to secure or obtain prior or exclusive rights to valued resources rest on perceptions of entitlement and infringement, but are also backed—to varying degrees—by the institutions of immigration and citizenship policies.[92]

Nativism was created by self-identified natives, exclusively with European privileged white colonizer/settler groups, for the purpose of sustaining and protecting their national interests in a colonial context. Even when European colonization ended and moved to a postcolonial era, nativism was still used to foster colonial interests. By using foreignness as a negation tactic to define who they are not, natives try to secure their exclusive rights, demand entitlement, and exercise control over the gate in a postcolonial context. The concept of nativism promotes self-identified natives to invent the colonial patriotic notion of "one of us," whereas it automatically designates the concept of alien as immigrants to identify the oppositional notion of "not one of us." Defining "we" in opposition to foreignness is the most crucial colonial strategy to promote nativism. This binary approach between one of us and not one of us allows nativism to register various differences, including differences of physical appearance, history, culture, religion, sex/gender, race, and nationality as foreignness. When foreignness is discovered in these differences, the definition of natives allows neither foreignness nor differences to enter the boundary of one of us. It tends to stay in a monopatriotic identity. Drawing the line between self-identified natives and forcefully classified aliens, nativism intensifies foreignness as a divisive device to play a critical role in negating nonwhite and nonblack racial ethnic others as the absolute other. As pointed out in the previous section, it is interesting to note that self-identified natives often include blacks as natives within both black/white and native/alien binary divides. White hegemony uses black groups as a defense to protect white rationales in excluding nonwhite and nonblack groups. In their rationales, as long as they keep black groups on their side, they do not have to take any blame for exploiting other groups. As long as they keep the clear distinction between white and black within the black/white binary divide, keeping a monopatriotic identity within the native/alien binary divide has the double effect of excluding nonwhite and nonblack groups. Developing both black/white and native/alien binary divides is a careful political consideration to not share white privileges and benefits.

The concept of nativism originated from the colonial mentality of territorial control. Controlling territories is the most important colonial resource to increase the benefits of natives. Territories are constantly occupied by colonial power in the form of national borders. Territories are the place of exercising political power and controlling both in colonial and postcolonial contexts. Depending on who controls territories, the identities of natives change. What makes natives is closely connected with the issue of "territorial belonging."[93] When territory is the subject of nativism, it is not about who is born in the land or who arrives here first. Natives' birth rights and benefits are not the subject of nativism anymore. It is really about power to control the land. Whoever controls the land as their territory self-identifies as native. Self-identified natives who use nativism as a tool to control territories and their innate resources are not often existing inhabitants. Especially in the colonial era, self-identified natives were exclusively white colonizers. The concept of who natives are is not created by natives in their colonized countries. It is created by white colonizers who want to control the colony. When white colonizers occupied territory by using colonial force and violence, they sought to find the validity of their invasion. And their validity of invasion was always claimed as protecting their national interests in their motherlands.

To protect and expand their national interests beyond their national borders in the context of colonial patriotism, they needed cheap human capital and new territories. They controlled the resources in colonies as they controlled mobility to move the colonized people around between the colonizers' lands and colonies. At first, the colonizers brought the colonized from the colonies to their motherlands. They used the colonized to build the country. When they built the nation for certain projects, they recruited specifically targeted colonized groups to do these projects. If the project was about building railroads or digging mines, they recruited young male laborers. If the project was about providing domestic labor, they recruited young female laborers and experienced women laborers. The reason to claim nativism at this point was to legitimate drafting physical laborers from colonized groups to build the nation.

When they finished the projects and gained the benefits from the achieved projects, they sent those groups back to the colonies. They recruited the colonized from the colonies, moved them to the colonizers' lands and/or pulled them back from the colonizer's lands as they needed. Meanwhile, the colonized lands were destroyed, and resources were exhausted. Because of these horrible exploitations, some immigrants from the colonies resisted going back to their home countries. However, colonizers forced these immigrants to leave their lands. They did not want to extend any benefits or credits that the colonized worked for. As they used violence to recruit these people, they also used violence to banish them from their lands. They sent the colonized back to the colonies that they plundered and exploited. They used nativism as a valid rationale to remove the colonized from their motherlands. Nativism, at this point, claimed to protect natives' rights and the benefits of the colonizers from the colonized, who were now seen as thieves and free riders instead of nation builders. The meaning of protecting the rights and benefits of native-born and existing inhabitants is only referred to by colonizers. Nativism is never used to grant rights to the native-born descendants of the colonized in the colonizers' lands or to existing colonized inhabitants in the colonies. In this sense, nativism is not about protecting the rights and benefits of native-born and existing inhabitants. It is about protecting the rights and benefits of the colonizers.

When these rights and benefits are claimed as natives' in the U.S. context, they are claimed by European Anglo-Saxon white immigrants. They see the land of the United States as new territory to claim. Under the heavy colonial minds of territorial belongingness, they adopted territorial senses of nativism. The history of Native Americans is the prime example of this colonial exchange. For white European immigrants, the land was the place to invade and occupy. It did not matter whether they were born in that land or not. As long as they had power to occupy the space, they claimed to be natives in that land and exercised the rights and benefits for themselves as natives. In their colonial minds, the land was not associated with any spiritual or psychological sentiment. It was purely the subject of conquest. It was a place to control. It was a commodity to sell and trade. However, for Native Americans, the land was a spiritual concept. It was a space to connect people with the divine. It was a sacred place to be, not to have. The land symbolized a spiritual power. Land was considered the "specific portion of Spirit Earth on which a particular nation resides."[94] Native Americans have a deep-rooted spiritual sense of land. For them, the land was not the object to sell but to revere and protect. Because of this understanding, they had no concept of owning land.

When European immigrants encountered Native Americans in their land, they disdained the concept of Native Americans' land and took away all land rights from Native Americans. By designing the United States' legal system to support their colonial invasion, they criticized the different views of Native Americans' concepts of land as the subject of civilization and education. This attitude is clearly shown in the case of *Caldwell v. the State of Alabama* (1832). The legal decision was made that Native Americans have no right to own any lands, but have a right of occupancy only, whereas the rights of European colonizers was claimed as "right of discovery" to have ownership of the land.[95]

> The issue was whether the white government of the State of Alabama had jurisdiction in Creek Territory. The Creek Tribe claimed jurisdiction based on prior occupancy and governmental sovereignty. The tribe asserted that "possession acquired by force conferred no right" to Alabama since the state violated the "paramount natural right of the original occupants." Chief Justice Lipscomb dismissed the Creek claims with contempt. "We will examine this high pretention to savage sovereignty. If a people are found in the possession of a territory, in the practice of the arts of civilization, employed in the cultivation of the soil, and with an organized government, no matter what may be its form, they form an independent community; their rights shall be respected and their territorial limits not encroached on." Notwithstanding that the Creek Nation could thus be described in 1832, the justice declared that they were one of a number of "savage tribes without a written language, or established form of government, and wholly ignorant of the customs and usages of civil society, (and) are not capable of appreciating the principles of their code." Extending his remarks to include all Native American nations, in spite of the fact that he was ignorant of the governmental structure of the Creek Nation, he declared all tribes to be wandering hunters (not even descriptive of the Creek Tribe) and one might just as well make a treaty with "the beast of the same forest that he inhabits."
>
> Justice Taylor reinforced, in a more scholarly way, the views of Justice Lipscomb. He asserted the right of European immigrants to take land from the original inhabitants of the American continent by appealing to the "right of discovery," the doctrine that John Marshall enunciated in the McIntosh decision. He also asserted the right of military conquest as a means of acquiring land from Native people when needed on other occasions, and the right to acquire by purchase from Native tribes.[96]

European immigrants stole the land from Native Americans and claimed it as their territory. Here, nativism is not claimed as protecting the rights of native-born and existing inhabitants. Rather, it is claimed as right of discovery. Right of discovery itself is a clear product of colonialism. It is a superseded right of native-born and existing inhabitants. Whoever has power to take land has priority to claim the ownership of the land. It presents a pure intention of colonial nationalism. Creating the U.S. legal system, European immigrants declared the right of discovery as a right of the United States government. Their group's interests equated with national interests. They claimed that their needs were the needs of the nation and its sovereignty. They identified themselves as the nation itself. Even though Native Americans claimed their right as native-born and existing inhabitants, their claim was treated as disturbing the national interests. Their rights were minimized and dismissed. Creating the image of Native Americans as the subjects of civilization and assimilation, white colonizer groups successfully manipulated the legal system to support their colonial violence and legally control the land. Between 1887 and 1934, the General Allotment Act, also known as the Dawes Act, was enacted and Native Americans lost 100 million acres of reservation land.[97] Many Native Americans who refused this policy lost their claims to land and could not receive any legal protection. Furthermore, even when their lands were assigned by this legal act, these lands were often taken by white immigrants.

> The Allotment Act was particularly destructive because Native people were caught in the breech between their traditional spiritual associations with land and American values of land as a commodity to be exploited for financial reasons. Most Native peoples were not aware that particular geographic areas in which they lived were being claimed by a foreign people as exclusive territories. Many adults who were aware of what was happening refused to participate in the allotment system and thus lost any claims to land. In Oklahoma a version of the Indian land allotment system known as the Indian Welfare Act was put into effect. The tribal rolls were closed and tribal territories were broken up into land parcels and assigned to tribal members without legal protection. Indian babies on the rolls received allotments and were assigned white guardians. By the time these infant assignees reached legal age, their land had often passed to the ownership of the "guardian."[98]

The rights of European white immigrants always overpower the rights of others. The colonial process of overpowerfulness always collides with guided legality. As they create rules and laws to protect their privileges, their overpowerfulness is treated as protecting their national interests. Their individual and private interests become national interests. When they stole the land from Native Americans, they claimed their roles as the guardians or protectors of the nation. In a similar manner, when they invaded other lands outside of the U.S., they claimed their roles as the global leaders and peacemakers. European white immigrants legalized nativism in the name of their right of discovery to own the lands as their new territories over Native Americans, while they legitimated their colonial/postcolonial invasion as teaching civilization and sharing economic advancement. The logic of nativism changes depending on the contexts. However, it repeatedly affirms that nativism is invented for protecting the rights and benefits of the people who control territories. The rights of whoever controls territories are protected and legitimated.

What Makes Them Natives? Reinvention of Territorial Racism into Nativism

Nativism is constructed under the logic of the native/alien paradigm to discriminate against those who are "not one of us" in order to control territories and economic resources. This colonial notion of nativism within the native/alien binary paradigm is intrinsically connected with territorial racism. As European white colonizers became white settlers in the United States, they occupied new territories and claimed these territories as their own through the right of discovery. These actions of nativism were validated through the use of the native/alien paradigm. This paradigm generated racism to dismiss the presence of other racial ethnic groups in these territories. Racism originated from colonial obsession with territorial belongingness that was racially coded and territorially marked. Philip Kretsedemas calls this racism *territorial racism*. He understands that "territorial racism justifies discriminatory treatment by using racially coded, territorial distinctions to identify those who authentically belong to the territory and those who do not."[99] Territorial racism was invented to position people in the hierarchical order of race. In order to justify territorial belonging, territorial racism is used to discriminate against others who are supposedly different or inferior.

> Territorial racism sensitizes people to how "their group" is distributed and organized in a given space in relation to other groups that are presumed to be racially and culturally different from theirs. As a result, territorial distinctions become another way of expressing power relations through racialized categories. The fear of losing control of territory is really a concern about changing power and

status of the racialized categories of people who inhabit this territory. Conversely, the desire for territorial control is about achieving an optimal level of status and power for "your group" (which is
always being defined relative to the perceived status and power of
the others).[100]

Territorial racism was created to categorize various racial ethnic groups in
hierarchical order and control resources to protect the privileges and power
of the colonizers. It is a product of colonial practice from the fear of losing
control of territory after its colonial invasion and postcolonial occupation.
Because occupying territory does not automatically secure the colonizers'
position of power, territorial racism was invented and practiced as a way to
secure power and rule the colonized. As European white immigrants differentiate themselves from other racial immigrant groups, the logic of territorial
racism invented white superiority as the norm. Implanting racial categories
into racism, they claim their racial superiority as a reason to control territory. Based on their racial superiority and advancement of knowledge, they
claim the necessity to control other immigrant groups and resources for the
betterment of all people. They use racism and white superiority as essential
devices to control territory. However, racism and white superiority are not
enough to convince other racial groups to accept colonial control, including
their own white middle-class liberals in the postcolonial context. They need
a stronger political device to support their legitimacy to control the territory
beyond geographical occupation. Nativism, in the name of national security
and benefits, was adopted from this need. They adopted nativism to create a
stronger ideology to control human capital and resources. It became one of
the strongest apparatuses to reintensify territorial racism.

To understand territorial racism in the postcolonial context, even in
the absence of physical colonial territorial occupation, it is very important
to see how the native/alien binary divide reinvents territorial racism into
nativism. Investigating the relationship between territorial control, capitalism, and the modern state, Kretsedemas claims that territorial racism is the
main problem of the native/alien paradigm and "race and class inequality in
the US continues to be defined by patterns of white/black and black/non-
black stratification" through territorial racism.[101] As he analyzes patterns of
residential segregation, evaluating household wealth and collecting data for
employment and incarceration rates, he powerfully demonstrates how the
privileged white group controls not only themselves but also others: where
to live, with whom to live, how to live, and what to do for a living. The privileged white group uses territorial racism as the established norm to control
others and territorial resources. By transferring territorial racism in the colonial context to nativism in the postcolonial context, this group legitimates

territorial invasion and attempts to have total control over the territory and normalizes this process as the way things are.

Under the strong influences of territorial racism and its postcolonial impacts, race and class inequality between the privileged white group and other racial ethnic groups, including all immigrant groups, is easily justified within the white/black and black/nonblack binary approaches, which work side by side with the native/alien binary approach. Kretsedemas points out that this territorial racism has designated immigrants as "removable people" from the very beginning of their arrival in the U.S. and always legitimately puts them in a position to possibly "become illegal."[102] Positioning immigrants in the native/alien paradigm, black/white paradigm, citizen/noncitizen divide, and/ or legal/illegal distinction, territorial racism locates nativism as the center of a rising anti-immigrant mentality and puts immigrants in the margins of all these aspects. As territorial racism becomes a part of nativism, nativism becomes a part of territorial racism. The interaction between territorial racism and nativism intensifies their control over all immigrant groups in the name of national interests and security. Socioeconomic and political control, with or without geographical occupancy, always has been the main purpose of this territorial belongingness. To make sure that the immigrants are socioeconomically poor and politically powerless, territorial racism is constantly affirmed and exercised in the name of national interests in company with nativism.

Even though territorial racism has been in company with anti-immigrant racism historically and culturally, both territorial and anti-immigrant racism are not regarded as real racism and do not carry the same weight as black/ white binary racism. Rather, black/white binary racism is overused to minimize the issues of immigrants within the native/alien paradigm. Exhorting color blindness and cultural blindness, the native/alien binary construction grants nativism and excessively promotes racial discrimination under the black/white binary system. Within the native/alien binary divide, cultural blindness is justified and equalized with nativism. Within the black/white binary divide, color blindness is promoted and racism among nonwhite and nonblack groups is minimized. As nativism promotes cultural blindness against nonblack and nonwhite groups in the native/alien binary divide, racism keeps its boundary within black/white color blindness from nonblack and nonwhite groups.

Many nonwhite and nonblack immigrants, especially Asian immigrants, are caught in between. On the one hand, Asian immigrants are outsiders of the black/white binary divide. They are totally dismissed in this paradigm. Even if some Latinx and black groups can pass as white because of their light skin color and Western physical appearance, Asian immigrants do not have the possibility of passing as white because of their Asian appearance. They are treated as the people who belong to neither white nor black groups. They do not have any rights of discovery like white groups, and they do not claim any rights from building this country like black groups. In fact, they are not given any credit for building this country but are the people who received the payment. It is believed that they are *paid*.

The notion that "they are paid" has three assumptions in the native/alien divide. First, it is assumed that they are paid for what they came for. They are compensated for their work. They are just temporary employees who have no credits to claim. They work for the exact amounts of money that they are paid. There is no territory that they can claim in this nation. They have no right to claim they built this nation. Second, "they are paid" assumes that this country treats these workers fairly. It means that this country has no obligation to provide them any protections or give them any rights. They are temporary workers who need to go back to their motherlands. Third, "they are paid" means that immigrants should be grateful for their payment. It is believed that immigrants steal jobs from natives and get the payment instead of them. Based on this misbelief, the discussion of rights and bene- fits for their well-being is considered disgraceful. It implies that they need to show gratitude rather than demanding rights and benefits. Despite their cheap labor and hard work, their well-being and opportunities to improve their lives are ignored and even disdained. They are simply assumed to be aliens and immigrants who do not belong to this country. Immigrants are immigrants—not citizens, not a race. Because Asian immigrants are paid and compensated, it is understood that there is no need to have any further dis- cussion of their *foreign* problems. The permanent status or image of being "temporary workers" excludes Asian immigrants from any socioeconomic and political racial discourse, especially within the black/white divide.

On the other hand, Asian immigrants are perceived as permanent aliens within the native/alien binary paradigm. In fact, they had no legal rights to permanently stay in the United States until 1965 (Immigration and Nation- ality Act of 1965). It was not just the image that Asian immigrants carried as forever foreigners. Legally, they were permanently foreigners in this country for a long time. They could not be natives in the U.S. legal system. Their exis- tence has been systemically and culturally denied. Because it is believed that they are paid, it follows that natives have rights to remove them. Asian immi- grants are considered removable laborers. In this paradigm, Asian immi- grants are the people who are always expected to leave. They are removable laborers, commodities, who inevitably have to go back to their motherlands, regardless. Furthermore, within this native/alien divide, there is another layer that many Asian immigrant groups uniquely face. In the recent immi- grant situations, the native/alien binary presents immigrants' issues as exclu- sively Latinx issues. Many immigrant movements are organized by Latinx populations and led by Latinx immigrant leaders. When immigrant rights are discussed in public, it becomes heavily Latinx issues only.[103] Exclusively framing immigrant issues as Latinx issues, the native/alien binary paradigm gives more attention to Latinx immigrants and conveniently ignores other immigrants' difficulties. Lifting up Latinx groups as the only immigrant group, this paradigm dismisses the voices of other immigrant groups, including Asian immigrant groups. Asian immigrant groups are immigrants, but not immigrants enough in the native/alien divide.

As the black/white binary divide depicts black groups as the targeted group to dismiss other racial sufferings, the native/alien binary divide casts Latinx groups as the targeted group to dismiss other racial immigrant problems. The issues and difficulties of Asian immigrants are not considered in either binary divide. Both binary divides intentionally erase the issues of Asian immigrants in public. Their concerns are silenced and presented as the issues of foreigners and visitors, not even immigrants. When they raise their experience of racism with black and white groups, their voices become either the echoes of black experiences or the defense of white privileges. When they share the concerns of Asian immigrant issues, their immigrant experience is coded with the minority model myth and used to mute Latinx immigrant issues. In the intersection between black/white and native/alien binary divides, Asian immigrant groups stand as neither white nor black and as neither completely natives nor completely aliens. Both divides deny the presence of Asian immigrant groups and locate them in an ambiguous position to be marginalized and often conveniently used for blame. Their struggles against racism within the black/white binary paradigm are minimized, and their issues of immigrant struggles within the native/alien binary paradigm are treated as visitors' complaints. Their in-betweenness continues, not only in the black/white binary, but also in the native/alien binary in the end.

Both black/white and native/alien binary constructions have eradicated the voices of Asian immigrants from any political issues. These constructions impose the images of Asian immigrants on invisible natives and visible foreigners. Even though they become legalized as citizens in law and change their status as existing inhabitants in this country, their existence is still perceived as temporary visitors and workers. Their physical and cultural presence is perceived as distinctive foreignness, displayed for public mockery. In fact, their visible foreign presence is often covered with "voice-over narratives."[104] Their native languages are voiced over with English captions, and their accents are used for mimicry and mockery in the form of humor.[105] Even if they might be on screen as the main actors, their actions and performances are already evaluated and narrated with "voice-over interpretation." Inequality between the power of English and the subjugation of immigrants' languages legitimates not only voice-over narratives but also voice-over interpretation. They are pictured as foreigners, and their voices are muted in the intersection between black/white and native/alien binary divides. Their

Asianness becomes the shadow for the black and white stage. Both black/ white and native/alien binary constructions generate voice-over narratives and voice-over interpretations to marginalize the presence of Asian immigrants in the public square. They create distorted and disfigured images of Asian immigrants as a group who does not deserve equal rights and opportunities, but have already taken and enjoy these rights and opportunities. Their struggle against racial discrimination is interpreted as the desire to have white privileges and/or a threat of dismissing black suffering. As long as these voice-over narratives and voice-over interpretations guide immigrant problems as Latinx problems in the native/alien divide, and as long as African Americans are seen as "the real aliens"[106] in the black/white binary paradigm, both black/ white and native/alien binary constructions can efficaciously carry out the mission: white colonial and postcolonial domination against all groups is forgotten, forgiven, and justified.

In summary, "'nativism' is associated with an exclusionary impulse directed toward the foreigner within; it suggests animosity or bias, in other words, toward *immigrants*, or toward aspiring immigrants."[107] It tries to establish the dangerously clear line between natives and immigrants. It always claims that it serves national interests. In the colonial and postcolonial contexts, serving national interests means justifying colonial invasion and exploitation to extend colonizers' territory. To protect the interests of natives who were white colonizers/settlers in a colonial era, white colonizers/settlers forcibly captured the colonized and used their labor in and outside of the colony. In the postcolonial era, European white settlers/immigrants control the formally colonized groups and non-white immigrant groups to work toward building their nations. As soon as these white groups control their new territories, they self-identify as natives of the territories and claim their exclusive rights as rights of natives. Natives in this sense are not the people who are born in the new territories or existing inhabitants but the people who invade and control the territories. They now become natives, whereas existing inhabitants become aliens from their own lands and become immigrants in the colonizers' lands. This colonial and postcolonial mind uses nativism as a political strategy to control the others. It installs the native/alien binary divide as a paradigm to distinguish white and nonwhite groups. It is another powerful form of white hegemony to legitimate their discrimination against nonwhite racial ethnic groups. As nonwhite racial ethnic immigrants become the complete other, the native/alien paradigm becomes the most powerful postcolonial apparatus to dismiss the presence of many nonwhite immigrants, including Asian immigrants.

Within the intersections of black/white and native/alien binary divides, the problems of African American groups are presented as the issues of justice and reconciliation, and the conflicts of Latinx immigrant groups are introduced as the issues of human rights at the expense of each other. As the black/white binary dismisses the issues of racial discriminations against nonwhite and nonblack groups as a threat to national security over black lives, the native/alien binary erases the issues of black lives as the second priority over immigrant problems. Separating the racial issues of African Americans from other racial groups, the black/white binary paradigm successfully achieves its goal: dismissing nonwhite groups, including black groups, as the other. It minimizes various problems and conflicts of various racial groups into one single foreigner problem. It mismarks African Americans as *the* problem of society and discharges other racial groups from the discussion table of justice and equality. Separating the immigrant issues of Latinx immigrant groups from other immigrant groups, the native/alien binary paradigm also completes the same mission, dismissing nonwhite groups as the other. It supresses various immigrant issues into the single issue of Latinx problems and dismisses other immigrant voices. Both black/white and native/alien binary divides cultivate suspicion in each group and raise fear against each other in the mode of competition.

Under the intersection of these binary divides, Asian immigrant voices are minimized and turned into voice-over metanarratives that "valorize" their Asian immigrant lives. Various problems related to institutional and structural racism are muted and denied.[108] These binary constructions dominate the ears of the public and prohibit Asian immigrant voices from speaking. Exclusively emphasizing black/white racism and Latinx immigrant problems as a focus of attention, these constructions foster racial "alienation."[109] The function of both binary concepts is the same to Asian immigrants. It is the elimination of Asian immigrants' presence in public. It puts them in the position of in-betweenness and marginality. As Asian immigrants are seen as neither white nor black in the black/white binary divide, and as they are seen as neither completely natives nor completely aliens in the native/alien binary divide, they experience double marginalization. As the black/white binary construction accelerates and complicates relationships among nonwhite and nonblack groups, Asian immigrants are either ignored by white and black groups or bullied by both groups. Even within the native/alien binary divide, their position of in-betweenness continues. Asian immigrants are often trapped in the intersections of black/white and native/alien binary divides, which collide to discriminate against them. However, this trap is always hidden and never discussed in public. Both binary paradigms successfully use Asian immigrants to blind the public and protect white privilege and negate nonwhite groups.

These multiple complications jeopardize Asian immigrants' relationships with other racial groups. However, the in-betweenness of black/white and native/alien binary divides is not the only predicament that Asian immigrant groups are in. Among the many predicaments, four issues will be addressed in the next chapter: racial triangulation, anti-Asian immigrant sentiment, the minority versus nonminority debate, and the difficulties faced in coalition work with other racial groups. Combining the black/white binary divide with the native/alien binary divide, these four points produce more complications for Asian immigrants. These impediments put Asian immigrants in an impossible situation as they attempt to build their relationships with other groups equally and harmoniously.

CHAPTER 2

Unique Relational Challenges for Asian Immigrants

Racial Triangulation

Triangulation is "the tracing and measurement of a series or network of triangles in order to survey and map out a territory or region, *spec.* by measuring the angles and one side of each triangle."[1] In order to know where the object is or what the object is, it is important to have three elements, including the object itself. Triangulation is a necessary technique to define not only the location of the object but also the relationship with other objects. It assumes four things. First, triangulation is about the proof of existence. Existence itself is not a concern for this concept. It is about how to *prove* its existence. If it cannot be proved, it does not matter whether the object really exists or not. Second, existence itself does not need any proof to exist; but in order to prove one's existence in certain space and certain time, it requires certain elements: three objects and the relations of these three objects. Three objects in these relations are the precondition to prove one's existence. Each object exists in a condition of simultaneous presence (certain time) of three objects and their relations (certain space). Without three objects in certain space and certain time, it cannot prove that each object is in existence. Togetherness requires each object to be in the same place and time. It gives the object public validity for its own existence. Third, without one object in a different position, two objects are not comparable in value. Two objects can compare each other and claim their own subjectivity. However, with only two objects, there is no objectivity that can be claimed. In other words, two objects can compare and argue, but there is no conclusion or judgment to be made without the third element. The third element brings the validity of truth. Fourth, when three elements are provided, two elements are often used to measure values of the third element. It assumes that two elements are used as the proved axiom to evaluate the third element. The goal of triangulation is to give two elements authority of their existence and measure the third element in relative objectivity. The third element is often the subjectivity of the measurement, and two other elements are used as the norm to compare. In other words, depending on the values that two other elements have built, the value of the third element is decided. With these assumptions in place, triangulation is often used to measure one's own subjectivity in agreement with two other elements.

In philosophy and language, triangulation was introduced as an analogy by Donald Davidson. He refers to triangulation in this way: "The basic situation is one that involves two or more creatures simultaneously in interaction with each other and with the world that they share."[2] Triangulation reflects relationships among creatures, which creates a social condition in human society. In his paper, "Rational Animals," Davidson argues that in order to prove belief, it is necessary to commend subjective-objective contrast. However, the "*only* way one could come to have the subjective-objective contrast is through having the concept of intersubjective truth."[3] He claims that intersubjective truth is the only truth that one can discover. Belief is from the concept of each person's personal truth. Everyone holds one's truth, which is subjective truth, even though people often claim their personal truth as the objective truth. In order to find or create *the* truth, the objective truth, it is necessary to share their beliefs by communication, language, culture, experience, and so forth. However, by sharing their differences and contrasts through communication, what people find is a "shared world, an intersubjective world,"[4] not the objective truth. Even if they remain in disagreement at the conclusion of the discussion, the process of disagreement still requires sharing their thoughts and understanding the world before they agree or disagree. On what they agree or disagree is not the objective truth, but the intersubjective truth that they often claim as the objective truth. Within the logic of triangulation, intersubjective truth is the only truth that people can find.

This intersubjective truth originates from differences. From different perspectives, experiences, and beliefs, it creates a common shared space, world, and vision. Triangulation is not a process of becoming the same. It is a simultaneous process of finding similarities and understanding differences. Difference becomes the intersubjective truth itself in a shared world. Difference can be the main source of creating the intersubjective truth. Finding intersubjective truth is not about discovering the Truth in the proof of existence, even though it is always used to legitimate the intersubjective truth as the Truth in human relationships. It is a process of finding, creating, and/ or re-creating truths in the form of existing. Intersubjective truth is always moving and changing. It is not the Truth in a fixed form, but truths in a consistent and concomitant process. By representing differences as unique truths, triangulation proves values of the intersubjective truth.

In this process, triangulation shows that thoughts can be empirical objects. It "is presented both as a condition on empirical reference and as a principle for the determination of empirical referents."[5] When triangulation becomes a condition and a principle, it holds the power of interpretation and communication. It interprets empirical reference as a social condition and communicates between empirical referents in the position of comparison. When the concept of triangulation is employed by sociology, anthropology, religious studies, cultural studies, immigrant studies, postcolonial studies, and other fields of study, the neutrality of triangulation is seriously challenged. The common concept of triangulation assumes neutrality among three elements. The three elements interact but do not have the power to eliminate each other in theory. Rather, this interaction expects the process of "circularity" and "mutual knowledge."[6] It claims a certain equality. Three elements are presented in equal power to create the intersubjective truth. The power of objectivity in triangulation comes from this positional equality. This positional equality holds the power of objectivity. As long as three elements play in equal power positions, the intersubjective truth can be accepted and presented equally. In other words, if three elements are not in an equal position, the intersubjective truth cannot be created equally. This means that the intersubjective truth can be dominated by one perspective that holds more power even though it would still be presented in public as the intersubjective truth in a process of equal collaboration.

When the concept of triangulation is adopted in racial discourse, neutrality of triangulation is broken because three or more races interact with each other with different power and privileges under unequal social conditions. They interact but react with different perspectives based on different social conditions and power. As we observe the colonial past and postcolonial present, their different perspectives are not equally voiced. The voice of white colonizers/settlers and their descendants dominates, and the voices of other groups are voiced over with a white colonial and postcolonial metanarrative. The intersubjective truth is controlled by these white groups. It itself becomes a voice-over interpretation. Racial triangulation never stays in a neutral position to define who people are equally. As it circulates, it attempts to eliminate certain races or put them in certain positions. Instead of providing mutual knowledge to share from all races in equal power, the racial triangulation process is controlled by white colonial power. It selects or produces certain manipulated knowledge and delivers it as shared knowledge. In this circulative process, the intersubjective truth is narrated by white morality and coded in the white colonial past and postcolonial present. It usually tries to hypnotize nonwhite and nonblack races to believe white normativity is the way things are in the rules of U.S. society. Triangulation is used as an apparatus of racism to legitimate white normativity.

When triangulation interacts with the black/white binary divide, this interaction repeatedly puts nonblack and nonwhite immigrant groups, especially Asian immigrant groups, in a triangular position between whites and blacks. Even though Asian immigrants are often invisible in this binary paradigm and are treated as a group outside of this binary structure, they are usually caught up in the position of triangulation. Holding blacks and whites as the points of measurement objectives, they are used to maintain and support the dominant structure for whites. At the same time, they are perceived as pseudowhites, honorary whites, or a model minority, and they receive a lot of criticism for mimicking whiteness separate from black, Latinx, and other racial groups. This is a crucial element, and the impact on model minority theory will be more thoroughly discussed in a later section. Racial triangulation becomes the beachhead to isolate Asian immigrants from both white and nonwhite groups. It places Asian immigrants in a double marginalized position within the black/white binary system.

Racial triangulation uses blacks as the point of *differentiation from* in the black/white binary divide, just as it uses Asian immigrants as the point of *dissociation from* in the native/alien binary divide. Within the black/nonblack binary divide, black groups are used as the object from which to differentiate. Nonblack groups, including white groups, try to demonstrate how different they are from black groups. From skin color to socioeconomic behaviors, nonblack groups try to illustrate their nonblackness. In this binary, Asian immigrants also try to distinguish themselves from blacks. As discussed above in the section on the black/white binary divide, Asian immigrants are forced to adopt racial triangulation by making the point that they are not blacks in the black/nonblack binary framework. They are forced to erase their identities and accept a nonblack identity as their identity. Claiming that they are not blacks and better than blacks, Asian immigrants present themselves as near whites, as seen in the case of Chinese immigrants in the Mississippi Delta. Before 1952, without any possibility of becoming citizens in this country, Asian immigrants had to find a strategy to survive in the U.S. black/white context. As they observed and experienced the heavy oppressive influences of the black/white and native/alien binary paradigms, they tried to put themselves nearer to white than black and made an intentional differentiation from blacks to advance their lives. They employed racial triangulation as a survival strategy.

Within the native/alien binary paradigm, it is not blacks but Asian immigrants who are the object from which to dissociate for both white and black citizens. They are perceived as foreigners who cannot be associated with. In the native/alien binary divide, Asian immigrants are not the object to prove how different they are from black groups because their foreignness already proves that they are neither black nor white. Their foreignness supersedes blackness in this divide. They are the object with which both white and black groups cannot associate. Their difference is marked as foreignness, and this foreignness is impossible to associate with. It does not matter that they are not black or better than black. It does not matter how similar they are to white. It is perceived as something dangerous to associate with in terms of national security and interests. In this perception, Asian immigrants become the object that both white and black groups have to dissociate from.

Racial triangulation locates Asian immigrants in-between and in-neither whiteness and blackness in black/white and native/alien binary divides. Claire Jean Kim's model of racial triangulation is a good example to explain this simultaneous dynamic. She illustrates the process of racial triangulation for Asian Americans with two types.

> Racial triangulation occurs by means of two types of simultaneous, linked processes: (1) processes of " relative valorization," whereby dominant group A (Whites) valorizes subordinate group B (Asian Americans) relative to subordinate group C (Blacks) on cultural and/or racial grounds in order to dominate both groups, but especially the latter, and (2) processes of "civic ostracism," whereby dominant group A (Whites) constructs subordinate group B (Asian Americans) as immutable foreign and unassimilable with Whites on cultural and/or racial grounds in order to ostracize them from the body politic and civic membership.[7]

Describing how white colonial/postcolonial racial dominance exercises its power historically and sociopolitically in concert with colorblindness from the mid-1800s to the twentieth century, Kim shows that racial triangulation is used as a critical device to exclude Asian immigrants from any political and social participation in society and to ensure white privileges.[8] As she claims, racial triangulation is a "simultaneous, linked process." When whites valorize Asians over blacks, they simultaneously ostracize Asians. I argue that this simultaneous process is accelerated within the intersection between black/white and native/alien binary divides because whites valorize Asian immigrants in comparison with blacks in both divides. At the same time, the native/alien binary divide ostracizes Asian immigrants as foreigners and unassimilable aliens. Even though it is the black groups who are mainly targeted for domination in the black/white binary divide, it is Asian immigrant groups who are mainly used to criticize black groups in the dynamics of racial triangulation. Racial triangulation targets Asian immigrants to be representatives of nonblack groups who become whites instead of whites judging nonblack groups.

Asian immigrant groups are the main object of racial triangulation. As soon as Asian immigrants stepped on U.S. soil, they were framed by racial triangulation under colonial/postcolonial white power. The purpose of framing Asian immigrant groups under racial triangulation is to establish racial hierarchy and confirm racial superiority for whites. The function of racial triangulation tries to ensure that black and white racial lines exist. It holds racial lines as the intersubjective or the objective truth. The black/white binary paradigm utilizes racial triangulation to stabilize the hierarchy of whites at the top and blacks at the bottom. Locating the position of Asian immigrants in between a black/white binary order, it treats Asian immigrants as intermediary groups: not so superior to whites, not so inferior to blacks, not so equal with whites, not so deserving rights like blacks, but still not so average either. Even though they are "supposed to be in the middle position" in this black/white binary system of hierarchy, being in the middle position is not attainable because the goal of racial triangulation is not putting Asian immigrants in the middle of the hierarchy. Rather, racial triangulation uses them as the object of comparison to support the black/white binary divide and casts Asians as substitution for cheap labor.

Asian immigrant sexuality is another good example of this racial triangulation. When Chinese immigration started, many young Chinese male immigrants came to the U.S. without their wives and children. However, by law, they were neither allowed to marry any other races nor to bring any women from China. This situation shaped Asian men's sexuality as undersexed. Racial triangulation presents this situation in a more complicated manner. In the comparison with overemphasis on black male hypersexuality and masculinity, Asian men's sexuality is understood as "undersexed," "effeminate," "asexual" and/or "homosexual."[9] In comparison with white male domination in terms of sexuality and masculinity, Asian men's sexuality is understood as "not real men" who "must be refused access to white women, lest they threaten the purity of the race."[10] Whites valorize Asian men to work better than black men, whereas they ridicule Asian men's sexuality in comparison with black men. While whites within the black/white binary structure give "validation" to Asian men as hard workers, they make sure that Asian men's sexuality is incomplete in comparison with white men. As they control Asian men's sexuality, they exploit Asian men's cheap labor.

Relative valorization is used as a trap to control both Asian immigrant groups and African American groups. Validating the presence of Asian immigrant groups over disdaining the presence of African American groups is a toxic racial triangulation strategy to secure the path of white supremacy. Both of these groups are victimized and marginalized in this process. As Asian immigrants are put in a mode of hideous competition with African American groups, they are forced to show their loyalty to white society. Prioritizing white dominance is the main goal of racial triangulation. Employing racial triangulation, the black/white binary structure recognizes the existence of Asian immigrant groups in comparison between blacks and whites but does not recognize the existence of Asian immigrants by themselves. By using the existence of blacks, whites, and Asian immigrants, existence of each race is proved, but by interactions of these races in unequal social conditions, the existence of Asian immigrants is continuously contested.

Whether Asian immigrant groups accept white racism against blacks voluntarily or not, the black/white binary structure lures them into believing white racism as the way it is. In between, differentiating from blacks and assimilating with whites, Asian immigrant groups have to learn how to stay and not to stay in between. Witnessing the mistreatment of blacks, they strategize how to distinguish themselves from blacks and how not to be treated like blacks. Observing the impossibility of assimilation with whites, they maneuver how to stay out of white territories and boundaries. They are taught to accept relative valorization as compensation for their middle position. Relative valorization validates racial triangulation as a way to show how Asian immigrant groups achieve better statuses. By measuring certain Asian elite immigrant groups' economic achievement in comparison with black groups, relative valorization presents Asian immigrant groups as evidence to praise white ways of colonization and modernization. Because the goal of racial triangulation is supporting white dominant normativity, after its use, civic ostracism of Asian immigrants naturally follows. As Asian immigrants distinguish themselves from blacks, it proves that they are different from whites simultaneously. Their distinctiveness from both blacks and whites in the logic of racial triangulation is used as an evidence to prove their unassimilable foreignness. Racial triangulation uses their foreignness as the point of difference from blacks and whites, but at the same time as the point of invalidity in black/white relations. It locates Asian immigrants as the object of ostracization.

This racial triangulation is not just measured in a monodimension. As Kim uses "fields of racial position"[11] to move beyond a linear singular approach to understand black/white racial dynamics, fields of racial position extend its measures with various multidimensional approaches. Jun Xu and Jennifer C. Lee provide multidimensional racial triangulation approaches to show how Asian immigrants are recognized in various social conditions. They believe that a singular hierarchical approach cannot provide the proper picture of the Asian immigrant position in the black/white binary system. From multidimensional racial triangulation approaches, they suggest that "on average whites are more likely than blacks to have more favorable views of the relative positions of Asians, particularly for family commitment, nonviolence, wealth, but blacks are more likely to assume racially egalitarian views than do whites."[12] In this research, Asian immigrants are perceived as the model minority at the top of the hierarchy in certain areas, rather than in the middle of the hierarchy. However, at the same time, they are viewed as low in certain areas, such as the feeling thermometer, desirability in living in the same community, marriageability, and patriotism.[13] Especially regarding civic ostracism, Asian immigrant groups are seen in a similar position as blacks.[14]

Xu and Lee's research demonstrates how whites and blacks show different attitudes toward Asian immigrants on certain issues. When racial triangulation measures for relative valorization and civic ostracism in various areas, it shows different results. In the measure of relative valorization, Asian immigrants are measured high in certain areas, but in the measure of civic ostracism, they are measured low. In the process of racial triangulation, what Asian immigrants find is discriminations from both white and black groups. They are often instructed by white society on where to stand and how to obey. They try to stay in line with whites. At the same time, they are often in a conflict between blacks and Latinx groups but stay with them in shared social conditions. In the eyes of other racial groups, they are perceived as nearly white. In the eyes of whites, they are perceived as nonwhite. In their own eyes, they are confused by their new immigrant identities.

Politics is another example of unique challenges that only Asian immigrant groups experience. When Asian Americans run for political office, Min Hee Go argues, they experience racial triangulation during the election. For example, when the issue of welfare in general comes to the public's attention, it is usually approached as a white issue, whereas when this issue comes to certain welfare programs like Medicaid, it becomes a black issue.[15] In a similar manner, immigration issues are perceived more as Latinx issues than as Asian immigrant issues. Racial triangulation puts Asian political candidates in a weaker position to compete with other candidates. In this process they are politically triangulated and relationally marginalized. "The bottom line is that Asian Americans and Blacks experience inequality between each other, tension with each other, while simultaneously serving as referents to each other."[16] From labor and employment markets, housing segregation, political election, and education opportunities to religious and cultural ostracism from the political social economic sphere to the individual private sphere, racial triangulation exercises its power to maintain and fortify current white domination.

However, in this racial triangulation schema, the presence of whiteness is invisible. It disappears from the main stage but controls the main stage from the backstage. White groups are not the object of comparison. They are not the groups to compare. They are the standard. What people see on the stage are the struggles between other racial groups. What they hear is the voice-over narrative from white public speakers. Racial triangulation is played as a voice-over interpretation to justify white privilege as the way things are and to disregard the conflicts between other racial groups. It is controlled by white voice-over narratives in both public and private spheres without contesting the discriminatory practices that other racial groups experience under white dominant culture.

Racial triangulation is adopted by both black/white and native/alien binary paradigms. It is part of the strategy that these paradigms develop. Both paradigms function as two correlated elements to frame racial triangulation to measure Asian immigrants as the third object. When Asian immigrants are racially triangulated between black/white and native/alien paradigms, they are perceived as adversaries from both sides. Not because they are located in the middle between black groups, Latinx groups, and white groups but because they are neither white nor black nor Latinx, they are negated by black, Latinx, and white groups. Not because they are foreigners but because of their perceived foreignness, they are negated as aliens. Not because they are neither natives nor aliens but because they are neither completely natives nor completely aliens, they are negated by black, white, and Latinx groups. Both paradigms triangulate Asian immigrant groups. These paradigms claim their own knowledge as mutual knowledge and their perspective as a shared perspective. However, this shared perspective and mutual knowledge are provided by the dominant white structure between the dynamics of these two paradigms. Under the dynamics of these paradigms, racial triangulation negates the presence of Asian immigrants. It claims this negation as the objective truth. As the black/white binary paradigm positions Asian immigrants as common adversaries from both sides, the native/alien paradigm puts Asian immigrants in a position of outsiders and temporary insiders simultaneously. Within the intersection of black/white and native/alien paradigms, Asian immigrant groups are doubly discriminated against. Racial triangulation dismisses discrimination against Asian immigrants because it perpetuates black/white and native/alien binary divides to legitimate discrimination against Asian immigrants as the intersubjective truth. The process of these simultaneous intersections and interactions of racial triangulation makes the presence of Asian immigrants more problematic and vulnerable. Their perceived foreignness is used as a reason to refortify the circular racial triangulation process. As it is circulated, it becomes more distinctive and challenging. It evokes more competition and discrimination among all racial groups, including whites. In consequence, anti-Asian immigrant sentiment is cultivated through this circular process of racial triangulation colliding with black/white and native/alien binary paradigms.

Anti-Asian Immigrant Sentiment

The news web site MSNBC is apologizing for a headline that seemed to suggest figure skater Michelle Kwan was not an American. Asian-American groups were taken aback by the headline, "American Beats Out Kwan," saying it suggests a reluctance to acknowledge that they are United States citizens. "It's simply an indication of how far we still have to go in this country to understand that we are a diverse society," said Herbert Yamanishi, national director of the Japanese American Citizens League. "Maybe there's a little progress in that they don't see (figure skater Tara) Lipinski as a foreign name anymore, as they used to," he added, tongue in cheek. "It's an error for which they apologize," said Sandra Michioku, executive director of the Asian American Journalists Association, "but it still showed an insensitivity and encourages the stereotype of Asian Americans as foreigners. Anyone who knows Michelle Kwan knows she is an American."[17]

When Rep. David Wu (D-Ore.), the only Chinese American ever elected to Congress, attempted to enter the building Wednesday to give a speech to Asian Americans in celebration of Asian Pacific American Heritage Month, two guards refused to admit him. He was asked three times if he was an American, his office said, and the guards refused to accept Wu's congressional identification for admittance. . . . After about 15 minutes, the Hill folks asked for a supervisor and a lieutenant came over to straighten things out. The explanation was that congressional IDs are easy to fake, so one can never be too careful. But Wu communications director Holly Armstrong says Capitol Police recall only one incident of possible congressional ID forgery, 20 years ago and never proven. Wu mentioned the encounter to his pal, Rep. Michael E. Capuano (D-Mass.), who went to the Energy Department yesterday to test security. Capuano and two aides signed in, checked the form asking if they were Americans and entered with no trouble, Armstrong said. "There was a mix-up" involving Wu, said DOE spokeswoman Jeanne Lopatto. Wu came in through the basement and his escort was waiting on the first floor, she said. But "everyone who comes to the building has to check the form as to whether they are Americans," she said. "Our security people did exactly what they were supposed to do. The Department of Energy takes security matters very seriously and we will continue to do so." Both congressmen, she said, were treated "exactly the same."[18]

Even though the actual headline, "American Beats Out Kwan," ran about 15 minutes, 85,000 subscribers received news alert service.[19] This headline revealed the secret that Asian immigrants did not belong to U.S society yet and never would. This incident can be interpreted through two points. First, it clearly implies that Michelle Kwan is not an American. She is treated as a foreigner who was defeated by an American.[20] The native/alien binary brings about the perception that Kwan is a foreigner because she is perceived only as an Asian. In this binary, she is unconsciously and consciously classified as a foreigner. The black/white binary brings about the perception that she is not a person of color because she is an Asian. "Why should we allow foreigners to claim they are minorities?"[21] Only blacks are allowed as people of color minorities. In this paradigm, she is classified as neither white nor black but just a foreigner, embodying the nonpersonhood of minority status. In the intersection between the black/white and native/alien binary, she can be recognized neither as an American nor as a person of color minority. Second, it can be described in a racialized context that Kwan, an Asian American woman, was beaten by a white American woman. Within the black/white binary paradigm, Kwan was treated as an Asian woman who should not beat a *white* woman. Within the native/alien binary paradigm, she was perceived as an alien woman who should not beat a white *American* woman. Even though Kwan was the representative of the U.S. Olympics, her Asian body was interpreted as a foreign body; therefore, her citizenship was dropped.

In a similar manner, Wu is perceived as a foreigner, a noncitizen. It is assumed that there is no possibility that he can be a U.S. representative or a U.S. citizen. His Asian figuration precedes his legal documentation. His identification was not recognized as the proper documentation, even though it was indeed the only proper documentation that security would accept in that space. His being in an Asian body was not accepted in Congress. His "supposed to be a foreign presence" is not allowed in U.S. politics. Even though it was proven that his white colleague was treated better the next day, it was said that it was "exactly the same" treatment. The "better treatment" was the fact, but it was denied. Rather, voice-over interpretation hid the fact. The better treatment was hidden, and authority figures claimed the two received the same treatment. In this context, the same treatment means the better treatment for white groups and the discriminative treatment for Asian immigrants. If white groups and Asian immigrant groups are treated equally, it is not "the same treatment." Both privileges and discrimination were concealed and presented as "exactly the same." White privileges are equalized with discrimination against Asian immigrants. Both white privileges and discrimination against immigrants are understood as the same treatment in the eyes of the white dominant society. For white groups, access is granted. They have freedom to be anywhere and everywhere they want to be. Their freedom is their privilege. However, it is not recognized as privilege, but as the way things are. For Asian immigrants, access is denied. They do not have freedom to be anywhere, but occasionally freedom is given over a limited amount of time and temporary access is granted for specific places. It is not recognized as discrimination but as the way things are. In the eyes of white domination, this limited accessibility is the *normal* treatment for Asian immigrant groups. In this context, "exactly the same treatment" means that privileges are granted only for white groups not as an exception but as the way things are. White privileges equate with discrimination against Asian immigrant groups. In the eyes of white institutions, discrimination against immigrants is not discrimination. It is claimed as a necessary and proper procedure to protect a common good. Even though this common good is achieved at the expense of discrimination and alienation against Asian immigrant groups, it is claimed that institutional discrimination never exists. There is no discrimination against any groups in the eyes of white institutions. If discrimination ever occurs and is ever caught, it is usually dismissed as an individual mistake or a mix-up. It is treated as the people's personal sensitivity or overreaction.

Black/white binary and native/alien binary paradigms dismiss the existence of discrimination against Asian immigrants and cultivate anti-Asian sentiment. The suffering of Asian immigrants is denied. Existence of anti-Asian sentiment or racial discrimination against Asian immigrants is not registered in the public domain. Anti-Asian sentiment is conveniently recognized as individual mistakes. Because of this atmosphere, anti-Asian sentiment does not draw any attention in the media and public discussion. It is not treated seriously as injustice. It is quickly erased and easily forgotten. Anti-Asian sentiment is always perceived as a matter of individual dispute. However, this sentiment is not a recent phenomenon. It has existed from the first day of Asian immigrants' arrivals to the U.S.

When Chinese immigrants were brought to the United States to supply cheap labor as the substitute for the free labor of slaves, they suffered from bigotry and discrimination. They were treated as slaves. The case of *In re Ah Yup* in 1878 revealed the clear legal discrimination against Chinese immigrants. The Ninth Circuit Court in California ruled that "Mongolian" petition of citizenship could not be granted because Chinese (Mongolian) persons are not white. This verdict was greatly affirmed by white groups to ensure that "only white immigrants—'Caucasians'—could become citizens."[22] The Chinese Exclusion Act of 1882 was granted and remained effective until 1943. This act had a huge impact on Asian immigrant populations. It started as a temporary exclusion act but was extended and became permanent. The permanent exclusion was sanctioned. All ethnic minority races were permanently excluded from membership in U.S. society. Knowing the vulnerability of Asian immigrant statuses and recognizing their difference as foreignness, white domination created serious anti-Asian sentiment.

The serious impacts of this law have continued even after this law was abolished in 1943. In fact, many discriminatory laws and policies against Asian immigration were not changed until 1952, when the McCarran-Walter Act granted naturalization for Asian immigrants.[23] Because of the Chinese Exclusion Act, not only Chinese immigrants but also all Asian immigrants have been discriminated against and marginalized under anti-immigrant sentiment. The common perception about Chinese and/or Asian immigrants was and still is that they are temporary residents, even in the twenty-first century. Not only Chinese immigrants but also other Asian immigrants have been treated as people who could not and should not stay in the U.S. and must go back to their own countries. They are legally used by white society to provide labor and also legally forced to return to their motherlands. The bird of passage was created legally and legitimately. This legal immigrant history has intensely and intentionally cultivated the images of the perpetual foreigner and alien toward Asian immigrants and makes them the subject of discrimination and violence.

Anti-Japanese sentiment is another form of discrimination that Japanese Americans suffered. It showed the clear white racist nature to cultivate anti-Asian sentiment. During the Second World War, crimes against Japanese immigrants were officially and legally committed. Without any charges or trials, but by order of law, all civilians of Japanese ancestry experienced suffering at the hands of the military. Anti-Asian sentiment was shamelessly discussed and irreversibly confirmed in public. Legislation was ordered and signed.

> WHEREAS, The successful prosecution of the war requires every possible protection against espionage and against sabotage. . . .
> NOW THEREFORE, By virtue of authority vested in me as President of the United States, and Commander in Chief of the Army and Navy, I hereby authorize and direct the Secretary of War, and the Military Commanders whom he may from time to time designate, whenever he or any designated Commander deems such action necessary or desirable, to prescribe military areas in such places and of such extent as he or the appropriate Military Commander may determine, from which any or all persons may be excluded, and with respect to which, the right of any person to enter, remain in, or leave shall be subject to whatever restriction the Secretary of War, or the appropriate Military Commander may impose in his discretion. . . .
> I hereby further authorize and direct the Secretary of War . . . to enforce compliance with the restrictions . . . including the use of

Federal troops. . . . I hereby further authorize . . . to assist the Sec-
retary of War . . . in . . . prescribing regulations for the conduct and
control of alien enemies.[24]

The action was justified by President Franklin Roosevelt and delivered by
the military in the form of violence in 1942. About 120,000 Japanese immigrants who were of Japanese origin and ancestry were permanently removed
from their homes and workplaces and incarcerated.[25] Even though most of
them were U.S. citizens, the wartime legal discourse turned them into alien
enemies and treated them like traitors to the country. They were accused of
being betrayers of the country. Interestingly, this document did not spec-
ify any Japanese Americans as the target of this violence even though every
action was committed against Japanese "racial origin" and "ancestry." Anti-
Japanese sentiment was legalized and codified in the name of national security. The violence that was committed in internment camps was kept secret
until 1980.[26] Even though an official apology was made in 1982 with $20,000
compensation to each surviving internee and their violence was confessed as
"racial prejudice, war hysteria, and a failure of political leadership,"[27] anti-
Japanese sentiment did not disappear. Rather, the stigma of this unlawful discrimination generates more of society's exclusionary reactions and violence
against Asian immigrants.[28] This incarceration was interpreted as a point of
reference for raising the suspicion of national loyalty toward all Asian immigrants. This violence was introduced as a national defense to contest the
assumption that all Asian immigrants are more Asian than American.[29] Japanese Americans were Japanese, not American. Asian Americans were Asian,
not American. This assumption did not change but uninterruptedly continued without many challenges in public. The cases of Kwan and Wu that were
discussed above are good examples of this assumption. It is an unspoken, but
not hidden, assumption about Asian immigrants in public. Since then, Asian
immigrants' loyalty to national identity is always in question. As discussed
in racial triangulation, their attitude toward national loyalty (patriotism) is
evaluated as low. Their identity as citizens is consistently contested and suspected. Anti-Japanese sentiment reinforces anti-Asian immigrant sentiment
more deeply and broadly.

From the beginning of Asian immigrants' arrival to the current years,
anti-Asian sentiment, including anti-Chinese, anti-Japanese, and anti-Korean
sentiments, has been inherited and empowered by white dominant discourse. Countless cases of Asian immigrant violence were continuously committed without any proper punishment.

The Chinese Massacre of 1885 also took place in the context of
a struggling economy and a growing nativist movement. In Rock

Springs, Wyoming, a mob of white miners, angered by the Chinese miners' refusal to join their strike, killed twenty-eight Chinese laborers, wounded fifteen, and chased several hundred out of town. A grand jury failed to indict a single person.[30]

Vincent Chin was the Chinese American killed in 1982 by Detroit autoworkers Ronald Ebens and Michael Nitz. Ebens, according to one witness, said "that it was because of people like Chin—Ebens apparently mistook him for a Japanese—that he and his fellow employees were losing their jobs." The two men pleaded guilty to manslaughter and were each given three years' probation and fines of $3,780. They did not serve a single day in jail for the killing of Vincent Chin.[31]

(Navroze) Mody was an Asian Indian who was beaten to death in 1987 in Jersey City by a gang of eleven youths. The gang did not harm Mody's white friend. No murder or bias charges were brought; three of the assailants were convicted of assault while one was convicted of aggravated assault.[32]

As documented by the Philadelphia Weekly, Asian American students in Philadelphia high schools have been subject to not only "name-calling, verbal threats, petty robberies, random punches in the head while walking down stairwells, and general intimidation" but also "massive rumbles where outnumbered Asian students were pummeled by packs of teens, sending several of the victims to hospitals." As one Philadelphia student named Wei Chen put it, "They don't even know you. . . . They just hit because you're Asian." In the SF [San Francisco] Bay area, notable cases of violence against Asian Americans include that of Tian Sheng Yu, a 59 year-old man who was beaten to death by two youths in Oakland; Huan Chen, an 83 year-old man who was attacked when leaving a transport stop and died three months afterwards; and a 52 year-old woman identified as a "Mrs. Cheng" who was hit and then thrown off a transportation platform at the same street corner in San Francisco.[33]

From the 1880s to now, violence and discrimination against Asian immigrants has persisted, but this phenomenon is much less known in the public square. These crimes do not draw attention from the media and do not count as anti-Asian immigrant sentiment. They are not taken seriously. Rather, they are always concealed and counted as individual incidents. This violence is trivialized and minimized as individual and personal matters. As the cases above have shown, there were no serious charges against people who killed and/or assaulted Asian immigrants. Public attention was not given, and public attitudes toward Asian immigrants were less favored.

When anti-Chinese and anti-Japanese sentiments were shamed and condemned by public eyes and international political relations, anti-Asian sentiments found another Asian group to target with discrimination: Korean immigrants. Anti-Korean sentiment is more complicated and severe. It did not just come from discrimination against Asian foreignness. Anti-Chinese, anti-Japanese, and anti-Korean sentiments all came from anti-Asian foreignness and international relations. However, in the case of anti-Korean sentiment, there is one more layer to analyze. Anti-Korean sentiment specifically came from racial triangulation in relation to black groups. Unlike Chinese and Japanese immigrant groups, Korean immigrant groups were seen as not just foreigners but also as groups who disrespected black groups. They became the group who oppressed and abused black groups. Instead of white privileged groups, Korean immigrants were depicted as the group to blame for the suffering of black groups in public. Unlike other immigrant groups, Korean immigrant groups are often cast as greedy merchants and disgraceful money makers in media. In the film *Menace II Society*, they are described as the people who scorn African American youth and disrespect black culture. The price for their scorn is death. Their death is justified by black groups' "righteous" violence. Not only films and songs but also numerous actual boycotts and much violence between black and Korean immigrant groups have brought public attention.

A Los Angeles incident in 1992 is the most famous example. Both Korean immigrants and black groups displayed their prejudice against each other in this incident. Korean immigrant groups' homogenous Korean culture, difficulties with English, and racism against black groups were described as arrogant and rude character traits in terms of nationality. Before Korean immigrants move to the United States, they are already exposed to racism against black groups from American movies, music, TV dramas, and so on. Being one homogenous race and being formally colonized, Koreans fear other races and nations. When they move to the United States under the great influences of racism and colonialism, and in the intersection between black/white and native/alien binary divides, racism against black groups has already been learned and embodied. As discussed in the black/nonblack binary divide, they learn how to be different from black groups. Without knowing the deeper meaning of slave history and understanding the accurate context of discriminatory laws like Jim Crow, they adopt prejudices against black groups for being thieves and lazy. In a similar manner, black groups' perception about Korean immigrants is also from a form of racism that the native/alien binary divide cultivates. Without knowing the Korean colonial and postcolonial history and understanding Korean culture, black groups see Korean immigrant groups as job stealers and foreigners. Especially when their black nationalism intertwines with the native/alien binary divide, Korean merchants are easy targets to provoke black righteous vindication. They racially treat Korean immigrant groups as outsiders. They exhibit racial discrimination behaviors and anti-immigrant sentiment.[34] They claim that Korean merchants are barriers to their economic success and social mobility. They accuse not the white store owners in bigger business but the Korean immigrant owners in smaller business as the groups who steal their economic opportunities and prevent their social advancement. They blame Korean immigrant groups for their economic disadvantages.[35]

Pyong Gap Min argues that this relationship should also be understood within the dynamics of class differences between the middle class among Korean immigrants and the working class among black groups.[36] In other words, there is less conflict between middle-class Korean immigrant groups and middle-class black groups. The conflicts between working-class black groups and middle-class Korean immigrant groups are exaggerated by the media as the conflict between the entirety of black groups and Korean immigrant groups. Jennifer Lee finds from her interviews that "responses from interviewed customers about Korean merchants and the perception of mistreatment showed that not all black customers felt Korean merchants disrespected them."[37] Even though the conflicts between black customers and Korean immigrant merchants occurred, it is not true that all black customers hated Korean merchants. However, it was the media that manipulated and exaggerated the conflicts. It generates images of Korean immigrants as the groups who are ignorant about racism and are morally immature, thus demonstrating disrespect to black groups. Korean immigrant groups are designated as a group to take all the blame in the intersection between the two binary divides.

Furthermore, Dae Young Kim and L. Janelle Dance argue that it is important to have both structural and business-related perspectives in this conflict between Korean immigrant groups and black groups. In terms of structural perspective, there are three factors to consider: the socioeconomic circumstances, the demographic changes of inner-city dynamics, and the competitions among nonwhite racial groups. In terms of the business-related perspective, it needs to be understood that the merchant-customer relationship has different perspectives on the price and quality of service. Unlike ordinary economic transactions, when other factors such as racial, immigrant, and cultural differences are added to transactional disputes, merchant-customer disputes turn into immigrant problems. Blacks may understand these disputes "in racial terms, reasoning that the merchants' refusal to exchange or refund is due to prejudice held by 'foreigners' doing business in their community," whereas Korean merchants may understand foul language and yelling from black groups as a sign of impertinence and hate against Asian immigrants.[38] Without critical analysis of structural, business-related, sociopolitical, and cultural approaches, the conflict between Korean immigrant merchants and black customers easily turns into racial conflicts between entire Korean immigrant groups and entire black groups. Then this conflict can be presented in public as anti-Asian sentiment and/or racism against black groups.

Even though anti-Chinese and anti-Japanese sentiments clearly exist, white society tries to hide or deny these sentiments. They dismiss this discrimination as the misunderstanding and oversensitivity of Asian immigrants. However, the case of anti-Korean sentiment is the opposite. Anti-Korean sentiment is displayed in the media as a result of foreigners' arrogance and greed. They are pictured as merciless and immoral foreigners who take advantage of the natives. It is believed that Korean immigrant groups bring anti-Korean sentiment on themselves because they are the problem for causing the suffering of the natives, such as black groups. White domination creates anti-Korean sentiment as a strategy, not to take the blame but to cover white domination without showing the presence of whiteness. The conflicts between Korean groups and black groups are exaggerated and heightened by the media as a problem between natives and aliens. The media frames black groups as powerless citizen-victims and Korean immigrant groups as greedy foreign plaintiffs. The media, the white metanarrative, successfully controls the public to blame the suffering of black people from white domination on Korean immigrants. Korean immigrants "serve as a buffer against the demands and claims made from other powerless groups to power elites."[39] They are a "scapegoat" and "middleman" in the black/white binary system.[40] Anti-Korean sentiment extends anti-Asian sentiment to a bigger circle with more complicities and complications. Korean immigrants are an easy target to be used to cultivate anti-Asian sentiment. Anti-Asian sentiment exists but is not proven. It is presented as a defense of natives who fight against Asian "foreigners" for their survival.

As the recent crisis of the coronavirus pandemic is occurring, anti-Asian sentiment has taken a different and more complicated turn. Not only is the defense for natives' survival unashamedly used to push anti-Asian sentiment but also the suffering of all groups is blamed solely on Asian immigrant groups. As anti-Korean sentiment blames Korean immigrants as the cause of black groups' suffering, anti-Asian sentiment blames Asian immigrants as the cause of COVID-19 suffering. As former president Donald Trump called COVID-19 the Chinese virus, it led people to blame Asian and Asian immigrant groups as the dangerous foreigners who brought the coronavirus to threaten national safety. After this public condemnation against China, anti-Asian prejudice rapidly rose to the surface. Asian culture was immediately disdained as barbarian culture and Asian people were presented as ignorant savages. Anti-Asian violence is now literally practiced as a defense to protect natives by intentionally eradicating the presence of Asian immigrant groups in public. Suddenly, there are no Asian Americans, but Asian foreigners only.

On March 16, 2020, Trump started to refer to COVID-19 as the Chinese virus:

> "The United States will be powerfully supporting those industries, like airlines and others, that are particularly affected by the Chinese virus. We will be stronger than ever before!" read one tweet 16 March, the first time he referred to the illness as "Chinese virus" online. . . . Trump doubled down on the name at a press conference on Wednesday, insisting that using the term is not racist. "It comes from China, that's why. It comes from China. I want to be accurate," Trump said. Trump has received support from his allies who have defended the president for giving coronavirus a new name. "China is to blame because the culture where people eat bats and snakes and dogs and things like that . . . that's why China has been a source of a lot of these viruses," John Cornyn, a Republican senator from Texas, told a reporter when asked if the name was inappropriate. Trump's new name for coronavirus comes after weeks of racist attacks against Asian Americans seen across the country.[41]

As many political leaders cultivate fear of the Asian presence, the media delivers representations to the public to see Asian immigrant groups as dangerous foreigners who can kill natives. Then the native/alien binary divide escalates fear against Asian immigrant groups as the dangerous foreigners who need to be removed. Even though it is claimed that "we are in this together," Asian immigrant groups are certainly not seen as one of "us" who suffers together. They do not belong to "we" in this coronavirus pandemic. The native/alien paradigm enunciates Asian immigrant groups not just as the foreigners but as the dangerous foreigners who are like enemies who deserve punishment. Violence against Asian immigrant groups is demonstrated as punishment to attack the enemy.

> The vicious stabbing of an Asian-American family, including a 2-year-old girl, at a Sam's Club in Texas earlier this month has been deemed a hate crime by the feds, as authorities continue to raise

alarm bells about a potential surge in racially motivated crimes amid the coronavirus outbreak. Jose L. Gomez, 19, confessed to authorities that he attempted to murder three Asian-American family members, including the toddler and a 6-year-old, on March 14 at the Midland, Texas store, according to the Midland Police Department. Gomez, who stabbed the individuals and a Sam's Club employee, is now facing several charges, including three counts of attempted capital murder and one count of aggravated assault. He is being held on several bonds totaling $1 million. "The suspect indicated that he stabbed the family because he thought the family was Chinese, and infecting people with coronavirus," according to an FBI analysis report obtained by ABC News.[42]

An Asian woman in New York City wearing a face mask was assaulted and called "diseased" in early February by a stranger in a subway station. In Los Angeles, a man directed a racist rant about coronavirus to a fellow passenger, who is Asian. One family in Fresno, California, had their car tagged with the word "Fuck Asions . . . and coronavirus." A middle school student in California was told by his teacher to go to the nurse's office after he coughed, though he told his teacher that he choked on water and was not sick. When he asked his teacher why he didn't ask non-Asian students to go to the nurse after coughing, he was told to "let it go and move on."[43]

Violence against Asian immigrant groups has been illustrated in many ways, from barring them from establishments, barring them from transportation, coughing/spitting on them, online and physical assault, shunning, verbal harassment, workplace discrimination to other forms of discrimination. Verbal harassment, followed by shunning and physical assault, is the most common discriminatory incident that many Asian immigrants experienced.[44] Even though anti-Asian sentiment has existed from the beginning of U.S. history, the existence of this sentiment, as it is described above, was denied or hidden in public. However, during the coronavirus pandemic, anti-Asian sentiment has been displayed and even promoted by white political leaders on every level. The level of extreme hate from other groups is impudently expressed in public. In this period, many Asian individuals live in fear of being attacked in their daily lives on the street, in grocery stores, and in any public spaces.

"I feel like I'm being invaded by this hatred," said the man, Edward, who asked that his last name not be used because he feared attracting more attention. "It's everywhere. It's silent. It's as deadly as this disease." He said he had tried to hide the details of what happened from his mother, who moved to the United States from China in the 1970s. But there was one thing he did tell her. "I told her, whatever you do, you can't go shopping," he said. "She needed to know there's a problem and we can't act like it's normal anymore."[45]

From eye rolling to stabbing and gun shots, anti-Asian violence seriously impacts and profoundly shapes the Asian immigrant groups' daily life. Every move that they make is watched by many other individuals with fear and caution. Their presence is rejected and abhorred in both individual spaces and public spaces. Asian immigrant groups experience this hatred in hostile silence and indifference. Anti-Asian sentiment is blatantly turned into hate crimes/incidents, including physical and psychological violence. Asian women are more targeted in this violence than Asian men.[46]

> Hundreds of New Yorkers took the [*sic*] to the streets of Benson-hurst on Saturday to show their support for an 89-year-old Asian woman who was attacked by a stranger—and to condemn the police's decision not to classify the incident as a hate crime. "I said to myself, 'This is too close to home, and enough is enough, and I have to do something about this,'" said China Mac, a Brooklyn-born rapper who helped organize the march. "We have to go into Brooklyn and take a stance and make people uncomfortable." The 89-year-old victim was approached by two unknown men on 77th Street and 16th Avenue shortly after she left her Bensonhurst home on the evening of July 14, authorities said. One assailant slapped her in the face, and moments later, her shirt was lit on fire by a match or a lighter, police said. The victim raised her hair and rubbed her back on a nearby wall to put out the flames, she told ABC7, preventing her from suffering serious injuries. Police have made no arrests and an investigation remains ongoing, a police spokesman said. The incident had not been deemed a hate crime as of Aug. 4.[47]

When the eighty-nine-year-old Asian woman had this horrific incident, the police refused to call it a hate crime. Many anti-Asian violence cases like this case are not seen as hate crimes/incidents, but considered as personal misfortune. Because it is believed for a long time that there is no concept of hate crimes against Asians, unlike Jewish groups and black groups, there is no violence against Asian immigrant groups in public. Even though "close to 3,800 incidents were reported from March 19, 2020 to February 28, (2021)" and "roughly 503 incidents took place in 2021 alone," naming anti-Asian violence as the racism is still a tough discussion to bring within the intersections of both the black/white and the native/alien binaries.[48]

The coronavirus pandemic is being used to deepen the gap between Asian immigrant groups and other groups and to isolate Asian immigrant groups in the position of blame. As black and Latinx groups are announced as the most vulnerable victims of coronavirus,[49] both the black/white and the native/alien binary divides seek to find the group to blame. Asian immigrant groups are immediately targeted. The more these divides highlight the death of black and Latinx groups as the major victims of coronavirus, the more conflicts between Asian immigrant groups and other groups surface. Rather than providing reasons of racial discrepancy in coronavirus situations, this binary divide implicates the necessity of removing Asian immigrant groups from the natives' land. Their Asianness is again perceived as dangerous foreignness to be removed.

At the same time, the black/white divide is using this pandemic to call out Asian immigrant groups as the sinners who are the main cause for the suffering of others, and the native/alien divide is constructing Asian immigrant groups as the dangerous foreigners/enemies of society. As the black/white binary divide sees Asian immigrant groups as the group who brought barbaric unclean uncivilized culture that makes not only black groups but also white groups suffer, the native/alien binary divide frames Asian immigrant groups as the dangerous and foreign group who threatens the safety of the natives. The logic is because of their uncleanness and foreignness, the coronavirus pandemic started. Their foreign uncleanness makes people sick. Making people sick is their sin. Because they make people sick, they should be at least morally responsible for the cause of this crisis. However, because they have no ability to take responsibility, even morally, they are bad. Because they are bad, they cannot be morally good. Because they cannot be good, they are worthy of blame. The logic of the black/white divide calls Asian immigrant groups not only bodily unclean but also morally unclean. It disdains both their physical and psychological existence. The native/alien divide exhibits the similar but different logic. The logic of the native/alien divide calls them dangerous because it is believed that their foreign presence makes people fear. Their alien body is contaminated and infected. Making people fear is what foreigners/enemies intend to do to natives. Within the logic of the native/alien divide, Asian immigrant groups are dangerous and a critical threat to society. For this reason, this divide tries to erase their presence in public. Using the pandemic as the cause of blame against Asian immigrants, the black/white binary divide announces them in public as the sinners, and the native/alien divide locks them in a box of being diseased, of being dangerous.

In the intersection of black/white and native/alien divides, they are labeled as the dangerous foreigners, the sinners, the unclean, and the infected who are ultimately blamed for this coronavirus pandemic. Their presence is asked to be erased and removed. Instead of analyzing the problems of systematic injustice to black and Latinx groups in terms of a lack of privileges in accessing the health care system and social classism structure,[50] these divides activate anti-Asian sentiment as the defense of white structures. They scapegoat Asian immigrant groups as the target of blame, covering their poor white leadership and white privileged system. Under black/white and native/alien binary divides, Asian immigrant groups are urged to remain as outsiders who need to take the blame and who threaten insiders. As these divides position Asian immigrant groups to take the blame, anti-Asian sentiment is understood as the natural reaction out of fear in public. It is widely accepted as self-defense without guilt.

In summary, anti-Asian sentiment has always existed throughout U.S. immigrant history. It is very commonly expressed in public but never recognized as a form of discrimination and violence. It is almost always treated as a private matter on the individual level and as a native's defense against dangerous foreigners in the public domain. Even in the coronavirus pandemic, anti-Asian sentiment is recognized as the natural reaction out of fear. In order to defend the poor white leadership and its system, anti-Asian sentiment is used and manipulated by both the black/white and native/alien divides. Because Asian immigrant groups are not perceived as insiders and citizens in the native/alien binary, the violence against Asian immigrants is understood as a national defense to protect natives against dangerous foreigners, the enemy, and disease. Because they are perceived as sinners who make people suffer in the black/white binary, the violence against Asian immigrants is justified as a punishment against sinners. In the intersection of these binary divides, anti-Asian sentiment is easily justified not only as the communal and individual defense out of fear but also as legitimate punishment against the dangerous other. The action of anti-Asian sentiment demands the complete absenteeism of Asian immigrant groups.

Minority/Nonminority Debate

Are Asian immigrants minorities? Are they racial ethnic minorities? Who are minorities? How do people define minorities? How do people perceive minorities? Within the black/white binary paradigm, Asian immigrants are not classified as a minority. Within the native/alien binary paradigm, they are classified as immigrants but not a minority. The common mentality of "Why should we allow foreigners to claim they are minorities?"[51] implies that the matter of race discourse does not apply to Asian immigrants. Both black/white binary and native/alien binary paradigms simply categorize Asian immigrants as a nonminority.

The debate of minority/nonminority has been one of the main controversial issues regarding Asian immigrants. Specifically, after affirmative action policies became effective, this issue was heatedly debated.

SFFA (Students for Fair Admissions, Inc.) filed its Complaint with this Court on November 17, 2014 [ECF No. 1], and Harvard (Harvard College) filed its Answer on February 18, 2015 [ECF No. 17]. SFFA's Complaint sets forth two types of allegations. First, *103 SFFA contends that the general manner in which Harvard considers race in its undergraduate admissions program violates the Equal Protection Clause. As opposed to using race as a mere "plus" factor in admissions decisions, SFFA claims that Harvard engages in prohibited "racial balancing." Second, SFFA alleges that Harvard's policies invidiously discriminate against Asian-American applicants in particular because, by admitting only a limited number of Asian-American applicants each year, Harvard, in effect, forces Asian-American applicants to compete against each other for those spots. Consequently, a large number of otherwise highly-qualified Asian-American applicants are allegedly denied admission to Harvard on the basis of their race or ethnicity.[52]

Students for Fair Admissions v. Harvard (SFFA, 2015) is one of the cases that represents how the minority/nonminority issue for Asian immigrants is debated in public with respect to the prestigious higher education admission process. SFFA claims that Asian American students are severely discriminated against in Harvard's policies. However, this claim is not the first case that highlights discrimination against Asian Americans. In fact, there is a long history of discrimination against Asian Americans in admission processes in other elite higher education institutions.[53]

This issue is deeply linked with the issue of affirmative action. In 1965, President Lyndon B. Johnson introduced affirmative action as "a method of redressing discrimination that had persisted in spite of civil rights laws and constitutional guarantees."[54] In order to realistically implant civil rights and equality for racial minorities, this policy was adopted and instituted by many institutions, such as higher education institutions and companies. For equal opportunities in education and employment and to promote ethnic minority groups, this policy was encouraged in public. However, this policy is repeatedly disputed by both conservatives and liberals due to its own complexities. For conservatives, this policy is interpreted as closing the door for whites and their equal opportunity. Unqualified minority groups get preferential treatment for a free or easy ride, whereas poor white groups lose their opportunity to advance despite their hard work.[55] For liberals, it is interpreted as justice for racial minorities, especially for blacks who suffered severe racism. Recognizing white privileges embedded in the current social structure, they claim that affirmative action would give an equal opportunity for whites to dismantle white privileges and promote diversity.

The case of the University of Michigan in 2003 was one of the most famous cases in affirmative action history. The U.S. Supreme Court decided to uphold the right of affirmative action. The Supreme Court endorsed that race should be considered as one of the factors for school admission. It ruled that even though affirmative action could not justify compensating past oppressive history and injustice, it could "promote a 'compelling state interest' in diversity at all levels of society."[56] Affirmation action was confirmed in higher education because it is believed to include all groups equally and proportionately.

However, affirmative action does not usually include Asian Americans as the benefactors of this policy. They are excluded in this discussion. There are two reasons that explain this exclusion. First, Asian Americans are the highest interest group in education. Among all racial groups, they are the largest groups who enter higher education. Many Asian students take more opportunities for higher education even without affirmative action. If affirmative action is applied to Asian immigrants, it makes Asian immigrant groups even larger in number than they currently are. It means that Asian immigrants will be the most dominant group to occupy higher education.[57] Second, they are the model minority. It is interpreted that because they achieve socioeconomic advancement, they need to compete not with other racial groups but with whites. Because they made it to the top or near the top, they should not take any more advantages to advance their lives. Asian Americans are seen as the group that does not need any special treatment or protection.

Affirmative action rules out Asian Americans for fear of both losing blacks (and Latinxs) and whites. On the one hand, when affirmative action includes Asian Americans as a racial minority, it implies that when every single Asian American is accepted as a racial minority, black (or Latinx) students would lose their seats for admission.[58] In other words, when Asian Americans are included, racial minority groups have to compete with each other. Therefore, it is better for higher education institutions to classify Asian students in the nonracial minority category. By this logic, in order to secure the way for racial minority group members, it is necessary for Asian Americans to yield their privileges. Positioning Asian Americans as a nonethnic minority in this policy, institutions claim that racial minorities could have more room to secure their admission. Here, Asian Americans are used as the group who paved the way for racial minority groups, but they are not included in the group. They are a minority but should not be claimed as a minority in order to protect the equality of other minorities. Their minority status is denounced by affirmative action to support other racial groups' equal opportunities. Other racial equal opportunities are secured at the expense of Asian immigrants within the white structure. However, the truth is that institutions can provide secure admission for racial minority groups without excluding Asian Americans.[59]

On the other hand, when Asian Americans are excluded from affirmative action, they are used as the group who actually paved the way for whites, not other racial minority groups.[60] In fact, affirmative action grants not only the seats of racial minorities but also the seats of whites. As this policy sets the boundary for racial minorities using the quota system, it protects the boundary for the admission of whites. It is not black or Latinx students who get the benefits. It is actually whites who are granted certain numbers of admission. Locking in a certain number of racial group members, whites can secure their seats for safe admission. It means that Asian Americans are the group who is left out in this policy. Without any acknowledgement of anti-Asian sentiment and discrimination, they are put in a position of competing with whites unequally. They are subjected to "the unfavorable treatment of Asian Americans relative to Whites" which is called "negative action."[61] Asian immigrants are compared with whites in the course of negative action, which ends with discrimination in the name of equal treatment.

In the research of Thomas J. Espenshade and Chang J. Chung in 2005, they found that affirmative action greatly benefited African American students and, to an extent, Latinx students but resulted in negative action against Asian American students. They claimed that "eliminating affirmative action would substantially reduce the share of African Americans and Hispanics among admitted students."[62] They noted that Asian American students received a disadvantage in comparison with white, African American, and Hispanic students.[63] In their 2009 research, Espenshade, Alexandria Walton Radford, and Chang Young Chung confirmed that if racial preference and "Asian penalty" are removed, the admission rates of Asian American students would be changed from less than 25 percent in current policies to 40 percent of all admitted students.[64]

> With these assumptions (racial preference and "Asian penalty" in race-neutral policy), acceptance rates for minority students would decline even more—to less than 11 percent for blacks and to 16 percent for Hispanics. Minority shares among admitted students would fall to under 8 percent, less than half their overall proportion under current practice. White applicants would also suffer. Their acceptance rate would drop to 23 percent—less than the average acceptance rate of 24 percent and lower than the white rate under racial affirmative action (25 percent). Asian students would be affected the most. Nearly three out of every ten Asian applicants would be accepted under a race-neutral policy, compared to fewer than two out of every ten in 1997. Asian candidates could be expected to comprise nearly 40 percent of all accepted students, compared to less than 25 percent under current policies.[65]

Both these studies revealed the existence of Asian penalty as negative action against Asian Americans. Asian American students have to achieve higher scores than any other racial groups in order to enter the same school. If they achieve the same level, they have no opportunity to be admitted to the same school. Asian American students have suffered from this negative action in admission processes. A double standard is asked and required. Despite these disadvantages, many Asian American students still enter elite schools. However, their presence at these schools is not interpreted as positive efforts. Rather, it provokes negative action from both whites and racial immigrant groups. Excluding Asian Americans from affirmative action, it confirms again that Asian immigrants are "neither American nor minorities."[66] Positioning Asian Americans in competition with whites, blacks, and Latinxs, negative action has been consciously and unconsciously practiced by many politicians who "use [an] admission ceiling on Asian American applicants as an incisive tool to criticize all race-based policies as morally bankrupt."[67]

Despite double oppression with and without affirmative action, the rates of Asian Americans in higher education have increased. Many Asian Americans show great interest in education. In fact, because of the Immigration Act of 1965, which favored highly educated immigrants, immigration for highly educated Asian immigrants is intentionally supported and selected.[68] However, despite higher education achievement, it is claimed that there is still a serious glass ceiling above Asian immigrants. The education of first-generation Asian immigrants is often discounted, and their Asian higher educational credentials are not fully recognized in U.S. society. Moreover, because of a lack of English proficiency and adjustment to cultural differences and anti-Asian sentiment, they tend to have positions that result in lower social status and salary in comparison with positions they had in their native countries. They experience downward social mobility in general. Because of this, they often show the higher pattern of self-employment than the second generation.[69] For second- and third-generation Asian immigrants, they also have suffered racial discrimination and experienced slow promotion, or a glass ceiling. Even though higher percentages of both first and second/third generations obtain college degrees and enter various places of industries, a very small percentage of Asian immigrants reach high-level leadership positions.[70] After they finish higher education and make a successful landing in entry-level positions, they experience slow promotion and an impenetrable glass ceiling.

Using a novel EPI approach to compare representation of South and East Asians in the leadership pipeline, the Ascend report uncovers surprising new insights about the role of race and gender in Silicon Valley: Although both race and gender are factors that contribute to a glass ceiling, the impact of race is 3.7 times more significant than the impact of gender as a negative factor for the Asian workforce within the companies examined. While white men are 42% more likely than white women to be an executive in these companies, they are 149% percent more likely than Asian men to be an executive, and 260% more likely than Asian women to be an executive. For Asian women in these companies, this translates into a "double whammy" race-plus-gender problem: Only 1 of every 285 Asian women is an executive, less than half the ratio for the entire workforce of 1 executive per 118 professionals.[71]

It is a fact that both race and gender are the main factors of a glass ceiling for Asian Americans and other racial groups. However, for Asian immigrants, there is a unique challenge in terms of the glass ceiling. Under the model minority myth, they suffer double prejudices between both whites and other racial groups. The widely accepted model minority myth says that Asian immigrants are doing well and even beat white competitors in certain industries. This myth advertises Asian immigrants as the model minority, "superminority,"[72] outperformer, "a trophy population,"[73] and "exemplars of hope."[74] It is believed that they are greatly successful despite racial barriers and achieve the American Dream.

There are several problems with this model minority myth. First, making Asian immigrants the example of color-blind neutral society denies the existence of structural racism. If Asians can make it, why not others? This myth is commonly used to criticize the predicament of other racial groups as their individual personal failure. As Asian immigrants become the model minority, other racial immigrants become the problem of society. In this logic, it is not the unjust structure that generates poverty but the people who cannot assimilate and work hard. It is not the structure to blame but the individuals who should take responsibility. Second, the model minority myth dismisses the suffering of Asian immigrants. "You are prospering and overachieving. You are doing too well no matter what. Why do you still complain?" Even though Asian immigrants experience racial discrimination and double oppression under the white/black binary and the native/alien binary paradigms, these discriminations and oppressions are easily ignored and dismissed. Their suffering does not count as suffering but unnecessary complaint. It conceals their unjust social condition and suppresses their suffering by voice-over narratives. Their voice is muted with voice-over interpretation. Third, the model minority myth turns Asian immigrants into whites even though they are not whites and will never be treated as whites. When the model minority myth leads to color blindness, Asian immigrants are identical with whites except that they are not white. It deceives in alluding that anyone can be white even without privileges. White privilege is interpreted to not be very significant in terms of personal advancement. It justifies a color-blind or color-neutral policy as the just policy and supports white privilege as something to easily overcome. Fourth, the model minority myth refortifies a clear boundary between minority and majority. "Asian immigrants are model *minority*, even though they are *model* minority." This myth makes sure that Asian immigrants stay in the boundary of minority, not majority. It states that they are good enough to be a model for the minority but not for the majority. As long as Asian immigrants who are successful stay within the boundaries of minority, it is interpreted that whites are the majority because they are still better. Locating Asian immigrants as the minority confirms white superiority.

When the model minority myth encounters the problem of promotion against Asian immigrants, it creates another complication. By emphasizing Asian immigrants' successful advancement in education and into the entry-level workforce, discrimination against the promotion of Asian immigrants is treated as nonexistent. It is understood as something that does not actually exist. It is said that if Asian immigrants have been successful this far, it is their limitation that they cannot make further advancement in terms of higher social positions and leadership. The logic is this: they can assimilate, but they cannot assimilate completely. They can get out of the bottom of the class system, but they cannot make a class at the top. Because there are problems in the Asian race, they cannot reach the top. They are short of being the first class. They belong to the second class.

This logic delivers two additional problems to Asian immigrants. First, it leads the public to believe that Asian immigrants made it all the way through, but not to the top. It is commonly believed that lack of executive top positions and leadership is the only problem that Asian immigrants have. Is it really true? In the analysis of authority attainment, Zhen Zeng claims that discrimination against Asian immigrants when it comes to work promotions exists not just at the top of the hierarchy. This research shows that downward mobility still plays a significant part in obtaining authority positions for Asian immigrant men and other racial immigrant groups, and disadvantages against Asian immigrants are not just concentrated at the top but actually in the bottom- to middle-level transition.[75] This logic minimizes the actual problems of lack of promotion for Asian immigrants. It sets up the limit that there are obstacles for Asian immigrants' promotion only at the top. It implies that there is no more discrimination or barriers for Asian Americans in terms of economic advancement except achieving executive positions.

Second, it explains discrimination against Asian immigrants in terms of promotion as their individual problems of leadership. As communication skills are considered one of the most essential leadership skills, they are one of the most important measurements in the promotion process. However, it is interesting to observe that both first- and second-/third-generation Asian immigrants are commonly criticized in their performance evaluations for lack of communication skills or leadership. Kuris Takamine introduced seven reasons why Asian immigrants are not considered for high-level positions:

1. APAs (Asian-Pacific American) are deficient in necessary communication skills.
2. Minority candidates do not interview and test well for promotional opportunities.
3. Minority candidates do not have adequate social networks.
4. Minorities do not have adequate mentorship and sponsorship experience.
5. Minorities do not have the necessary exposure to "line" positions.
6. Minority middle managers are still "in the pipeline."
7. Minorities are not "aggressive" enough.[76]

As this study indicates, the common criticism of Asian immigrants' leadership is lack of communication and relationships. Asian immigrants are often seen as the groups who cannot communicate effectively with others. In particular, their English efficacy, accents, and manners of communication are often evaluated as a lack of communication and ineffectiveness in cultivating relationships. When an accent "serves as a marker of race,"[77] it is understood as a signifier of communication. Later, it becomes communication itself. Then their skills of communication, not their accent, are perceived as something not trainable but innate. Then their communication, not their accent, seems an unfixable quality for Asian immigrants to perform in leadership. This logic forces the model minority myth to confirm the lack of communication skills as an innate problem of Asian immigrants. It leads the public to conclude that Asian immigrants deserve to stay in the second class.

In summary, the minority/nonminority debate is another form of discrimination against Asian immigrants. Are Asian immigrants as minorities included in affirmative action policy? No, they are not. They are treated as whites and compete with whites in higher education and work entry. They experience double disadvantages between both whites and other racial immigrant groups. They are used as the group to protect white domination. Are they minorities in the model minority myth? Yes, they are. They are treated as the minority who is the model but cannot be the majority. They are treated as a racial minority and compared with other racial immigrant groups under the model minority myth. They are used as the group to oppress other racial immigrant minorities and justify discrimination against all racial groups. Are they minorities? Yes and no. They are treated as minorities and nonminorities simultaneously. Depending on the needs of white dominance, they are systematically excluded and included. When there is a need to protect white privileges and structures, they are excluded from the status of being a minority and encouraged to compete with whites under the rationale of protecting other racial minorities and their equal opportunity. When there is a need to prove the nonexistence of racial discrimination, they are included as being the model minority and encouraged to compete with other minorities. The minority/nonminority debate for Asian immigrant groups generates dual negation. From the viewpoint of whites, Asian immigrants are seen as a threat to take away white privileges. From the viewpoint of other racial minority groups, Asian immigrants are understood as honorary whites who take away limited opportunities from them. It locates Asian immigrants in an impossible negotiation between whites and other racial groups.

When this debate intersects with the black/white binary and the native/alien binary paradigms, it refortifies discrimination against Asian immigrants and dismisses their suffering further. It makes the black/white binary more polarized and the native/alien binary more intensified. At both ends, Asian immigrants are used as the group protecting white privileges and justifying color-blind policy in affirmative action. They are used as a group to dismiss other racial groups in the model minority myth. In the intersection between affirmative action policy and the model minority myth, they are treated as a group that should remain in the second class due to their own limits and inability. Asian immigrant groups are doubly excluded and marginalized in this intersection. Minimization and marginalization are commonly practiced and justified. Under the dual dynamics of the black/white and the native/alien binary paradigms, this minority/nonminority debate intensifies the invisibility of Asian immigrants' suffering. As a consequence, it creates more anti-Asian sentiment in public and produces unconscious self-blame and lack of self-confidence inside Asian immigrant groups.

Both the black/white binary and the native/alien binary paradigms are the predominant discourses of the colonial/postcolonial paradigm to establish and maintain white privileges and Eurocentric sociocultural construction. These two binary paradigms are two main wheels of discrimination against all racial immigrant groups in the U.S. context. Controlling the dynamics of these racial and cultural relations under these two paradigms, white domination constantly discriminates against Asian immigrant groups. They have to go through the hoops of racial triangulation, anti-Asian sentiment, and the minority/nonminority debate and sacrifice their immigrant lives without recognition. The colonial and postcolonial discourse collides with these black/white and native/alien binary paradigms on a deeper level not only politically and socioculturally but also psychologically and spiritually.

Internal Struggles within Asian Immigrant Groups

Along with the intersection between the black/white and the native/alien binary divides, racial triangulation, anti-Asian sentiment, and the minority/nonminority debate against Asian immigrant groups refortify the marginalization of Asian immigrant groups among racial groups. Both white and nonwhite groups treat Asian immigrant groups not as allies but as competitors. Specifically, when nonwhite groups and Asian immigrant groups try to improve their positions within the black/white binary paradigm, they often compete with and hurt each other at their own expense. At the same time, as white groups fear the success of Asian immigrant groups, they make sure that Asian immigrant groups remain second-class citizens. As both white and other racial groups see Asian immigrant groups as competitors, in some political cases, both groups coalesce with each other. "In fact, xenophobic native-born blacks often united with white nativists to oppose social justice for Asians, whether native-born or immigrant, instead of joining forces to challenge the racial hierarchy that subordinates them."[78]

However, when both groups need to demonstrate their coalition work in public, such as immigrant movements and human rights movements, they expect to have collaborative efforts from Asian immigrant groups. Because it is important to show a multicultural atmosphere in these movements, the presence of Asian immigrant groups is politically necessary. However, even though the presence of Asian immigrant groups is required, it does not require any active leadership roles for Asian immigrant groups to participate. Rather, it is perceived that it is better for them to be participants, not the leaders of the movement. Still, because of their minimal participation and lack of leadership in coalitions, they receive criticism from both white groups and nonwhite groups again. Theories of racial triangulation, anti-Asian sentiment, and minority/nonminority models within black/white and native/alien binary divides are some explanations for this criticism. However, there are more complications and barriers that Asian immigrant groups experience. If black/white and native/alien binary divides, racial triangulation, anti-Asian sentiment and minority/nonminority issues are external factors that cause serious barriers for Asian immigrant groups to join this society, there are internal factors that Asian immigrant groups struggle with among themselves. Among many internal factors, two explanations will be discussed in this section.

First, Asian immigrant groups live in a dilemma between going back to their motherlands someday and staying in the U.S. permanently. They left their motherlands for various reasons, such as poverty, political freedom, study, colonial/postcolonial political situations. Whatever reason they come to the U.S., many of them have strong connections with their motherlands.

Some immigrants come to the U.S. to work to support their families finan-
cially. They send money to their families regularly until their families secure
better living situations, hoping one day they can return home. If they come
to the U.S. to escape from their motherlands for political reasons, they keep
watching their communities and connect with these communities, hoping
that they can go back to their communities after political situations get better. Specifically, first-generation immigrants give more attention to concerns
about political issues of their motherlands than political and social justice
issues in the U.S. such as racism. Sometimes, it takes more than several years
to go back to their families and communities. Other times, they never have
a chance to go back. As their circumstances change, they settle down and try
to make this place their home. However, even if they never have a chance to
go back, they always have deep concerns and sympathy for their families and
communities in their motherlands. Because they are uncertain whether they
will stay in the U.S. and are homesick for their motherlands, they continue
to intend to go back to their motherlands for a long time. Even after they
secure their legal statuses and become citizens of the United States, many
of them are still deeply connected to people in their motherlands. They are
transnational citizens from the beginning of their immigrant lives. In some
cases, even after they become citizens of the U.S., after they retire, they go
back to their motherlands eventually.

Meanwhile, they also deal with the message from the U.S. to go back
to their motherlands. Even if they decide to live in the U.S. permanently
because of life circumstances and even if they finally give up their dream to
go back to their motherlands, they realize that they are not fully accepted as
members of this society. They are always treated as temporary visitors and foreigners. This society expects that they are permanent guests who need to go
back to their motherlands. They feel that they do not belong to U.S. society.

Because of these simultaneous internal and external struggles, their
sociopolitical and psychological status always remains ambiguous. On the
one hand, as described above, Asian immigrant groups are treated as forever foreigners who never belong to the U.S. They are ignored by white
and nonwhite groups. They are asked to go back to their motherlands. The
atmosphere of the U.S. cultivates anti-Asian sentiment. It controls Asian
immigrant groups to accept their foreignness as legitimately less qualified
to be members of this society. It pushes them to be in the second class in a
sociopolitical hierarchy. On the other hand, Asian immigrant groups themselves always maintain the intention to go back to their motherlands because
of their family and community members. Because of this intention, they
want to keep their memberships in their motherlands and postpone obtaining citizenship in the U.S. Some of them are reluctant to join the U.S. as
citizens and just want to keep resident status permanently. Until they realize

that they do not have a chance to go back to their motherlands, they do not want to obtain full citizenship. Others become undocumented immigrants at some point and have a hard time regaining legal status. This long reluctance prevents them from being full members of the U.S. Because many of them are not legal citizens of the U.S., such as many green card holders and those who are legal visa holders, they do not feel that they are full members of this society. They feel that they are still guests in this society. Because of their unbelongingness in this society, they tend to stay back from racism and social justice issues. In the case of undocumented Asian immigrants, they are more reclusive from any public activities. Even if they become U.S. citizens, because of a long path being treated as permanent guests legally and psychologically, they do not feel like real citizens of the U.S. Living in between the motherland and the U.S. is the major cause of stress that Asian immigrant groups experience. Living in betweenness is a dilemma that especially the first-generation immigrants experience intensely. Many of them experience this dilemma for the rest of their lives. This dilemma causes not only psychological trauma and physical symptoms but also difficulty in obtaining legal sociopolitical status.

As Asian immigrant groups experience this dilemma, they do not see racism and other social justice issues in the same ways that other racial groups see them. As they are treated as visitors and as they feel themselves to be guests in the U.S., they feel that they are not invited to take these issues as their own. Many first-generation immigrants understand that these issues are not their issues to join. Some of them see these issues as black/white issues in a way that the black/white binary divide intends. Others begin to gradually recognize these issues after they settle down in the U.S. and learn U.S. history and culture more. Learning and understanding U.S. slavery history and white culture, they observe the problems of racism. However, unlike the second- and the third-generation immigrant groups who are educated in the U.S., most first-generation Asian immigrants do not have many opportunities to learn history and culture in the U.S. educational system. Their daily experience does not give them enough opportunities to learn how other racial groups, such as black, Native American, and Latinx groups, experience the U.S. Their recognition of the importance of these issues takes a very slow path. When they decide to be citizens of the U.S., that is when many of them make the first step to recognize the problems of racism.

Still, there is another barrier that some Asian immigrant groups do not share with other ethic immigrant groups. That is a class issue. U.S. immigration selectively chose Asian immigrants who were from the middle class in their motherlands: "Merchants and foreign students, not laborers before 1965, and urban professionals until the 1980s" who denounce communism and socialism.[79] Many of them come from the upper and middle classes and join conservative Republicans.[80] They are mostly educated elite middle-class groups who admire white civilization as the model of their society and want to achieve better economic advancement for themselves. Under the heavy white colonial and postcolonial influences, they tend to accept whiteness as the norm and make their best efforts to assimilate with white society. As they experience keeping their privileges as the middle class in their motherlands by obeying the colonial rules of their society, their colonial minds move them to learn how to keep their privileges by accepting white rules and adopting white culture. As they witness white colonial power and survive under it by cooperation, their middle-class mentality easily accepts these rules and observes white culture to achieve better treatment. Their middle-class attitudes show respect to the current institutional structures and desire white privileges. Their middle-class minds also seek advancing their privileges and security by differentiating themselves from poor blacks within the black/ nonblack binary paradigm. They agree with or even appreciate being in the middle position not only in the economic hierarchy but also in the racial political hierarchy in the U.S. This middle-class mindset fails for Asian immigrant groups to join in solidarity with other racial ethnic groups and, rather, reinforces racial hierarchy.[81]

At the same time, "for a large number of Asian Americans, especially of the recent immigrant generation that escaped from war, political upheaval, colonization, and barriers to social and economic mobility in the homeland, America has meant 'promised land' or 'dream country.'"[82] The recent Asian immigrant groups are not necessarily from the middle class only. After the 1980s, various Asian immigrant class groups arrived for various reasons. For many of them, the U.S. was the country that saved them from their political and economic problems. It is the country that they should thank. In their belief, white rules and cultures are the ones to follow and obey, not to criticize. As it is taught that they did not have rights to discover the lands like white groups, they feel it is important not to claim any rights. As it is believed that they did not build the country like black groups, they feel it is important not to claim any credits. They cannot claim any belongingness to this land like Native Americans, who are the real natives in this land. They have no ground to claim their standings. Rather, the attitudes that Asian immigrant groups bear are more toward gratitude for the U.S. white society than criticism of social justice issues such as human rights and racism. Their colonial minds lead them to appreciate the current structures and laws. Instead of joining with other racial groups in coalition work to fight for social justice, they tend to stay out of this coalition work and remain silent.

Immigrants from South Korea are a good example of this. As Korean colonial history with Japan is recognized, there are strong tensions between Koreans and Japanese. These tensions are not hidden. In fact, these groups hardly interact with each other. After long and hideous colonial oppression from Japan, Korean immigrants still see Japanese immigrants as the colonizer's group. They observe a political relationship between Korea and Japan when they interact with Japanese immigrant groups. They follow the reactions and responses of their motherland. Even though they recognize the injustice of Japanese Americans' internment, many first-generation Korean immigrants hardly pay attention to this case. Rather, they give more attention to the fight for an apology and compensation for Koreans from Japan, such as that owed to comfort women. Even the younger generation Korean immigrants who did not experience colonial violence from Japan directly are exposed to this anti-Japanese sentiment when they grow up under the influence of their first-generation immigrant parents. From their colonial historical relations with Japan, they see the United States as a savior country. Many first-generation Korean immigrant groups from South Korea believe that the United States saved South Korea from Japanese colonial occupation and North Korea's communism. Without support from the U.S., they believe that they still would not have independence. As they admire the U.S., they admire white groups. They identify white groups as their supporters and helpers. They have gratitude for white groups. Because of this gratitude, they prefer to work with white groups and support them. These Korean immigrants intensely watch global political relations between the United States, Japan, China, and North Korea rather than giving more attention to working with other ethnic racial groups for racial justice issues within the U.S. As this case illustrates, various Asian immigrant groups support white normativity and protect white privileges in order to secure their survival and privileges.

Furthermore, there is another political complication that Asian immigrants experience. Many Asian immigrant groups are often used as the political subject of negotiation between their motherlands and the U.S. Elaine H. Kim explains their in-betweenness in a political situation between U.S. homeland politics and racism.

> Yet Asian American interests and issues were most often cast aside as they were squeezed between U.S. racism and homeland politics. Any Japanese Americans who hoped that Japan would help them when they were interned during World War II were bound to be disappointed; Japan was interested in using them as pawns in a propaganda campaign against the U.S. or as bargaining chips for Japanese prisoners of war. . . . Filipino Americans were not exempt from the long arm of the Marcos government and its blacklist. Today, a huge amount of Vietnamese American attention has been focused on the dream of "taking back" Vietnam from the Communists. During the past 15 years, many Vietnamese Americans have been murdered in

cold blood for making what were regarded as leftist statement. . . . Historically, Asian American involvement in homeland politics, for whatever its effects on the fate of the homeland, has for the most part distracted Asian American attention from U.S. issues, including coalition work with other people of color against racism and social justice in this country. Perhaps, too, the focus on homeland class and gender hierarchies, often making it difficult for working-class Asian Americans and Asian American women to participate fully in community politics.[83]

U.S. homeland politics and racism always use Asian Americans in their global politics in relations with Asian countries. Whenever any political incidents and issues arise, Asian immigrant groups have to figure out where they need to stand and how they support their motherlands or the U.S. accordingly. As discussed previously in this section, many first-generation immigrants are more sensitive to their motherland's politics than racial issues in the U.S. because they are often more concerned for their families and communities in their motherlands than for themselves in the context of racial discrimination in the U.S. Their communal sense of belongingness and sense of sympathy for social justice issues are often with families and communities in their motherlands more than other racial communities in the U.S. Because they are the first-generation immigrants who already embodied history and culture in their motherlands and because they do not have time to learn U.S. history and culture like the second- and third-generation Asian immigrants, it is easier for them not to recognize the importance of coalition work but to focus on only the difficulties that they experience living in between their motherlands and the U.S. This living in betweenness causes more inner struggles for them, occupies their attention, and makes them more isolated from other racial groups.

Second, Asian immigrant groups do not feel solidarity among themselves in the same or similar ways that black groups, Native American groups, and Latinx groups do among themselves. Asian immigrant groups are not one group. They do not share the same history, culture, language, and so on. Some Asian immigrants are from former colonizer countries, while other Asian immigrants are from former colonized countries. As they carry their motherlands' colonial history to the United States, when they encounter other Asian immigrant groups, they show different attitudes upon meeting them. In fact, some Asian immigrant groups find their closest adversaries within Asian immigrant groups. The relationships between Korea and Japan or between immigrant groups from the People's Republic of China and immigrant groups from Taiwan is a good example. Because of different historical backgrounds and cultures, they do not feel much solidarity within

Asian immigrant groups. Working with other Asian immigrant groups produces the same level of connection as working with non-Asian immigrant groups. In some cases, working with other racial ethnic groups is preferred over working with other Asian immigrant groups. When Asians migrate to the U.S., they bring their colonial past with them. Many Asian immigrant groups remember their colonial past and carry the wounds to the U.S. Their colonial wounds are the major barriers for their coalition work with other Asian immigrant groups. In order to understand the entangled relationships among Asian immigrant groups, it is important to understand each nation's colonial history in Asia.

Under these entangled colonial relationships, there is another crucial factor that creates difficulty in achieving solidarity. That is a lack of common language for communication between Asian immigrant groups. Asian immigrant groups do not have a common language other than English. They do not communicate the way African American and Latinx groups communicate. Furthermore, many Asian immigrant groups have a hard time understanding and speaking English. Unlike Spanish and other European languages that are similar to English, Asian languages have totally different linguistic structures and vocabularies. Many Asian immigrants who spend more than ten or twenty years in the U.S. still do not have much confidence in their English and avoid any critical interactions with other groups in English communication. Some 1.5-generation Asian immigrants even confess that their accents are still corrected by their children and feel so frustrated speaking English. Others report that they experience discrimination in terms of jobs and promotion because of English inefficiency.[84]

The lack of English proficiency is one of the strongest challenges that most Asian immigrant groups experience. Before their arrival, they hardly imagined fear in speaking. However, upon their arrival, they start to experience difficulties in communication. They fear speaking English. As they fear speaking, they fear developing any relationships outside of their own ethnic groups. As they tend to stay with their own ethnic groups, they do not work with other groups. Coalition work is out of their comfort zone. Not only the strange environment but also speaking and understanding English makes Asian immigrant groups much less active in relationships outside of their ethnic groups. They lose confidence in having certain interactions and engaging in certain activities. Their broken English is the target of discrimination. Hyung Chol Yoo, Gilbert C. Gee, and David Takeuchi claim that language discrimination is critically related to Asian immigrant groups' health.[85] It is well known that racism causes harm to all racial ethnic groups and causes physical and psychological health problems.[86] However, it is not commonly known that language discrimination causes more health problems to Asian immigrant groups specifically. For Asian immigrants, besides anti-Asian racism, language discrimination produces more barriers for them to collaboratively work with other groups. "The relationship between language discrimination and chronic conditions was stronger for Asian immigrants living in the USA 10 years or more compared to more recently arrived immigrants."[87] Asian immigrants who live in the U.S. more than 10 years develop chronic conditions in relation to language discrimination. As Asian immigrant groups are more exposed to language discrimination than other immigrant groups, they experience more physical and psychological health problems.

Language discrimination is one of the most significant forms of discrimination that Asian immigrant groups are exposed to exclusively within the native/alien binary divide. "Underlying the intersection of language and race is a language ideology that we call the *ideology of nativeness*, an Us versus Them division of the linguistic world in which native and nonnative speakers of a language are thought to be mutually exclusive, uncontested, identifiable groups."[88] It is a significant subdivide under the native/alien binary divide. It creates a subtle but clear division between natives and aliens without directly identifying natives as whites. "This discourse coincides with, and is often used to justify, exclusionary practices that perpetuate the normalization of Whiteness, Americanness, and nativeness in certain prestige varieties of English."[89] Learning English is another form of colonial normalization. As people learn English, they learn whiteness as the normal standard way of communication and equalize it with Americanness and nativeness. Even though English as a language does not carry nationality specifically, English in the U.S. and European contexts delivers the power of colonialism over nationalities. Learning and speaking English guarantees certain privileges and prestige. It opens access to these privileges and opportunities. It is power not just to survive and communicate but also to obtain certain hierarchical sociopolitical statuses. However, it does not guarantee complete equal status. Rather, English serves as the object to distinguish nativeness and Americanness from Asian immigrants. This language is a postcolonial imperative to support the native/alien binary divide. In the U.S. specifically, it turns into nationalism. It conveys postcolonial nationalism and reinforces that nationalism in white domination and normalization as the way things are. It is recognized as the normal and natural way to believe that everyone should speak English only. It assumes that natives are native English speakers, and native English speakers are equalized with natives. It means that whoever speaks different languages or speaks English with accents are not treated as natives or citizens. Even if their English is perfect in terms of grammar and structure, English with accents does not count as speaking perfect English. Especially if someone speaks English with an Asian accent, it is interpreted as second-class English. It evokes discrimination. The native/alien divide employs English as a way to make Asian immigrant groups distinct from natives and other racial groups. It is profoundly related to racism in systematic ways.[90]

As Asian immigrant groups live in the face of a dilemma between returning to their motherlands and settling down in the U.S., and as they live in the face of a dilemma between bearing multiple barriers of coalition work and keeping solidarity with the communities in their motherlands, they are in constant struggle internally and externally. Within the intersections of black/white, black/nonblack, and native/alien binary relations, and within the layers of internal and external struggles that are discussed above, Asian immigrant groups experience very complex, subtle, almost unexplainable and unrecognizable discrimination. It is almost unexplainable because it is very complicated and multilayered. It is unrecognizable because it is unknown and exists in interstitial spaces. However, despite their struggle in these complexities, they have changed and transformed their immigrant lives along with their failures and critical problems. As they learn and support white domination, they also try to unlearn and relearn how to challenge white power and create a new way to live with others at the same time.

CHAPTER 3

Asian Immigrants as the Third Other

The Imperfect Otherness

There are many Asian immigrants who came to the U.S. with great dreams but left with empty hands and heavy hearts. Many went back to their motherlands. Of those who returned, some could not obtain proper documents and legal status, while others could not find any jobs to maintain their living. Many of them desperately tried to stay and secure their lives; however, they could not find a way to stay. They had to leave. They were seen as visitors after all. There are also many other Asian immigrants who came and stayed. They persist in their efforts to follow the rules and obtain proper documents. They have found jobs and make a living. They make this new place their home and find a way to survive. They stay. They are understood as permanent residents and citizens. There are other Asian immigrant groups who have tried to follow the rules but cannot obtain proper documents. Instead of leaving the U.S., they decide to stay without legal documentation. They are called "undocumented immigrants." There is another group who lives in between. They can leave or stay. Either they hold temporary legal documents and risk illegality in the future, or they do not have legal documents at the moment but apply for legal status. They believe that they will achieve legality in the future. Their life is uncertain and unknown. Depending on their individual situations, many Asian immigrants hold varying socioeconomic political statuses. However, most of them bear uncertainties at some points in their lifetime as they go through several transitions of socioeconomic and political status as immigrants. They have to learn how to walk with uncertainty. They have to know how to live without hope. They must wait with great patience whenever they move another step in their immigrant lives. These experiences differ profoundly across generations.

As the first-generation immigrant groups wait and settle into their new immigrant lives, they are immediately asked to dive into repressive binary structures. Second- and third-generation immigrant groups are born and raised in these structures. However, despite many of them diving into or living in black/white, native/alien, host/guest, racial triangulation, anti-Asian sentiment, minority/nonminority, assimilation/resistance, disconnectedness/connectedness, and other binary spaces, it is difficult for them to be consciously aware of these structures. They are taught to see these structures as the way things are. Because of this normalization process, many Asian immigrant groups often do not know how to describe what they experience. Especially in the early years of their immigrant lives, first-generation immigrant groups experience losing not only the ability of speaking but also the ability to describe their indescribable suffering. Even if they are aware of these structural problems, they do not know how to name them in this culture and language.

Racism training is one example in which Asian immigrant groups often experience binary structures but do not know how to describe them. They are often asked to choose between white and black groups and urged to stand in between these relations. Although they try to explain what they experience through their lens as Asian immigrants, their experience is easily dismissed and trivialized. *They experience differently.* However, their different experiences are not understood. They have different backgrounds, histories, cultures, sociopolitical positions, psychological understandings, and so forth that make them experience and express racism differently. However, binary paradigms repress their experience and saturate them with binary debates. Their language is covered with voice-over narratives and metanarrative interpretations that are representative of binary paradigms. They are urged to learn how to speak and what to speak to assimilate into, accommodate, and support this binary system. They are asked to learn how to think and what to think in certain ways. The power of binary thinking controls their language and thoughts.

When many Asian immigrant groups sought a better life and decided to move to a new nation, with new neighbors and a new culture, they did not expect these binary barriers and discriminations. They did not know how these divides would function and lock them in a box of binary constructions in the form of rules, laws, customs, and history before the immigration. However, as they started their immigrant lives in the U.S., they experienced newness and also marginalization and hardship in the intersections and interactions of binary paradigms, often without critical awareness. Regardless of their socioeconomic and political status, within these intersections and interactions, they were treated as the imperfect, incomplete other. The effects continue to exist. They are neither completely black nor white. They are neither near white nor near black. They are neither completely aliens nor natives. They are neither completely minorities nor nonminorities. They are never recognized as the complete other. Rather, they are treated as the invisible other who exists but never identified as the other at the opposite end. They are *the imperfect other*. Their "otherness" is a different other. It is as much a political, repressive other as it is an economic, indispensable other, but not the other whose presence requires absolute political correctness and economic oppression. Their otherness is not treated even as the other in binary paradigms. Existence of their otherness is denied. Binary paradigms dismiss their otherness as nonotherness because their otherness is positioned as the middle in binary relations and in third space in multirelations. I call it *the third other*. Asian immigrants are the third other. Their otherness is different from otherness in a binary sense. They are the other in a third sense. They are the other in between spaces. Their otherness is not the reflection of "I" or "the other." The third other is not the "shadow other" behind "I" and "the other," even though sometimes it does stand behind. Asian immigrant groups' otherness exists in interstitial spaces. Their otherness exists beyond the space of the other. It is otherness in margins and peripheries that do not hold the strong binary sense of otherness but picture the otherness in a saturated sense in limited capacity. Their otherness is saturated in the form of permanent guests and invisible citizens from multiplications and intersections of binary paradigms. This saturated otherness is presented in the sense of temporary, fragmented, localized universalities and repressive sociopolitical structures.

When some Asian immigrants fail and cannot "meet" legal or social conditions, their otherness is saturated, and they are seen as dangerous foreigners. Their being immigrants in the past is not recognized. Their past is quickly forgotten and fragmented. Their presence is terminated and even criminalized. They became dangerous others. They urgently need to remove themselves from where they used to be. When they hold temporary legal status, their otherness is saturated, and they are labeled as temporary workers. They are allowed to be there, but only temporarily. They are expected to "go back" at some point. Their temporary stay is conditional and provisional. They are under constant supervision and control. They are seen as temporary visitors. When Asian immigrant groups hold permanent resident status, their otherness is saturated, and they are presented as permanent guests or unwelcomed residents. They are invited as guests to stay legally but not welcomed as cohabitants. They experience strong sociopolitical repression and live in between social and political spaces. When they finally become citizens, their otherness is saturated, and they are recognized as invisible citizens. Their presence is individually localized and personally imperceptible. Their advancement and promotion are often underevaluated and stopped. They are often criticized for lack of communication skills and leadership skills. Then their otherness is saturated and universalized as lack of public leadership. As dangerous foreigners, temporary visitors, permanent guests, unwelcomed residents, and/or invisible citizens, their saturated otherness is emphasized and temporarily highlighted. At the same time, their presence is trivialized and dismissed. Their third otherness is vaporized in binary paradigms.

What does this third otherness mean in Asian immigrant contexts? How is Asian immigrants' third otherness perceived and practiced? What are the realities of their third otherness in institutions and social justice movements? How does being the third other impact their individual and communal psychology? How does the third otherness function, and how is it challenged?

The Third Other in Institutional Practice: Assimilation

As black/white, black/nonblack, and native/alien binary divides are invented, they become a paradigm for people to believe and accept as the norm. As black/white relations dominate racial discourses in public, they draw the line for nonwhite groups and nonblack groups to follow and not cross. This line determines the space and institutionalized strategies to define them. Assimilation is one of the powerful practices that draws this line to fortify black/white, black/nonblack, and native/alien binary relations. The model of assimilation is not just a model that is imposed on nonwhite groups to follow and adopt. It is the model that fosters a dangerous interaction between white institutional colonial binary paradigms to protect white privileges and individual desires to obtain white privileges. Individual desire includes not only white groups keeping their privileges but also other ethnic groups pursuing white privileges. As black/white, black/nonblack, and native/alien binary divides control ethnic relations, this dangerous interaction produces assimilation as a way of intensifying these binary divides. Assimilation becomes not only a socioeconomic imperative of protecting white privileges but also a moral imperative of legitimating and pursuing white privileges. It controls ethnic relationships and supports these divides to guard white domination.

Asian immigrant groups are the main subjects to follow this institutional practice. Assimilation for Asian immigrants functions as a device to erase their identities and foreign presence, leaving them to develop a new adopted identity and accept invisible presence. It is a new identity process for Asian immigrant groups to erase their difference and assume invisible identifiers of the society. In the practice of assimilation, they are asked to dismiss their racial/national identities and rebuild new identities between white and/or black positions. The more they assimilate, the more they experience their unexplainable otherness. They are treated as the other but encouraged not to be the other in this assimilation process. They live in the contradicting message. They learn and accept that they are the other but not the absolute other. Assimilation as an institutional practice determines the position of Asian immigrants as the third other. How then does assimilation determine the position of Asian immigrants? How was and is this practice developed in institutional settings and perceived in Asian immigrant contexts? What are the interpretations of the assimilation theories that have developed and changed in terms of sociopolitical relations? How are Asian American groups as the third other understood in the assimilation process?

After massive immigration between the 1800s and 1900s, several anthropologists and sociologists observed phenomena of different cultural encounters and tried to define them. The Social Science Research Council Subcommittee on Acculturation defined these phenomena as acculturation "which result[s] when groups of individuals having different cultures come into continuous firsthand contact, with subsequent changes in the original cultural patterns of either or both groups."[1] They see different cultural encounters and their changes for either and/or both groups. This definition does not necessarily show any power differences between two groups but expects changes from either and/or both groups.

Robert E. Park and Ernest W. Burgess define assimilation as "a process of interpenetration and fusion in which persons and groups acquire the memories, sentiments, and attitudes of other persons or groups, and by sharing their experience and history, are incorporated with them in a common cultural life."[2] This definition assumes two things: a process of interpenetration and fusion among individuals and communities and the existence of a common cultural life. This definition is not clear regarding whether interpenetration and fusion contribute to a common cultural life or not. It can be interpreted in two ways. First, this definition can imply that the common cultural life exists before interpenetration and fusion. There was a common cultural life, and then different groups brought interpenetration and fusion to that common cultural life, or the common cultural life was already formed and established. Sharing of personal and communal experiences and history does not necessarily change the common cultural life in this definition. A process of interpenetration and fusion is, rather, treated as a monoprocess of a simple merger into a common cultural life. Interpenetration does not interpenetrate the common communal life. It does not change the common communal life. It assimilates to the common cultural life. Interpenetration and fusion simply mean assimilation. Second, it can also be assumed that interpenetration and fusion contribute to the common communal life. The memories, sentiments, and attitudes are shared and become part of a common cultural life. However, it is not clear how interpenetration and fusion contribute and impact the common communal life. What is clear in this definition is that interpenetration and fusion exist, whether it impacts the common cultural life or not. And they are identified as assimilation. Still, this definition does not necessarily acknowledge power differences of inter-penetration and fusion that different ethnic groups make or impacts on the common cultural life.

However, recognition of power differences among various ethnic rela-tions has been quickly raised and debated. Some scholars saw these different cultural encounters and began to analyze power dynamics among different immigrant groups more specifically. *Dictionary of Sociology* defines assimi-lation in this way:

> Social assimilation does not require the complete identification of all the unities, but such modifications as eliminate the charac-teristics of foreign origin, and enable them all to fit smoothly into the typical structure and functioning of the new cultural unit. . . . In essence, assimilation is the substitution of one nationality pat-tern for another. Ordinarily, the modification must be made by the weaker or numerically inferior group.[3]

It clearly states that assimilation is no longer understood as a simple merger of cultural diversities. It is a modification of weaker groups under stron-ger groups. It becomes a power game that stronger white groups dominate the assimilation process and encourage nonwhite immigrant groups to fit into certain features of common cultural life. At the end of the process of assimilation, it is expected that cultural differences disappear, and stronger groups dominate everything.[4] There are neither ethnic identities nor nation-alities. It assumes a loss of particular ethnic identities and a disappearance of racial ethnic differences.[5] Assimilation continues to pressure nonwhite racial groups to learn white norms and culture.

One of the most influential assimilation theories is Robert Ezra Park's theory of the race relations cycle. He introduces four stages of assimilation: contact, competition, accommodation, and assimilation.[6] He uses Orientals, especially Chinese and Japanese, as an example to describe how human contact has caused competition.[7] He claims that "competition, which had been personal, became racial, and race competition became race conflict."[8] In this explanation, when Orientals entered the U.S., competition occurred and became racial conflicts. Orientals were treated as the ones who started competition. They, as the strangers, were the triggers to bringing problems to the host society and starting competition among other immigrant groups in the U.S. The pursuits of their individual and personal desire to achieve better lives were considered not as personal competition but as racial compe-tition because they were not seen as individuals like white groups were. They were instead seen as the representatives of visible strangers. Because it is not considered personal but communal, competition cannot be introduced as competition, but instead conflict. Because of their communal presentation, "a new race consciousness" was raised.[9] Going through their individual competition and communal racial conflicts, Park suggests that they tried to accommodate and learn the culture and hoped to eventually assimilate. The process of accommodation was the process of learning white culture, which led these Orientals to assimilate, even though they could not assimilate. It was considered impossible for them to assimilate, but they were guided to mimic white culture. Asian immigrants are not the other who cannot assimilate completely, but the third other who can assimilate but cannot complete the process. In the model of Park's assimilation theory, competition means conflicts only within nonwhite ethnic immigrant groups. In white groups, competition is not considered. No one can compete with white groups for two reasons. First, competition implies achieving equal status. However, within black/white and native/alien binary paradigms, achieving equal status is not accepted. Second, free and fair competition is not possible systematically and institutionally. If anyone wants to compete and demands free and fair competition within these unequal systems and institutions, competition means that he/she/they challenge(s) the systems and institutions. In this sense, nonwhite groups' desire to compete for advancement in their lives is seen as a dangerous demand to challenge white dominant society. Instead of competition, they are guided by both binary paradigms to accommodate white culture. Accommodation means to adopt or agree with white domination. These immigrant groups are encouraged to win white privileges by accommodating and assimilating. In this sense, the final goal of assimilation is establishing and validating white privileges. Park's race relations cycle ends with eventual and complete assimilation with white society by all ethnic immigrant groups.

Emory S. Bogardus is another sociologist who discusses the race relations cycle. Whereas Park and Milton M. Gordon explain how immigrants assimilate to the dominant white society, Bogardus describes how the dominant white society reacts to immigrants. He introduces seven stages of the attitudes of "native" Americans toward Asian and Latinx immigrant groups, including Chinese, Japanese, Filipinos, and Mexicans.[10] Bogardus uses "native" Americans as an identifier for white American groups, not Native American indigenous groups, in this theory. The first stage is curiosity. Asian immigrant groups and Mexicans are viewed with curiosity for their *strangeness* and fewness in numbers. The second stage is economic welcoming. They are welcomed because they work long hours for lower wages. The third stage is industrial and social antagonism. As more immigrants come, prejudice against them arises. Their high birthrates and aggregative living styles disturb the individualistic white American style. It is considered "race invasions."[11] White American groups feel this as a threat. They show antagonism in the form of patriotism and chauvinism. The fourth stage is legislative antagonism. "A full-fledged campaign is organized against the 'undesirable' immigrants."[12] Systematic discrimination happens in the name of state and national concerns. This discrimination will continue until white American groups feel secure. The fifth stage is fair play tendencies. It is a countermovement against these antagonisms by other white groups. It comes from justice seeking. Even though this movement is not steady, it does occur. It tries not only to help immigrants but also to maintain a national reputation. The sixth stage is quiescence. After certain restrictions are institutionally established against certain immigrant groups, the antagonistic groups and organizations modify their activities and change their attitudes. Meanwhile the protagonists show sympathy and seek justice in the future. The seventh stage is second-generation difficulties. Bogardus raises this concern specifically for Japanese and Mexicans who come to the U.S. with their families.

The racial relations cycle is understood within the framework of assimilation theories. Some scholars, like Park, show how the racial relations cycle on the side of immigrant groups moves toward assimilation, and other scholars, like Bogardus, try to explain how racial relations cycle on the side of white groups or how white society sets up barriers to immigrants' assimilation. Assimilation is encouraged by both immigrant groups and white groups. However, it is simultaneously discouraged by both groups. Immigrant groups are encouraged to assimilate, but they themselves resist white domination by not achieving complete assimilation. White groups try to protect white domination by making sure that immigrant groups cannot assimilate completely. At the same time, they encourage other groups to assimilate so that other groups can taste white privileges and foster a desire to have them. As long as they have that desire, white privileges are protected.

Even though these groups show different approaches to emphasize assimilation, they understand assimilation as the guideline for Asian and Latinx immigrants to follow. When Bogardus and Park describe different levels or stages, they share common analyses to support each other. Bogardus believes that immigrants are first seen with curiosity and somewhat welcomed by white Americans for their cheap labor. For Park, this is the stage of contact. Both white groups and Asian groups interact with different purposes and expectations at this stage. On the side of Asian and Latinx immigrants, socioeconomic and political reasons are the main reasons to stay in the U.S. On the side of white groups, economic reasons are the main reasons to receive immigrant groups. As both of their needs are met, they come and interact. When competition begins not only among ethnic immigrant groups but also with white groups, industrial, social, and legislative antagonism arises among white groups. Thus, the meaning of competition in assimilation can be narrowly defined. White groups designate certain spaces for nonwhite groups to compete against each other, but not with them. Ironically, in order to avoid competition with other ethnic groups, white groups create these antagonistic barriers to win the competition. As white groups win the competition and create these antagonisms in all places systematically and institutionally, immigrant groups have to accommodate to these barriers as "the way things are" by accepting these antagonisms.

For immigrant groups, accommodation is a survival imperative in colonial and postcolonial immigrant spaces. Whether they want to accommodate the needs of white environments or not, they have to accommodate these needs. When immigrants are encouraged to learn how to accommodate white groups, they are guided to assimilate. For Park, assimilation is the final stage for immigrant groups to finally be ready to live in the U.S. The first three stages are the learning process to let go of their own authenticities. For Bogardus, assimilation is the result of immigrant groups being forced to accept industrial, social, and legislative antagonism. When immigrants accept assimilation, some white groups show sympathy and other white groups begin to calm down. Fair play tendencies are the side of white groups' defense to demonstrate good white morality. Bogardus believes that after white groups win the competition, establish the restrictions and barriers, and secure their places, they enter the stage of quiescence. However, this stage has not happened. There is no stage of quiescence. White groups never permit quiescence with other ethnic groups. They always are alert to and protective of their privileges. Whether immigrants want to assimilate or are forced to assimilate, until immigrant groups show an effort to assimilate and submit to white power, assimilation is emphasized as a way to control racial relations.

One of the most influential assimilation theories of the twentieth century is Milton M. Gordon's theory. Based on three axes—Anglo conformity, melting pot, and cultural pluralism—he develops seven stages of assimilation: cultural or behavior assimilation, structural assimilation, marital assimilation, identificational assimilation, attitude receptional assimilation, behavior receptional assimilation, and civic assimilation. Cultural or behavior assimilation is the first and the most basic assimilation. It is individual and communal interactions with common cultural lives. Gordon believes that immigrant groups will naturally change and adopt cultural patterns of host countries by assimilating to cultures and/or behaviors. The second stage, structural assimilation, is the most crucial assimilation stage for Gordon. He believes if structural assimilation happens, all other assimilations will naturally follow.[13] The ultimate stage of assimilation is civic assimilation. Without conflicts over value and power, immigrants will completely merge into the host society in this theory.

Gordon's assumption of assimilation is that the host society holds absolute power to change immigrant groups, and immigrant groups have no power to influence the host society. It seems that the host society feels no impacts or influences from immigrant groups. It is immigrant groups that are the subject of change. Gordon's concept of assimilation is unidirectional and binary. It does not allow any interactions and interdependences between the host society and immigrant groups. The host society and immigrant groups are separate entities and establish binary hierarchical relationships between them. Even though this theory indicates a merger for immigrant groups to dive into white society in every dimension, it reveals the impossibility of immigrant groups assimilating.

Assimilation has been a key to understanding relations among all ethnic and racial groups. It functions to keep Asian immigrant groups in the position of being the third other. Analyzing the theories of Park, Gordon, and Bogardus, I explain how racial relations are enacted and woven into black/ white, black/nonblack, and native/alien binary divides through assimilation theories. These scholars believe that whether it is by white power or the individual and communal desire of immigrant groups, assimilation occurs, and I argue it is encouraged by these binary divides. As these definitions and theories illustrate, assimilation theories demonstrate how Asian immigrants need to behave around white domination. They attempt to instruct how different racial ethnic groups need to develop a relationship with white power, and they intend to validate the current patterns of racial relations and practices. They provide the general and intentional guidance in ethnic immigrant relations to white society.

However, these theories are critically evaluated and debated. Scholars like Michael W. Foley and Dean R. Hoge point out that assimilation theories assume neither multidirectional nor interactional processes, but a unidirectional process.[14] These theories are based on the assumptions of the monolithic host society and monolithic white culture. The predominant view of assimilation does not allow different ways of going through the acculturation process but a monoway of imitation for adopting monowhite culture. It emphasizes white relations as the core of all relations. Most assimilation theories teach that the host society influences immigrants in a unidirectional way and that this way is not irreversible. Immigrants are the subjects of receiving influences from the white hosting society. They need to buy, accept, and even desire white ways of living. White domination and/or power are presented as the common life and common ground to start with in these theories. As the host society holds power to change immigrants, it does not expect any differences among them. The loss of the differences is expected and invigorated. In the end, assimilation means agreeing to white domination willingly.

The invention of the assimilation process is clear. Under black/white, black/nonblack, and native/alien divides, the assimilation process was created for nonwhite and nonblack ethnic groups to fit into these binary relations.

Specifically, for Asian groups, as it encourages them to accept these binary relations, it also urges them to dissimulate their Asian identities and cultures. The process propagates the legitimacy of white power and causes groups to disdain their Asianness. It negates their presence but recognizes their difference. Their foreignness is visible in binary divides, but their presence is forgotten in these same structures. Their third otherness exists in this dual visible and invisible presence through the process of assimilation. These binary structures recognize their presence as "who they are not" but does not recognize their existential being. Assimilation is "dissimulation" for Asian immigrants.[15] It challenges them not to be the other. At the same time, it locates them as the other. They are the other in reality, but not the other in political and social correctness. Their third otherness exists between this reality and sociopolitical correctness. They are by no means the perfect other but the imperfect other by any means necessary in this assimilation process. In their third otherness, assimilation is dissimulation of binary divides.

Institutions practice assimilation not as the goal for Asian immigrants to achieve but as the strategy for them to *realize* the impossibility of assimilation. This realization of being the third other is the goal of the assimilation process. The model of assimilation starts from two conflictive assumptions.

> The underlying assumption was, "You will become like us whether you want to or not." For people of color, however, the prevailing unspoken message was, "no matter how much like us you are, you will remain apart." Thus, the adversarial and oppositional dynamic of intergroup relations in racial pluralism began to develop on two fronts. At the same time that society pursued a policy aimed at the assimilation of recent arrivals from Europe, it also segregated people of color, who by virtue of their much longer history in the society had already contributed significantly to the shaping of a corporate culture in the United States. People of color were gradually silenced and marginalized by these two forces.[16]

On the one hand, assimilation is required for all racial ethnic groups, including even white immigrant groups, to accept and follow. All groups and individuals need to learn who whites are, what makes whiteness, and how to be white. It is important to teach what white is and to mark the territories of white power. As black/white and black/nonblack divides underline whiteness and blackness, assimilation to whiteness and not to blackness is carefully designed and implanted in the minds and consciousness of Asian immigrants. On the other hand, assimilation is not an achievable goal but a tool to force Asian immigrant groups to be silent. Hoping to achieve the American Dream, they try to assimilate, act like whites, speak like whites, look like whites, and be like whites. However, they know in the end that they cannot act, speak, look, and be like whites. Their efforts to be white are impossible tasks. From the beginning, it was set up for failure for all immigrant groups, including Asian immigrants, to dissimilate.

In these conflictive assumptions, the third otherness of Asian immigrant groups is born and raised. Their otherness is suppressed by desires to be white. Because they believe they can be white, this belief ignores the existence of their otherness. Their otherness is invisible by not only the society but also themselves. Their otherness is not completely accepted by both. It exists in denial. They are the other, but not completely the other because their otherness is seen only as the partial truth. Their incomplete otherness is recognized as temporary otherness that can be overcome. Their partial otherness is understood as only partially fragmented otherness that can be redeemed. This incomplete and partial otherness presents the third otherness. Their hope to be white persuades society and them to negate their otherness. Their triangulated position between the black/white binary and native/alien binary perceives this otherness as not the other but the nonanother. They are neither white nor black. Their double negated position does not allow their anotherness, their independent existence. Their third position of otherness confuses the binary assimilation process not to recognize their existence as an independent being, another being. It dismisses their presence as the disposable other who becomes the substitute in these binary structures.

Their third otherness exists not only as the reality but also as the result of the assimilation process. As this assimilation is continuously instructed toward the continuous flowing streams of immigrants, it is one of the most powerful institutional practices to perpetuate Asian immigrant groups as being the third other. It means that the assimilation process never ends for Asian immigrants, and their otherness is never completely revealed. Their otherness is covered with deceptive hope and unreachable goals to pursue. Because the assimilation process causes Asian immigrant groups to hold this dissimulated hope and goal as an achievable American Dream, it makes them implant their third otherness as the necessary developmental stage to pass. Their third otherness is incessantly discharged and unseen.

The Third Other in Social Justice Practice: Coalition Work

Whereas assimilation is set up by black/white, black/nonblack, and native/alien binary divides as an institutional practice to support white domination, coalition work is raised by many immigrant groups, including Asian immigrant groups, as a social justice practice to protect their own identities and survival. As assimilation is encouraged and forced on all ethnic groups, coalition work also increases among ethnic immigrant groups. If assimilation means to accept white ways of living, coalition work means to create their own ways of surviving/living, and it often occurs in the form of resistance.

The concept of resistance is fundamental in coalition work. Resistance often appears in sociopsychological identity development as a reaction/ response to naïve or acceptance stages.[17] From monoracial groups to multiracial and multicultural racial groups, resistance is often explained as the stage that many groups go through to recognize white oppression and cultivate their own ways to sustain themselves in U.S. society. Even though it is a fact that immigrants are "still adapting to microconditions that lie beyond their control," most immigrants resist, challenge, and creatively improve these conditions simultaneously.[18] As they are aware of the impacts of assimilation, they begin to suspect the way things are. Resistance starts with questions about the current status quo and continues with analyses of the assimilation process with reasonable doubt and suspicion. In the theories of identity development, resistance is often described as the second or third stage to pass.[19] It is the stage at which people are intentionally, consciously, and/or unintentionally and unconsciously aware of hidden and unhidden racism. They often feel rage. Resistance comes from the counterreaction that people have when they question the acceptance or assimilation they are taught to practice.

In these identity models, resistance is described as the immature stage or a stage to pass through, whereas integration is described as the final stage to achieve for any human development. Worded differently, resistance is described as passing through zones to obtain integration. It catches problems of acceptance but reacts to them in the form of rejection. Resistance is easily identified with rejection to white culture in a premature sense. It is not a form meant to exist as the final form. However, I argue that resistance is not the stage to pass through but the stage to live in continuously. It is not a complete refusal or rejection of white culture, but the part of integration and a mode of life that nonwhite groups often experience continuously. It is the *constant strength* to fight for better lives. It is one of the most vibrant practices against black/white, black/nonblack, and native/alien binary paradigms.

As institutional practice coerces Asian immigrant groups to assimilate, involvement in coalition work as social justice practice shows their natural, but intentional reaction/response to resist this institutional practice. They experience assimilation and resistance against assimilation simultaneously. Being in the position of the third other, they are asked to learn how to assimilate to whiteness and relearn how to dissimilate themselves beneath this assimilation process. As they assimilate, they learn about their ambiguous otherness. As they resist, they find their triangulative position as the ambiguous, incomplete other. Resistance in the form of coalition work is not necessarily the opposite of assimilation. It does not mean a complete refusal to understand immigrant reality. Rather, it is a creative way to adjust with their own consciousness. As they experience their incomplete nonbinary otherness (of which they might not consciously be aware), they collaborate with others in the form of social justice movements. Even though they are not treated as the binary other, their third otherness experience moves Asian immigrant groups to choose to join others. Their third otherness becomes a choice to be the other. As Asian immigrant groups experience the invisible otherness in their immigrant reality, they use their third otherness as a crucial imperative for coalition work with others. When Asian immigrant groups resist, their third otherness raises solidarity. It becomes a force to transform public institutional relations into individual and communal relationships. It encourages fixed and forced relations to move to organic and resilient relationships.

Coalition work is one form of resistance work that Asian immigrant groups demonstrate often. As we discussed, relations between Asian immigrant groups and African Americans are locked within black/white and black/nonblack binary systems, forcing them to be competitors. Asian immigrant groups are pictured as contemptible business merchants, whereas African Americans are stereotyped as dangerous poor customers. Los Angeles incidents and New York boycotts are the symbolic examples of these conflictive relationships. They see each other as opponents to obtain certain privileges and economic benefits in these systems. Yet, although it is not well known, Asian immigrant groups and African Americans have coalitions and work together in the form of coalition work. Asian immigrant groups work with African Americans to fight against racism. As they experienced injustice in terms of racism and prejudice against immigrants, they found their common ground to start their relationship as "ambivalent friends."[20] From the beginning of Asian immigrant history, African Americans and Asian immigrant groups formed ambivalent but sympathetic collaborative relationships. Their third other position evokes other racial groups to feel ambivalence and ambiguity about their otherness not as real otherness. In the eyes of other racial groups, the position of the third other is not specifically named, but it is partially identified. Asian immigrants' incomplete otherness gives other groups fear and doubt as well as trust and solidarity. The position of their third otherness is not completely accepted in this coalition work, but it is partially understood out of necessity. Under the strong power of binary paradigms, their relationship was often tested and became ambivalent because of their conflictive sociopolitical relationship. However, at the same time, as they had parallel racial discriminative experiences, they felt sympathy for each other and recognized the needs of solidarity. In their actions, they created collaborative work to make their lives better together. In this process, their individual and communal relationships were formed simultaneously. Their individual relationships were often crafted in the forms of friendship and interracial marriage, such as the case of Masumizu Kuninosuke, one of "the first Japanese settlers in California in 1869," "who married an African American woman," and Jean Ng, "an African American married to a Chinese American, was buried in a Chinese cemetery."[21] However, even these individual relationships went further than interracial marriages.

> In 1927, Lemon Lee Sing, a sixty-eight-year-old Chinese laundryman in New York City, filed to adopt Firman Smith, an African American child he had found sleeping in a hallway. Sam Lee, a Chinese restaurant owner in Washington D.C., refused to fire one of his African American employees despite threats on his life, while in Chicago, in 1929, a Chinese restaurant was dynamited for serving African Americans.[22]

These examples show that their individual solidarity extended to social justice activity and was deeply intertwined with sociopolitical struggles that they went through together. As individuals, they demonstrated amazing support and solidarity. They fought together to protect each other. They chose communal survival beyond individual disadvantages. Their admirable efforts changed their ethnic individual relations into *personal collaborative* relationships. As they deepened their individual relationships, they also built communal and sociopolitical relationships. They recognized their similar experiences of racism and worked to deteriorate white power. There are more examples of these sociopolitical relationships.

> Many African Americans opposed America's imperialism in the Philippines on the basis of racial solidarity with the Filipinos as oppressed people. . . . When management tried to displace Africans with Filipino Americans in 1925, the African American Brotherhood of Sleeping Car Porters welcomed Filipino Americans as members. Unlike the racist American Federation of Labor that excluded both African and Asian Americans, the Brotherhood reasoned, "We want our Filipino brothers to understand that it is necessary for them to join the Brotherhood in order to help secure conditions and wages which they too will benefit from."[23]

> In 1935 and 1937 the Filipino Community of Seattle, Inc., a coalition of clubs, lodges, and associations was created to increase Filipino influence in the Democratic Party, worked with Seattle civil rights organizations, progressive labor unions, and the Washington Commonwealth Federation to successfully block the intermarriage ban introduced in the state legislature.[24]

During World War II, amidst a racist war conducted in the Pacific and the mass detention of Japanese Americans at home, a majority of African Americans polled rejected discrimination against the Japanese.[25]

They gathered last week in front of the Department of Youth Services to do two things: to announce a coalition for fighting youth violence and to blast mainstream press for "race-baiting media coverage" that has characterized the Asian American and African American communities as violence-ridden. Led by the state commissions on Asian American and African American affairs and comprised of 44 local groups, the coalition issued a proclamation May 11 (1994) to work with media, government, law enforcement, schools and the business community to "end violence, increase peace and rebuild support structures for our families and communities."[26]

In the state of Washington, for example, effective political alliances have been formed between African and Asian American politicians, and several cities have multi-ethnic planning councils and cooperative groups. To disseminate and build these efforts, there is a need for both black and Asian intellectuals and activists to become more active in dispelling the destructive stereotypes, which the groups often have of one another, and to find new grounds for common understanding, common interests, and—possibly—common political action. A proactive communications and media strategy would be a part of this endeavor. Absent sustained "affirmative involvement," driven by a network of like-minded leading individuals focused on commonality rather than conflict, Asian black relations are likely to deteriorate further, to the disadvantage of both groups and of the American polity.[27]

Interethnic cooperation in politics has also emerged between blacks and Chinese Americans in Boston, Massachusetts.[28]

As these examples show, throughout history Asian immigrant groups and black groups have worked together even though Asian/black relations are complicated and conflictive. As they relate to each other, the relationship is formed in solidarity. They as individuals and communities tried to collaborate with each other despite their rivalrous situations. Recognizing the black/white binary paradigm, they understood the problems of racism and were determined to work together. However, their coalition work seemed weakened in the 1980s and 1990s. Under increasing influences from individualism and global capitalism, their coalition work seemed to disappear. Specifically, when middle-class Asian immigrant groups moved to the U.S. in the 1970s and 1980s, their relationships shifted from collaborative racial justice work to class conflicts.[29] The conflictive relations between black groups and Asian groups were presented as problematic and harmful. Many Asian immigrant groups such as Korean, Chinese, Vietnamese, and Latinx groups came to the U.S. "not as impoverished neocolonial immigrants, but as invited and assisted political pawns of the ideological war between capitalism and communism."[30] They brought their wealth, skill, education, and other resources from their motherlands. Because of this class conflict, Asian immigrants were criticized by both black groups and other nonwhite ethnic groups for not participating in coalition work in enthusiastically. As discussed before, it is partially true that Asian immigrants had less interest in coalition work because of this class issue, along with unique challenges and inner struggles that were discussed in the previous chapters. Many of them are still not aware of their third otherness and do not have much intention to work with other racial groups who experience absolute otherness in terms of sociohistorical and econopolitical hierarchies. At the same time, however, it is also true that they do coalition work continuously in a marginalized space and that their leadership is not necessarily invited in this multiethnic coalition work. Because of their unnamed, unidentified otherness, the third otherness, they still strive to work with others who share the positions of otherness.

Congregation-based community organizing is a good example. Congregation-based community organizing, or faith-based community organizing, is "a means for congregations to engage their members to connect with their neighbors and communities, and to address social inequalities while simultaneously transforming communities and congregational life."[31] This is a "mass-based progressive" movement that is different from "middle class progressive movements such as feminism, peace, and environmentalism."[32] This organizing movement was inspired by Saul Alinsky, who started to organize Chicago neighborhoods in 1939 and established the Industrial Areas Foundation (IAF) in 1940. He claimed, "Revolution by the Have-Nots has a way of inducing moral revelation among the Haves."[33] He believed power and leadership from the bottom can change the current structure that elite groups have built. His activism in faith-rooted community organization inspired many religious leaders to simultaneously work with community and religious institutions. Various ethnic religious groups organized their congregations and participated in this organizing movement. Based on the faith and teachings of Dr. Martin Luther King Jr. and the methodology of Alinsky, many religious organizations worked together for various issues, such as "healthcare access and reform, living wage ordinances, transportation equity, community benefits agreements, immigration reform, mass incarceration, bank lending and foreclosure practices, public school funding, affordable housing, crime reduction, and police accountability."[34]

In 1969, the Catholic bishops founded the Catholic Campaign for Human Development (CCHD) for churches to work with communities to support the poor and the marginalized through social justice initiatives and confronting poverty. In 2012, Brad Fulton's research showed that 189 organizations with 3,500 congregations in forty states were involved in this movement.[35] Currently, there are several national church-based community organizations in the United States: Direct Action and Research Training Center (DRAT), the Gamaliel Foundation, the IAF, InterValley Project (IVP), People Improving Communities through Organizing (the PICO National Network), and the National People's Action (NPA). Many diverse groups among white, black, and Latinx religious groups organize their congregations to participate in these organizations. The majority of groups are Catholic, Protestant, and Baptist: "Roman Catholic (35%), moderate/liberal Protestant (34%), Baptist (13%, mostly National, Missionary, and Primitive Baptists, thus mostly African American), historic black Protestant (5%), traditionalist Protestant (3%), Jewish (2%), Church of God in Christ (2%), Pentecostal (mostly African American), Unitarian-Universalist (2%), Other Christian (3%), Other non-Christian (1%)."[36] These organizations train clergy and lay leaders to organize their congregation and communities to engage with various issues in public meetings and campaigns. However, among these national church-based community organizations, Asian immigrant congregations (mostly interracial; less than 2 percent majority Asian, Pacific Islander, Native American) represent less than 2 percent of the racial makeup, whereas "38% white/European American, 33% African American, and 20% Hispanic (includes native-born and immigrant)" congregations sponsor these organizations.[37] From this statistic, it can be easily wrongly concluded that Asian American groups do not participant in multiethnic and multicultural coalition work. Missing Asian immigrant churches' presence and lack of leadership of Asian immigrant groups in this movement can be interpreted as the problem of foreigners who ignore or avoid coalition work.

However, if we look closer, there are several layers of complications that Asian immigrant groups experience in this movement. First, this movement is based on Christianity. Christianity is one of the most influential religions for many European, African American, and Hispanic groups, whereas it is not the most popular religion among Asian religious groups. While there are growing numbers of Christians in Asian immigrant groups, they are minorities in the tradition and are not necessarily recognized as minorities in this movement. Their third otherness does not cause them to be recognized as the religious other, but as nonparticipants who ignore coalition work. Currently, there are growing numbers of Christians in Asian immigrant groups, especially Korean and Chinese immigrant groups. Even though many Christians in Asian immigrant groups are conservative evangelical Christians who hesitate to participate in any sociopolitical social justice movements, among Asian immigrant Christian groups, Korean, Chinese, and Filipino church members are actively involved with local and regional congregation-based organizations like Clergy and Laity United for Economic Justice.[38] Furthermore, many Asian immigrant Christian churches, including conservative evangelical Christian churches, are very actively involved with missionary work to support people in other countries by providing educational opportunities, health care, and housing as a part of their church ministry. Regardless of denominations, many Asian immigrant Christian churches consider this work as God's mission to carry out for the poor and marginalized beyond their ethnic communities. Without considering Asian immigrant groups' religious background and Christian missiological history, Asian immigrant groups are simply seen as self-centered and self-interested communities who do not participate in collaborative coalition work. Thus, prejudice against Asian immigrant groups can easily occur. Their religious otherness in terms of Christianity is recognized as not the complete other, but the incomplete and ambiguous other whose solidarity and trust are questioned.

Second, most communication in this movement or any movement is done through English and/or Spanish. Because of large numbers of Latinx groups, Spanish translation can be offered,[39] but translations of other languages are rarely offered in congregation-based community-organizing meetings. As variations of English and Spanish function along a binary divide, many Asian languages are recognized as the third other. Because their otherness is not seriously recognized by the other, translation is not needed. Rather, their third otherness is expressed in public as muteness. Their otherness is recognized, but not recognized enough to translate. Even though their presence is needed in terms of multicultural diversity, their active participation is prevented because of this reason. As Asian immigrant groups fear speaking English and many of them have a hard time understanding English, they have a difficult time comprehending the political atmosphere and its agendas, creating shared understandings, and making a common ground to work for certain coalition issues and agendas. As a result, they show ignorance of social justice issues and abandon collaborative work. Furthermore, Asian immigrant groups who have no difficulty in speaking English still receive "microaggressions and subtle messages of racial bias" that "affect Asian American individuals' appraisals of present and future social interactions."[40] Regardless of their English skills, their communicative abilities are always under suspicion. Microaggressions and subtle racism are common barriers to their leadership and participation. They experience the third otherness between English and Spanish, and their own languages become the third discourse to dismiss.

Third, as mentioned in the previous chapter, Asian immigrant groups give more attention to social justice work for their mother countries. Their attentions are divided as their communities are transnationally divided. Transnational relationships are brought from the beginning of their immigrant lives and continue out of their individual and communal survival. Their third otherness starts to exist in these transnational contexts. As they intensify transnational connections and belongingness, they bring the otherness to the third space beyond the immigrant and motherland contexts. With and without awareness, they locate themselves in the third space apart from the "I" and "the other." Their third otherness is their choice and survival at the same time. It is formed by the circumstances but carried out by the will of Asian immigrant groups in this transnational context.

As white, black, and Latinx groups lead this coalition work, it is important to recognize that without extending intentional invitations to Asian immigrant groups from the current white, black, and Latinx leaders, it is harder for Asian Christian minority groups as the third other to join this movement. As Jacob Lesniewski and Marc Doussard describe, multicultural and multiracial movements have to diversify their memberships under the influences of civil rights movements, third-wave feminism, and social justice.[41] Without intentional diversification, this movement cannot yield multiracial and multicultural collaborative work for all. Multiracial and multicultural coalition work requires crossing the boundaries of individual and communal groups and including Asian immigrant groups.[42] It is easier to treat Asian immigrant groups as the groups that ignore coalition work than for white, black, and Latinx leaders to intentionally invite Asian immigrant groups to participate in and share leadership together.

Within native/alien binary discussions, Asian immigrant groups are often dismissed as invisible aliens, whereas Latinx groups are understood as visible aliens who need the most consideration for immigrant rights movements. As discussed in the previous chapter, immigrant issues become Latinx-dominated issues. When the native/alien binary paradigm frames Latinx issues as *the* immigrant issue, other racial immigrant issues are dismissed and silenced. As three groups—white, black, and Latinx—dominate leadership in this social justice immigrant movement,[43] it is important for them to intentionally include Asian immigrant groups and share leadership together. At the same time, Asian immigrant groups need to show more active participation and develop their leadership in this movement. Without considering the dynamics between these groups and inner Asian immigrant dynamics, Asian immigrant groups' invisibility in leadership and participation can be constantly criticized as arrogance and ignoring others as the groups remain in their racial ethnic enclave.

As this example illustrates, the third otherness of Asian immigrant groups has negated their collaborative work with other ethnic groups in the form of incompleteness and minimization in public. However, Asian immigrant groups' coalition work never stops. It is actually better presented in the form of pan-Asian coalition work. They use their experience of being the third other as the common ground to connect with others who experience otherness in the U.S. immigrant context. Their third otherness is transformed and functions differently in this social justice immigrant movement. Pan-Asian coalition work is one of the most popular types of coalition work in which many Asian immigrant groups have participated. Out of necessity and sociopolitical needs, Asian immigrant groups are encouraged to form a pan-Asian identity and lead and participate in pan-Asian coalition movements in the U.S. "Given that Asian Americans vary greatly by religion, language, and political ideology, structural factors appear to be the major contributors to a panethnic identity."[44] Structurally and systematically, Asian immigrant groups are expected to form some common Asian identities according to U.S. racial stratification. As they form common identities forcibly, unconsciously and consciously, and recognize the need for collaboration, they seek out ways to work together. Their third otherness functions as one of the common grounds that they share. Even though their third otherness is a given condition in this binary society, their being as the third other provides a common ground to hold various Asian immigrant groups doing coalition work continuously and independently among themselves. Crossing different Asian origins and interacting with other non-Asian ethnic immigrant groups, many Asian immigrant groups, especially the second- and the third-generation groups, show great participation in pan-Asian American coalition work. Through forming panethnic identities and building community based on religious and/or cultural institutions, they redress pan-Asian organizing movements. They free themselves from binary structures and choose the third way to empower coalition work. In the 1970s and 2010s, instead of doing coalition work between black groups and Asian immigrant groups, their coalition works continued in the works of multicultural coalitions and pan-Asian coalitions, such as the Asian American Legal Defense and Education Fund and Asian Americans Advancing Justice.

The Asian American Legal Defense and Education Fund (AALDEF) is a national organization that has worked for Asian American civil rights since 1974. It provides several programs, such as "Economic Justice for Workers, Immigrant Rights and Post 9/11 Civil Liberties, Voting Rights and Civic Participation, Educational Equality and Youth Rights, Anti-Trafficking Initiative, Housing and Environmental Justice, Affirmative Action, Anti-Asian Bias, and Leadership Development."[45] This organization cultivates economic and political justice and equal educational opportunities for various Asian immigrant groups. It seriously considers the advancement of Asian immigrant lives economically, politically, and educationally. The contradictory issues, such as affirmative action, anti-Asian sentiments, and leadership, are intentionally discussed and acted on.

Asian Americans Advancing Justice is another example. It was founded in 2013 and developed a network of four independent groups:

> Asian Americans Advancing Justice in Los Angeles (formerly the Asian Pacific American Legal Center), the largest legal organization serving Asian Americans; Asian Americans Advancing Justice in Chicago (formerly the Asian American Institute), the major pan-Asian American organization in the Midwest; Asian Americans Advancing Justice (AAJC, formerly the Asian American Justice Center), a civil rights and lobbying organization based in Washington, D.C.; and Asian Americans Advancing Justice-Asian Law Caucus (formerly the Asian Law Caucus) in San Francisco, the oldest legal organization devoted to defending Asian American civil rights.[46]

These groups have formed strong pan-Asian identities and are deeply involved with issues of religion, race, gender, and sexuality.[47] As they understand the current criticism of Asian immigrant groups being invisible in public leadership and lacking participation in the political legal domain, they present and try to protect Asian immigrant civil rights as equal and full members of this society. They see the importance of political power for Asian immigrants and intentionally provide more educational opportunities and cultivate belongingness. The research of Kim Geron, Enrique de la Cruz, Leland T. Saito, and Jaideep Singh indicates that many Asian immigrant groups recognize the importance of political power and create networks and resources from panethnic cooperation as they lead and participate in social justice movements, such as labor activism and language restriction on commercial signage.[48] The DREAM Act movement is another example of this pan-Asian organizing movement. Asian immigrant groups, especially student groups like Asian Students Promoting Immigrant Rights through Education (ASPIRE), work together to fight for immigrant rights and pursue equality for immigrants with other ethnic groups beyond their own ethnic groups.[49]

Even though it is difficult to work together, even among Asian immigrant groups, they see the need for collaboration as the third other, and they learn to collaborate with others. Through multiple channels of collaborative movements and leadership, Asian immigrant groups work and show collaborative effort. In fact, multicultural coalitions are now required and have been insisted on in recent years.[50] As members of multicultural communities,

Asian immigrant groups are required to be in solidarity with other groups. Even though their third otherness is formed by binary divides and structures, it functions as the common ground to initiate coalition action. Coalition work between Asian immigrant groups and nonwhite ethnic groups has the power to transform their static and conflictive relations into powerful and collaborative relationships. It moves Asian immigrant groups out of the third otherness, beyond marginalization, and leads them to be good allies, participants, and coleaders. As they transform their third otherness into resistance, receiving strength from their colonial past and postcolonial presence, they continue to resist and create new ways to overcome this otherness. They present challenges to create the better conditions for not only themselves but also others beyond the otherness. Even though their third otherness is not named and shared by other groups, they are understood by others and invited to share their experience of otherness. They are expected to share and develop common ground to work together. Their coalition work in the position of the third other takes different forms and requires different racial ethnic groups to move together. Their incomplete otherness encourages them to fight for freedom and justice together. Their desire for independence and freedom does not come from the leadership of the elite class but from below as the other and the third other. Building "people power" starts from connecting with others.[51] It changes their present and future. Not as individuals but as members of communities, they fight for their freedom and have achieved independence. Based on their third otherness and beyond it, Asian immigrant groups resisted, and they resisted together.

Community organizing is not new for Asian immigrant groups. They organize their religious institutions, local communities, and international affiliating institutes in the forms of rebellious groups, guerrillas, women's social groups, church prayer groups, Buddhist meditation groups, newspaper groups, book groups, social groups, and student groups to fight against colonial power. Their resistance in the form of community organizing has always existed in their colonial history. As they move to the U.S., their position as being the third other evokes their memories to pursue community organizing as the form of collaborative resistance that they embodied in their history. Many Asian immigrant groups resist and change the way of assimilation through coalitions. In the struggle of resistance, they understand that their challenge in the U.S. is to know how to build relationships "that can facilitate both the upward flow of influence and the exercise of collective power."[52] Even though their Asian cultures in their motherlands demonstrate top-down hierarchical leadership, they practice bottom-up rebellious community organizing movements, as many Asian historical events show. Learning both top-down and bottom-up relationships, they do struggle to balance how to facilitate both the upward flow of influence and cultivate collective power from the bottom. Their third other position holds them to meet this balance continuously in the U.S. immigrant context.

Because Asian immigrant groups as being the third other are encouraged to assimilate into black/white, black/nonblack, and native/alien binary divides, they forcibly accept these binary divides as the norm of this society. They forcibly and creatively adopt and adapt racial relations. At the same time, many Asian immigrant groups resist and challenge society to change the map of these binary relations to nonbinary relationships. Instead of accepting white domination, their third otherness destines Asian immigrant groups to work against white domination collaboratively and struggle together individually and communally toward justice and equality. As the third other, they live in between these simultaneous conflictive dynamics. Even though their leadership has been invisible in public and their presence in these coalition works is often marginalized because of their third otherness, Asian immigrant groups constantly have worked with black and other nonwhite ethnic groups in multicultural coalition and pan-Asian coalition works through the channels of religious communities and nonprofit organizational activities.

As their third otherness is revealed institutionally and sociopolitically in the public domain, it is also seriously revealed psychologically in the personal and communal domain. Their personal and communal psychological formation and transformation are radically formed by this third otherness experience. When they experience individual and communal negation from society, living the in-betweenness of black/white, black/nonblack, and native/alien binaries as the other but not the perfect other, they develop serious psychological mechanisms to survive. Their third other position greatly impacts the formation of their immigrant identities and finds a way to transform their relationships. Therefore, in the next section, it is important to explore how Asian immigrant groups struggle with their third otherness psychologically and try to overcome this otherness beyond binary social political constructions.

The Third Other in Psychological Practice: Belongingness

As Asian immigrant groups experience their third otherness institutionally and sociopolitically in the public domain, they undergo serious psychological transitions and transformations in the personal and communal domain within their own ethnic groups and beyond. In my previous work, *A Postcolonial Self: Korean Immigrant Theology and Church*, I introduced how a postcolonial self is constructed in the Korean immigrant context. Understanding their sense of communal identity, "we-ness," is denounced and shattered when they move to the new land. They encounter the individual "I" as the dominant identity. However, the more they mimic and assimilate into the dominant identity, the more they individually experience their identity as "I as the other." As permanent guests, their membership in society is denied. They realize they are never invited as "I as the center" with full membership. They recall their embedded memories of communal identity but realize this communal identity as "we as the other" in their immigrant reality. Their embodied we-ness reminds them to bring their communal identity in a new place even though it is not "we as the center," but "we as the other." Changing their communal ethnic-centered we-ness to immigrant other-ness is one of the most difficult traumatic experiences that not only Korean immigrants but also many other Asian immigrants have to go through. However, this change is often misrecognized and unrecognized by other groups.

> Our identity is partly shaped by recognition or its absence, often by the *mis*recognition of others, and so a person or group of people can suffer real damage, real distortion, if the people or society around them mirror back to them a confining or demeaning or contemptible picture of themselves. Nonrecognition or misrecognition can inflict harm, can be a form of oppression, imprisoning someone in a false, distorted, and reduced mode of being. Thus, some feminists have argued that women in patriarchal societies have been induced to adopt a depreciatory image of themselves. They have internalized a picture of their own inferiority . . . they are condemned to suffer the pain of low self-esteem. An analogous point has been made in relation to blacks: that white society has for generations projected a demeaning image of them, which some of them have been unable to resist adopting. Their own self-depreciation, on this view, becomes one of the most potent instruments of their own oppression. . . . Misrecognition shows not just a lack of due respect. It can inflict a grievous wound, saddling its victims with a crippling self-hatred. Due recognition is not just a courtesy we owe people. It is a vital human need.[53]

The institutional and social location of Asian immigrants as the third other misrecognizes or misplaces Asian immigrants as nontransferable immovable others. Seen as forever foreigners, their otherness is treated as not transferable and nonassimilable to be natives by any means. From this misrecognition or nonrecognition, Asian immigrant groups experience otherness as a part of their immigrant self. Even though this misrecognition is fundamentally constructed by their immigrant position as the third other, their third otherness cannot be easily explained or understood in current psychological immigrant identity formation processes for Asian immigrant groups. However, recognizing being the third other is one of the most complicated but crucial factors to understand Asian immigrant groups. Even though there are many important factors that need to be considered to understand Asian immigrant groups as the third other, in this chapter, belongingness is seriously discussed as the important example of revealing the third otherness of Asian immigrant groups.

When Asian immigrant groups try to find a way to settle down, they seek out the community where they feel belonging or want to belong. Heinz Kohut proposes belongingness as a third major self along with the two major selves, grandiosity and idealization.[54] This is an essential part of the human self. As Asian immigrant groups are disconnected from the motherlands and need to connect with the new land, they have a life-altering experience. "Immigration is a life-altering experience that may entail extensive loss of family and friends, customs and surroundings, and the need to adapt to a new cultural environment that often includes different moral values, standards and a new language."[55] Their whole world is changed and displaced. This life-altering experience drives them to develop a new sense of belongingness as quickly as possible for the sake of survival. However, developing a new sense of belongingness for Asian immigrant groups is often disguised as just restoring their past/old identities from motherlands or simply linking between the originality of persons and new nations. Restoring their belongingness in their motherlands or developing belongingness in the new land in this disguise is simply treated as a good remedy to establish a new sense of belongingness. However, developing a new sense of belongingness in Asian immigrant contexts is a very complicated process. It is not about making Asian immigrant groups be true to their individual originality or authenticity that they embodied from the homelands. It is not about simply answering "where are you from?" even though many scholars try to define or restore the immigrant identities from this question. At the same time, it is not about simply connecting with others beyond their ethnic groups in the new land. Their third otherness that they encounter in the U.S. immigrant reality has created a different dimension of understanding Asian immigrant groups and their sense of belongingness. It needs a serious restoration of time and space of belongingness.

In terms of time, this recognition of being the third other comes from their colonial past, continues in the present, but needs to transform in the future. Being the third other in the present is deeply connected with the position of their past. Before the colonial invasion, they were the center of "I" and "We" in their motherlands. They were always part of full members of their motherlands. Their existence was never questioned in terms of nativeness. Their beings were accepted and protected as natives in their motherlands. However, under colonial history, their full membership was invaded by colonizers. The validity of their membership was questioned. Their centered self was denied. They became the other. However, they did not accept their position as the other in their minds. In fact, it was their land. They had a deep sense of ownership. They as a community held their position as the center of their motherlands. They were treated as the other in the eyes of colonizers, but they did not recognize themselves as the other in their own lands. Their otherness existed in the colonial context, but not completely in the context of motherlands. They were the other, but not the other completely. The third otherness arose in their colonized motherlands.

Under the dominant white colonial history, many Asian immigrant groups move to new lands. However, immigration does not change their positions as the third other. Rather, their colonial past leads them to refortify their third otherness in the current immigrant context. Their colonial past and post-colonial present locate many Asian immigrants as the permanent incomplete third others in the global transnational context. In this sense, being the third other has been the position of many Asian immigrant groups from the past to the present. Their third otherness in terms of time belongs to both past and present. Their colonial past of being the third other is deeply connected with the postcolonial presence of their third otherness. Both past and present constitute the formation of being the third other under colonial and post-colonial power. The present has to understand its connectedness with the past. It means that ambiguity and uncertainty of how to understand the third other in their present needs critical examination of and reflection on the past. Depending on those examinations and reflections, Asian immigrant groups can connect and reconnect the future in different positions and with different power.

In terms of space, being the third other goes beyond linking between their motherlands and the new lands. Losing the sense of belongingness in their motherlands and regaining the sense of belongingness in a new land is a very difficult, traumatic, transitional experience. Many Asian immigrant groups start their immigrant journey from the experience of extensive loss of a sense of belongingness rather quickly but take a much longer time to rebuild a new sense of belongingness in both their motherlands and the new land. As they often experience disconnectedness from their motherlands, they encounter systematic and social discrimination in their new land, strug-gling between binary divides. They detect the absence of assurance of who they are and where they belong internally and externally. Recognition of who they are does not appear to be clear anymore, even within themselves. Rather, misrecognition of the others, especially within these multiple binary divides, becomes an indication of who they are in a new land. They are away from their familiar settings and are required to know and understand new settings. Not only misrecognition of the others but also uncertainty of new settings makes them vulnerable and confused. As their third otherness is given by these binary divides, they experience more vulnerability and con-fusion under these divides. In the process of remembering their origins and re-membering their identity in a new land, Asian immigrant groups feel dis-connected from both their motherlands and their new land and experience being the third other in both places.

When they are in their motherlands, they are the center of "we" in terms of belongingness. No one doubts that they belong to their motherlands. Motherlands recognize them as the center. However, as they move to the new land, their motherlands recognize them differently. Their motherlands do not recognize them as full members anymore. Their motherlands treat them only as semimembers. Because Asian immigrants are not foreigners in their motherlands, their motherlands do not treat them as complete for-eigners. It means that they are not the absolute others. However, the moth-erlands start to recognize them as the other, but not the complete other. Their motherlands see them as the third other. For immigrants, there is a similar process. When Asian immigrant groups disconnect themselves from their motherlands geographically, they also feel disconnected from their motherlands psychologically. They feel lost and disconnected consciously and unconsciously. Trying not to lose belongingness is the natural human response. When Asian immigrant groups feel the loss of connection, their psychological selves try to find a way to regain that connection on the same level of connectedness that they used to have before. However, having and feeling the same level of connectedness with the motherlands in a new land is not possible. They painfully realize that it is impossible to keep up with the same level of connectedness and relationships with their motherlands. As they recognize being the distant members of their motherlands, their third otherness is slowly and unconsciously recognized within themselves. This disconnectedness causes them deep wounds and profound frustration.

When Asian immigrant groups realize their being the third other in their motherlands, they seek compensation for their loss from the new land. As many scholars, such as M. D. Ainsworth and J. Bowlby see belongingness as attachment/connectedness, Asian immigrant groups cultivate belonging-ness by connecting with others. Through coalition work, they try to establish connection to the new lands. Developing new connections and networks is the most important way to foster belongingness in the new land. However, belongingness for Asian immigrant groups is not just connecting with oth-ers. It is also the act of avoiding loneliness and isolation. As C. Marangoni, W. Ickes, R. S. Weiss, D. Russell, C. E. Cutrona, J. Rose, K. Yurko, and oth-ers claim belongingness is avoiding loneliness, avoiding loneliness and isola-tion has been the main reason for Asian immigrant groups to accept or adopt assimilation. Because they are seen as strangers and foreigners, they desire to assimilate quickly in hopes that they will be treated as full members of society in the near future. They do not want to be lonely and isolated as strangers and foreigners. The act to avoid loneliness and isolation as being forever foreigners is a critical reason for Asian immigrant groups to develop belongingness.

However, developing belongingness in the new land requires more than connectedness and avoiding loneliness. It requires certain confirmations. It necessitates a legal and social recognition from institutions and a psychological assurance from individual and communal others. Richard M. Lee and Steve B. Robbins's research shows that social assurance and connectedness are highly correlated with a sense of belongingness. Without social assurance and connectedness, it is difficult to develop a sense of belongingness. However, being immigrants in the U.S., Asian immigrant groups have a hard time obtaining this confirmation, especially social assurance. Struggling with binary paradigms and their own challenges, their images are often seriously misplaced in public due to stereotyping and racial prejudices. Marginalization and loneliness occur, not only psychologically but also sociopolitically. Lee and Robbins state that "frustrations along any aspect in the development of belongingness may impair the person's ability to effectively function in life."[56] Frustrations in the development of belongingness are almost always required for Asian immigrant groups to suffer, especially because of the perception of their difference, foreignness. A lack of social assurance is a constant barrier for Asian immigrants to develop a new sense of belongingness. Institutional marginalization and isolation in terms of race, sex, gender, class, and so on cause serious damage to Asian immigrant groups' physical and psychological health. However, as Lee and Robbins, in agreement with Kohut claim, "People seek to confirm a subjective sense of belongingness or 'being a part of' in order to avoid feelings of loneliness and alienation."[57] Experiencing deep wounds and frustration, they still search for a way to find the sense of belongingness. Building new relationships with the new land is one of the most urgent and necessary ways for them to create a sense of new belongingness out of their survival and humanness.

Many Asian immigrant individuals start to build this new sense of belongingness through their ethnic communities that already existed in the new land. The research of McPherson et al., shows that homophily of racial groups is a stronger factor to foster close relationships than other personal identifiers such as class, education, gender, and religion.[58] Living in and connecting with similar racial ethnic immigrant groups shows better health benefits, such as lowering the risk for emotional and behavioral problems, and effective social behaviors, such as establishing friendships and networking.[59] Religious institutions play a very important role in providing this sense of belongingness. They nurture strong ethnic identities through not only religious faith but also sociocultural networks. Korean immigrant churches are an example.

For instance, Korean immigrant parents reported that transmitting religious values and beliefs to their children was one of the most important parenting practices. Korean American adolescents also reported finding Korean ethnic church youth groups safe places in which they feel a strong sense of belonging and experience personal growth and explorations of their identities by interacting with peers and mentors who share the same ethnic background and religious values and beliefs.[60]

Even though immigrants' ethnic communal living patterns are often criticized as a failure of assimilation and hiding in ethnic caves in the eyes of dominant white groups, they are proven as a healthy condition for immigrant groups themselves, including Asian immigrant groups. The more Asian immigrant groups nurture their ethnic connectedness, the more they are criticized by the dominant society, but the less they are frustrated and hurt in terms of their well-being. Through their ethnic communities, they practice maintaining connections with the motherlands and building new connections with the new lands that are equally important for Asian immigrants to have a new sense of belongingness. As they disconnect and reconnect with different times and spaces, they are urged to develop networks of individual and communal spaces.

Asian immigrants' sense of belongingness cannot be simply constituted by an individual desire to connect with their own ethnic members. If belongingness is an essential part of human behavior and human desire, staying within their ethnic boundary is not the final process of developing belongingness. Asian immigrant groups often start their belongingness from their own racial ethnic groups by remembering their past. When they find strong connectedness within themselves and fulfill their satisfaction to homophyly (love of one's race), they encounter two choices: either stay in their ethnic groups longer or connect with others outside of their racial groups. Staying in their ethnic groups should not necessarily be evaluated as a negative, immature behavior or stage. Depending on the abilities and given situations, they stay or move to build relationships beyond their ethnic groups. In many cases, many Asian immigrants develop relationships within their own ethnic groups first, and then move to have more relationship building outside of their ethnic communities.

"Connecting ability" is usually understood as a matter of individual ability of relationality in the Western concept of psychology. Depending on their individual ability and will, they develop relationships. However, making an effort to build relationships outside of their ethnic groups is very hard for Asian immigrant individuals. Actually, it takes communal power to build relationships beyond their ethnic groups. As they bring their communal cultural memories and experiences from their past, they deeply recognize their inter-dependence and interconnectedness within and beyond their ethnic immi-grant groups in the present. Especially when they experience these cultural memories in the forms of worship and practicing faith within their religious communities, they feel strong belongingness. They identify their religious communities as a core place to develop belongingness. Many Asian immi-grants learn, not only how to resist staying in the sense of a monoliner track of connectedness but also how to develop the sense of the dialogical multiple dimensions of connectedness beyond binary divides through religious ethnic communities. Their new sense of belongingness cannot be constructed with-out the teachings and practices of these religious ethnic communities in the sense of multiple belonging experiences. These religious ethnic communi-ties empower Asian immigrant groups to foster a new sense of belongingness in dialogical multiple dimensions of new times and places and guide them to see who they are and who they should be. By connection and disconnection from multiple places and times in various degrees, many Asian immigrant groups relearn the meaning of belongingness and underscore flexibilities and complexities of individual and communal connected abilities through these communities. From various gatherings and movements in these reli-gious communities, they can slowly connect with themselves and foster relationships with other groups and communities. Facilitating interreligious meetings, multicultural religious festivals, and immigrant coalition groups are great examples of this relationship building outside of each ethnic com-munity. Based on these religious ethnic community efforts, developing a new sense of belongingness naturally brings conflictive but consistent modes of developing a new sense of belongingness. It is conflictive because connect-edness and disconnectedness coexist and re-form constantly, and because recognition and misrecognition coexist and are reinterpreted simultaneously. It is consistent because this conflictiveness is constantly repeated and recur-ring simultaneously. Based on their religious communities and their transna-tional networks, they gain the communal power to resist disconnectedness and marginalization. Exercising communal power, Asian immigrant groups as a community feel more confident to cultivate relationships within and beyond their ethnic groups. This communal power leads them into fostering their belongingness as connected to multiple spaces and times beyond their knowledge and experience from their past and present.

In U.S. culture, it is believed that skills to develop relationships depend on individual ability and will. However, people's personal relationships and communal sociopolitical historical relationships are greatly conditioned by cultures, societies, nations, religions, and languages. Conditions of sociopolit-ical historical relationships largely constitute individual self. Individual rela-tionships are personally shaped and communally formed by these conditions.

These conditions create some commonalities that individual relationships carry on and form from these communal sociopolitical historical relationships. Any individual, *my* own, relationship is in fact not my own. My own relationship is never *my* individual independent development, especially for Asian immigrants. Particularities of individual Asian immigrant relationships are formed from a set of peculiar universalities that Asian immigrant groups inherit, and they are newly conditioned. Their third otherness is one of the newly given conditions as they enter the new land. This new land constitutes particularities of each Asian immigrant group and individual and communal positions as the third other. This individual and communal third otherness in each Asian immigrant group is dialogically derived and shaped by interactions and fluidity between their particular individual experiences of being the third other and peculiar universalities of the communal Asian immigrant position as the third other. Particularities of each Asian immigrant relationship are particularized by, not only each Asian immigrant group but also Asian immigrant groups as a whole in the U.S. in between black/white and native/alien power dynamics. Each immigrant context requires different cultural formation processes of relationship. At the same time, because of systematic and constitutional common binary conditions, pan-Asian peculiar universal identities are forged. Between these layers of particularities, their third otherness is "dialogically constituted"[61] and hybridized in the third space. Their collaborative coalition work and selective assimilation process become the necessity for their survival as the third other.

If there is a minimal level of security and tolerance of diverse identities within the cultural establishment of "recognizing competence, generating integrity, and supporting mutuality,"[62] the conflictive position of being the third other can be transformed as a source of cultivating belongingness among and beyond their own ethnic groups. Assuming will for collaboration and equality, Asian immigrant groups can use their third other position to be in solidarity with other groups. This position can aid Asian immigrant groups in demonstrating more active interactions and fluidity beyond binary systems and social structures. They "need relationships to fulfill, but not to define" their boundaries of relationships.[63] With these broken fragmentations but shared commonalities of being the third other, Asian immigrant groups connect with other groups and build a sense of belongingness in a new land. As they establish the sense of belongingness in multicultural and multiethnic immigrant contexts, they recognize their third otherness not as invisibility in a totalitarian sense of commonalities but as temporalities of their existence in solidarity. Their fragmentation, temporalities, and heterogeneity of being the third other are part of their memory of obliterated belongingness between past and present and between their motherlands and the new land. Each particularity of being the third other reflects a partial mirror of a peculiar universality of being the third other as a community. Their third otherness is not only their communal location but also their individual and personal positional existence.

However, being the third other is often used to support a difference-blind society that is dominated by black/white and native/alien binaries. These binary divides suppress each particular individual to be a part of the difference-blind society. "Consequently, the supposedly fair and difference-blind society is not only inhuman (because it suppresses identities) but also, in a subtle and unconscious way, itself highly discriminatory."[64] In a difference-blind society, their fragmentation, temporalities, and heterogeneity become permanent features of the otherness and their third otherness is in invisibility. However, even though white particularity and its infrastructures, such as these binary divides, control the difference-blind society, non-binary practices such as coalition work happen simultaneously. When Asian immigrant groups in these works are aware of these binary divides as the invention of white particularity, they can transform their third otherness into shared commonality with others in otherness. This transformation can raise the consciousness for strong connectedness within and beyond their ethnic boundaries and establish a new sense of belongingness in the new land. Being the third other in a sense of solidarity can determine the positions of connectedness outside of binary constructions and change the times and spaces of belongingness to transform their binary monomanufactured relationships into hybridized unpredictable, creative relationships.

CHAPTER 4

Conclusion

*Some Theological and Ethical Suggestions
on Postcolonial Relationships*

Tao Te Ching offers a theological model that connects mind, body, and spirit. In the concept of Tao Te Ching, there is no separation theory from action. According to Lao Tzu, "Tao means the integral truth of the universe, Te means the virtuous application of such high, subtle knowledge, and Ching means serious spiritual guidance." Therefore, Tao Te Ching reconciles the dichotomy of belief and action. Taoism as a paradigm can offer hope of recovering broken dimensions of humanity and nature, church and the world, other world and this world and male and female.[1]

Transforming binary relations to nonbinary relationships is a difficult, but ultimately essential task to fulfill. Many Western and Eastern women scholars have fought for this task using various strategies. Deconstructing dualistic approaches of white male patriarchy and colonialism, many white feminist scholars have serious arguments with patriarchal Christianity, sex, gender, class, and ecofeminism. Analyzing oppression in the intersection of race, sex and gender, many womanists have fought to reconstruct black/white binary racial structures and dualistic socioeconomic systems. Latina scholars lead this transformation by introducing their multicultural, rich religious traditions and mentoring future Latinx groups in education. Asian women scholars have struggled with Western binary colonial systems and white colonial/postcolonial power. They introduce various Eastern religious cultures and teachings as a way to embrace multicultural and intercultural movements and communal learnings. Young Lee Hertig's yinist feminism is a good example. Challenging a binary Western cultural paradigm, Hertig introduces Tao Te Ching as one of the most influential concepts for this transformation process. Providing yinist feminism as a theology of harmony, she demonstrates how Asian immigrant groups nurture belongingness to transform patriarchal binary thinking into integrative thinking and action. Many women of different colors, cultures, and immigrant contexts have challenged and introduced new ways to transform these binary constructions into nonbinary ones.

As these women scholars demonstrate how to deconstruct many forms of binary constructions, dominant ethnic relations have been guided by these binary constructions and are concomitantly challenged by these feminist nonbinary nonhierarchical thoughts and actions. Our ways of living and thinking were and are constructed with binary thinking—consciously and, especially, unconsciously. Our current binary racial relations are the maps of social constructions that are constructed by colonial past and current postcolonial sociopolitical, historical, cultural, internal, external, individual, and communal circumstances. These maps present the way things are, or the way things are supposed to be. As relations in the U.S. are mostly discussed within racial relations, Hazel M. McFerson summarizes these racial relations with three points: "(i) prevailing ideas about racial group superiority and inferiority as manifested in custom as well as in formal law; (ii) the role of race relative to the more conventional variables of stratification, e.g., class and culture; and (iii) the criteria used to classify racial groups, the resultant hierarchy of racial groups, and the centrality of the role of either genotypic or phenotypic definitions of race."[2] Relations in the U.S. context are organized in the order of racial hierarchy in these prevailing binary ideas and conventional variables of stratification. White superiority and nonwhite inferiority are played in formal/informal social cultural constructions and form a conscious/unconscious psychological reality. Treating race as a genetic biological, rather than sociopolitical, construction in every aspect of lives, for example, customs, formal laws, classes, and sex/gender, race relations, lies in establishing the hierarchy of class and culture and support this hierarchy as a permanent truth.

The position of Asian immigrants as the third other in the current U.S. context is the product of this racial hierarchy. As this racial hierarchy produces the positionality of Asian immigrants, the socioeconomic hierarchy of being the third other follows. It is seen as the representative of institutional standings for Asian immigrant groups to fit in. Racial relations became pillars of socioeconomic and political relations to not only Asian immigrant groups but also all racial groups. The white colonial past still dominates ethnic relations and leaves traces to direct how all groups relate to each other. These traces are presented in these binary divides as the norm of ethnic relations. They monitor how Asian immigrant groups relate and interact. White colonial power not only leaves traces but also draws the line for the map of relations. Many ethnic relations, including Asian immigrant relations, are greatly impacted by white colonial power and constructed by this line in every dimension. Along this line, Asian immigrants experience more unique challenges and have difficulties developing relationships outside of their ethnic groups.

However, even though these traces and lines guide and determine ethnic relations, these relations are also formed with individual and communal interactions and relationships. White dominant relations are not the only powerful relations. Various ethnic relations have shown their dynamic relationships and constantly challenge white relations in the form of resistance. Even though these binary constructions prevail and dominate racial relations, these individual and communal interactions and relationships form and reform to build new and different relationships simultaneously. This is what I call "postcolonial relationships."

A postcolonial relationship is not just a nonbinary relationship in opposition to a binary relationship. Being the third other is produced from binary relations, but their third otherness is not recognized in these binary relations because binary relations do not allow the existence of being the third other, as they emphasize the existence of binaries only. However, as Asian immigrant bodies exist, their existence in a binary relationship brings a contradiction because their existence cannot be denied. In fact, their existence is not a product of binary relations. They exist and they exist beyond the binary relations. Their existence itself demonstrates a possibility of a different relationship. It actively challenges binary relations and demands nonbinary, nonhierarchical, dialogical, dialectic, multirelational, interrelational, transnational-relational relationships. It demands nonbinary and nonhierarchical relations because the positionality of being the third other already requires more than binary, polarized, top-down relationships. Their existence demands dialogical movement because binary relations have to communicate with Asian immigrant groups in the third place. It also demands truly dialectical movement because there are always two or more concurrent conflicting understandings of positionality of Asian immigrants as being the third other. Because of this dialectic aspect, postcolonial relationships have to be multirelational and interrelational. Transnational relationships are also deeply involved. In fact, these relationships are the original relationships that many immigrant groups formed from the beginning of their immigrant lives. Transnational relationships are the foundation of other relationships that many Asian immigrant groups started with. These relationships also include ecorelationships between people and the earth and transrelationships between the living in the postcolonial present and the dead in the colonial past. Based on these relations and the existence of being the third other, a postcolonial relationship is requested.

Deconstructing the positionality of the third other, postcolonial relationships decultivate superior and inferior relationships beyond conventional variables of stratification and racial hierarchy. They cultivate nonbinary, nonhierarchical mutual and invitational relationships. They are interconnectional and interdependent relationships. They change the positions of relationships and demand sharing power and privileges. Postcolonial relationships are not the fixed maps, but the moving forces to change relations living in the postcolonial immigrant present and remembering the colonial past. These relationships are organic. They grow and withdraw. They assimilate and resist. They adopt, reject, and hybridize. They concurrently include and exclude. They deconstruct and reconstruct the map of relations at the same time. They disconnect, connect, and reconnect in multiple dimensions of their immigrant lives and communal and individual relationships. As these relationships grow and withdraw, they move to build new relationships beyond binary systems and structures. They connect and reconnect as they seek belongingness. They hold possibilities and impossibilities of conditional changes of relationships simultaneously. Even though white dominant relations limit the boundary of relationships and control the selections of relationships, postcolonial relationships can empower people's relatability and interactions individually and communally based on the postcolonial power that is embedded in people's power.[3] Considering the existing cultural-historical circumstances and individual and communal interactions, developing these relationships can lead Asian immigrant groups to learn, unlearn, and relearn ethnic relations, and to relate and interact with others equally and harmoniously in their postcolonial immigrant contexts. How, then, can the positionality of the third other be deconstructed and transformed? How can binary relations transform into postcolonial relationships? What are the main barriers for this transformation?

Sociopolitical misrecognition and systematic mistreatment accelerate the position of Asian immigrant groups as the third other, not only sociopolitically but also psychologically. In the intersections of these dynamics, they feel doubly helpless and marginalized. Without analyzing external and internal struggles of being the third other in various binary constructions, "many give in to the pressure of humiliating shame, injure their self-dignity, and develop false guilt-consciousness about their shortcomings, blaming themselves for being helpless."[4] Many Asian immigrant groups experience a lack of self-confidence and end up feeling shame. As they lose their connectedness from their families, communities, and motherlands, and cannot quickly gain a sense of belongingness in the new land, they experience the loss of their self and their confidence. In a frustrated hope to go back to their motherland someday, as they face their reality, they realize they cannot go back. They end up not only with frustration but also with shame about their inability to go back. At the same time, as they cannot establish new connections quickly, they also end up with double frustration and shame about their inability to connect in a new land. Shame emerges when people feel helplessness or have an inability to deliver.[5] As a consequence, Asian immigrant groups *see themselves* as unwanted foreigners and unwelcome guests. They constantly experience their being as the third other as white binary structures demand. This is one of the main barriers that needs to be challenged.

Many Asian immigrant groups struggle with being the third other, and go from dangerous foreigners, temporary visitors, permanent guests, unwelcome residents to invisible citizens. They try to assimilate, resist, collaborate, change, and transform this unrecognizable invisible third otherness in binary constructions to nonotherness in nonbinary open spaces. Transforming binary relations to the postcolonial relationship is one of the ways that Asian immigrant groups can transform their third otherness. As Asian immigrant groups develop their individual and communal relationality to go beyond binary relationships and hybrid "I," "we," and "others," a postcolonial self (I and we with others) can be formed, and a postcolonial relationship can begin.[6] Postcolonial relationships are the relationships of Asian immigrant groups as the third other that can imagine nonbinary, nonhierarchical, dialogical, dialectic, multirelational, interrelational, transnational-relational, and transworld relationships. As Asian immigrant groups learn how to understand and challenge binary relationships between "I" and "the other," they can form their third otherness in postcolonial relationships unlearning from the analysis of binary relations. As the individual and communal postcolonial self is nurtured and matured, individual and communal postcolonial relationships can grow and prosper.

However, transforming binary relations to the postcolonial relationship from the positions of being the third other is not a naturally occurring process. Rather, it is an intentional and risk-taking process for Asian immigrant communities and individual leaders to confront their third otherness in institutional structures. It is intentional because it needs will and power of the determined individual and communal Asian coleaders and coparticipants to challenge being the third other. It needs careful, deliberate attention and critical reflection on how to develop relationships more intentionally, analyzing the problems of binary structures. It is risk taking because it always challenges "the way things are" by dismantling the position of being the third other socially and politically. It contests normalization of the current beliefs and structures. It consciously questions the current systems and institutions as the subjects to reconstruct. Therefore, transforming binary relations to the postcolonial relationship is never an individual task. It is an individual, personal, and communal task. It needs individual and communal efforts to connect and collaboratively work together. It requires serious deliberate practices of examining binary social constructions and nurturing connectedness. However, it needs more than this examination and nurturing. In order to transform binary relations into postcolonial relationships, it requires certain practices. Even though there are many practices that can be named, I would like to suggest two practices in this conclusion: (1) forgiveness, and (2) hospitality. Considering their heavy involvement with religious communities, these practices cannot be fulfilled without religious leadership. In fact, religions are the most crucial influences for implanting these practices in Asian immigrant contexts to develop postcolonial relationships. Many religious institutions provide spaces to actually deliver these practices in their teachings and interpretations of their religious texts.

First, forgiveness is one of the urgent and necessary religious practices that Asian immigrant groups know and need to exercise in order to create postcolonial relationships. Understanding and analyzing the causes of feeling shame from the position of being the third other, Asian immigrant groups first need to learn how to forgive themselves and others in order to create postcolonial relationships. Their third otherness is often the first factor to make Asian immigrant groups feel shame without knowing it. Because of this unknown, unrecognized but experienced third otherness, they blame themselves for not fulfilling institutional and social expectations. At the same time, within binary constructions, they see other groups who hurt and ignore them. This leads them to blame themselves and see others as enemies or oppressors. They are isolated from themselves and from others simultaneously. In order to free them from this isolation, forgiveness of themselves and others is necessary. Without forgiveness, it is very hard for them to move on and connect with others.

Bryant S. Thompson and M. Audrey Korsgaard claim that forgiveness is one of the very most important factors to foster *stronger* relationships.[7] Practicing forgiveness can give Asian immigrant groups an opportunity to cultivate stronger relationships within themselves and with others. As they practice forgiveness, they learn how to let go of their shame and understand the new circumstances without blaming themselves and others. Andrew Sung Park suggests three steps to practice forgiving oneself and others: "brokenness with sorrow and grief, a willingness to let go, and the courage to envision a fresh image."[8] Recognizing brokenness with sorrow and grief is the first step for Asian immigrant groups to practice. It is a crucial step for initiating forgiveness. Without feeling and expressing their emotions and hurts, it is impossible to forgive. Without recognition of being the third other, they do not know how to let go of their pain, woundedness, anger, frustration, shame, and hatred, among other feelings. In order to let go, it is important for Asian immigrant groups to learn how to distinguish what their abilities are and what limits they experience institutionally. Understanding their ability and recognizing their limits are a crucial process, not only psychologically but also physically and economically. However, this process does not end there. It needs to go further.

Park claims that the act of letting go is beyond human capacity. In order to let go, he believes that connecting with God is required. Without connecting with God, the act of letting go is impossible. When human beings connect with God, they can transform shame into forgiveness. Only after restoring the relationship with God can they envision their new self, a fresh image.

Everett L. Worthington Jr. and Steven J. Sandage suggest similar phases of the forgiveness process. They introduce how to develop the ability of forgiveness in relation to healthy relational spirituality and propose four phases in the long term: (1) forming an attachment, (2) coconstructing a developmental crucible, (3) processing disappointment and grief, and (4) cultivating and extending differentiation of self.[9] When people form good relationships with their counselors, they can coconstruct a developmental crucible and process disappointment and grief successfully. As people cultivate and extend differentiation of self within themselves and with others, they can develop practices of forgiveness. Worthington and Sandage encourage people to nurture the values of relational hope that can expose people to encounter their reality of impossibility and to change their circumstances. This encouragement invites them to move into a recuperating process from disappointment and grief and to transform them to cultivate differentiation of self.[10] Despite any challenges, Worthington and Sandage demonstrate in their research that people can still hold hope to change when they process pain and grief at a deeper level. Religious faith, more specifically spiritual maturity, is a critical part of this forgiving practice. Worthington and Sandage note, "Differentiation of self has been found to mediate the relationship between forgiveness and mental and spiritual health and has been positively correlated with both hope and humility."[11] As people develop mature spiritual health and the sense of differentiation of self, they can cultivate a great ability to forgive.

Many religious faiths and theologies cultivate this spiritual maturity by teaching forgiveness. They confirm that forgiveness is one of the most important parts of spiritual practice that can transform the pain into spiritual growth and maturity. When pain is transformed, forgiveness is necessary.

> To suppress our pain is not the teaching of inclusiveness. We have to receive it, embrace it, and transform it. The only way to do this is to make our heart big. We look deeply in order to understand and forgive.[12]

> Nothing we do, however virtuous, can be accomplished alone; therefore we are saved by love. No virtuous act is quite as virtuous from the standpoint of our friend or foe as it is from our standpoint. Therefore, we must be saved by the final form of love which is forgiveness.[13]

Be on your guard! If another disciple sins, you must rebuke the offender, and if there is repentance, you must forgive. And if the same person sins against you seven times a day, and turns back to you seven times and says, "I repent," you must forgive.[14]

Forgiveness is virtue; forgiveness is sacrifice, forgiveness is the Vedas, forgiveness is the Shruti (revealed scripture). He that knoweth this is capable of forgiving everything. . . . Forgiveness is Brahma (God); forgiveness is truth; forgiveness is stored ascetic merit; forgiveness protecteth the ascetic merit of the future; forgiveness is asceticism; forgiveness is holiness; and by forgiveness is it that the universe is held together.[15]

Forgiveness is thus a central tenet of Hindu spirituality; it has been defined as mental strength in the face of offenses. . . . In modern age, people like Mahatma Gandhi, Indian political and spiritual leader, declared forgiveness as great virtue and stated that the weak can never forgive because forgiveness is the attributes of the strong.[16]

Based on these various religious traditions and theologies, many Asian immigrants are encouraged to learn and exercise the act of forgiveness. As people recognize pain, they try to learn how to embrace and transform it. Thich Nhat Hanh accurately describes above that pain does not disappear without understanding and forgiving, and "the only way to do this is to make our heart big."[17] Making our heart big requires understanding and forgiving. Without understanding and forgiving, human beings cannot grow. As they achieve spiritual maturity, they embrace forgiveness. Many religious beliefs and faiths teach forgiveness as the final form of love. It is the act of saving, not only for others but also for themselves. Because forgiveness is the act of saving, which means the act of victory over sin, religious teaching propagates the notion that it is the act of strength and the action of restoration for the future. Acts of forgiveness transform pain into restoration and growth as it transforms the weak to become stronger.

When Asian immigrant groups recognize experiences of racial triangulation, endure anti-Asian sentiments, deal with minority/nonminority debates, and struggle with their internal brokenness, they mourn the loss of themselves and the loss of their connections. Treated as being the third other, they have a hard time defining who they are and where they are. Without accurate awareness of being the third other, they often feel lost and oppressed. However, when they recognize the problems of binary structures and become aware of the position of being the third other, their relational hope challenges Asian immigrant groups to rethink the position of being the third other in the form of temporality. The condition of *temporality* gives them hope to *change*. It gives them strength to forgive despite the constant challenges of being called forever foreigners. By and within this hope, they try to restore the connection with themselves and others. Restoring the connection does not mean that it reconnects them with their selves and communities that they used to know at the same level of engagement. Rather, it requests new ways to develop various connections and networks. As Asian immigrant groups recognize racial triangulation, anti-Asian sentiment, minority/nonminority debates, and other experiences not as individual problems but as sociosystemic problems, they can start to forgive themselves. They can recognize their loss, not as their inability to connect but as their task to reestablish their relationships. When Asian immigrant groups recognize those problems and reconnect themselves as "cohosts" and "coguests" in this new land, they can stop feeling self-hatred and shame and restore their selves.[18] Through this restoration process, Asian immigrant groups can relinquish the negative images and reimagine the positive images of their selves. "Change means reworking, making peace with or putting an end to previous arrangements," letting go of the loss, accepting that whatever we choose would not bring the same life, and fostering courage to move forward by redefining who we are.[19] Transforming themselves as the third other from negative invisible presence to positive force of solidarity takes intensive mental will and sociopolitical support. This sociopolitical, psychological, and spiritual holistic transformation of Asian immigrant individuals is possible only when Asian immigrant communities work together to develop connectedness. Both individual and communal collaborative works can challenge the distorted current stereotypes and images of Asian immigrant groups and bring them courage to imagine who they can be.

Forgiveness is one of the most powerful ways to end conflictive relationships. It is "an efficient way for durably transforming, and even ending, interpersonal conflicts as well as intergroup conflicts."[20] However, not everyone has the ability to easily practice forgiveness. People are not naturally inclined to exercise it, unlike hostility and revenge.[21] Hostility and revenge are more natural responses in any human group. When conflicts occur, people often exercise hostility and revenge more strongly toward strangers. When Asian immigrant groups are seen and called strangers and foreigners, hostility and revenge are the feelings that they experience often from other groups and society. As they experience hostility and revenge, they respond to others similarly. Hostility and revenge occur in a vicious cycle for both parties. In order to go against these natural inclinations, forgiveness has to be intentional. It needs to be taught. Worthington and Sandage claim that even though forgiveness is an ability that requires a certain spiritual or moral maturity and psychological capacity of differentiation of self, it can be taught. Then how can people cultivate this ability?

Worthington and Sandage claim that the ability to forgive can be nurtured by many techniques and strategies. Among these techniques and strategies, one of their proposals is inviting empathy for others. When people imagine what others experience, it is easier for them to develop the ability to forgive. This proposal is similar to forming the sense of "we-ness" that A. Aron, E. N. Aron, and D. Smollan propose. In order to acquire the ability to forgive others, they suggest that it is important to form a sense of "we-ness."[22] When people include others as a part of their self, they forgive others easily. In other words, as people accept the other as we, a communal self, they develop a better ability to forgive others. In opposition, unforgiving behavior comes from polarized views of self and others.[23] When people experience a strong division between self and others, they cannot forgive others. *Cultivating forgiveness is cultivating communal self.* It connects "I" and "you" as "we," a part of oneself. This relational identification fosters stronger relationships. Bryant S. Thompson and M. Audrey Korsgaard claim in their research that "relational identification is positively associated with forgiveness" and "forgiveness is positively associated with relationship resilience."[24] Their research shows that when people identify others as a part of themself (we), they can forgive them and establish a stronger and resilient relationship with them.

Many Asian religious teachings and practices are among the powerful trainings that stop hostility and revenge and cultivate forgiveness. They always teach empathy for others and cultivate we-ness. These religious teachings and practices demonstrate how to stop this vicious cycle and how people can foster a strong will to survive and change the current status quo. Even though it is very difficult for Asian immigrant groups to practice forgiveness based on their circumstances and experiences as the third other in their immigrant contexts, it is also necessary for them to practice it as a way to reach out to and connect with others by transforming their third otherness into solidarity. Based on their religious faith and hope, they practice forgiveness. Reconstructing their third otherness, they need to exercise this practice intentionally. Understanding being the third other as the foundation of cultivating we, Asian immigrant groups can participate in coalition work, form pan-Asian identities, and connect with other groups. Using the position of the third other as the common ground to define we-ness, they can extend their boundaries of we-ness to other groups and exercise forgiveness to connect and reconnect with others. Even though it is their natural response to stay within their ethnic groups and define their sense of we-ness only in their ethnic groups, it is their religious practice to extend their we-ness, their communal self to others.

Through these religious practices, Asian immigrant groups are able to forgive others and connect with them as "significant others"[25] who provide and give a sense of belongingness as a part of we. In the sense of this we-ness, being the third other functions as one of the collective immigrant identities that "require(s) not just recognizing its existence but actually demonstrating respect for it."[26] Through religious institutions and ethnic communities, Asian immigrant groups learn forgiveness and exercise the real power to change static relations into living relationships. As Asian immigrant groups intentionally train themselves to extend their sense of self to include others as we, they form postcolonial relationships more easily.

Promoting forgiveness is not just a psychological development to connect with others but also part of religious nature for reconnecting with God. It is not only their psychological growth but also spiritual maturity to develop. As they forgive themselves, others, and even institutions, they gain the strength to fight for change and cultivate postcolonial relationships in their living contexts. Religious institutions can be the actual places to gain this strength and demonstrate "people power" to challenge the society.[27] They train people how to deepen the new sense of belongingness in relation to connectedness in times, spaces, and relationships. Through this training, Asian immigrant groups can connect and reconnect with their own selves, God, their communities in their motherlands, the communities in their new lands, and the spaces in the third place. As they forgive and restore relationships, their third otherness is deconstructed and reconstructed to transform their immigrant reality.

Second, hospitality is another important religious practice that needs to be intentionally cultivated for transforming binary relations to postcolonial relationships. With the act of hospitality, this transformation can be an impossible possibility for Asian immigrant groups to act on. It is impossible because these binary relations are still powerfully dominant, but it is still a possibility because postcolonial relationships happen through hospitality. Transforming the impossible possibility into conceivable actuality requires a radical move—hospitality—to break the vicious cycle of hostility, disconnectedness, isolation, and marginalization that Asian immigrant groups often experience between multiple binary divides. As Asian immigrant groups as the third other experience racial triangulation, anti-Asian sentiment, and minority/nonminority debates, they are exposed to hostility, revenge, isolation, and marginalization. They experience systematic and institutional discrimination. As they suffer from their internal struggles, they experience disconnectedness personally and communally. Isolation and marginalization occur, not only institutionally and systematically but also psychologically and socially. Their individual and communal wounds get deeper. Transformation of their immigrant life seems impossible based on their communal and individual experiences of hostility, disconnectedness, isolation, and marginalization.

However, these experiences are not the only experiences that they encounter. Their personal religious experiences and experiences they receive and learn from their religious institutions have sustained their immigrant life in hope and encouraged them to seek the possibility of transformation. The more they experience hostility, disconnectedness, isolation, and marginalization, the more they seek safety, comfort, belongingness, and connectedness in their religious communities. When Asian immigrant groups arrive in a new land, they seek these religious institutions, not only for practicing their faith but also for receiving the hospitality that they desperately need. When society sees them as unwelcome guests, they need to find a place to feel welcome and like they belong. They want to be recognized as welcome guests and as a part of the community. Based on the act of hospitality that many religious institutions provide, they feel welcome and belonging. Safety and comfort are immediately given. Belongingness and connectedness start to grow again.

Hospitality is a concept that all religious teachings promote actively and proactively. The object of hospitality is unconditional but expects mutuality in a sense that initiates relationships. It is one of the radical moves that Asian immigrant groups need to exercise intentionally. However, hospitality is not a strange concept to them. Actually, it is the practice that they have exercised in their Asian traditions and cultures from generation to generation. One of the most prominent features of hospitality that is exercised in Asian religious traditions is "guest as a god"[28] and host as powerless.

> Then the venerable Mahākāśyapa, understanding her thoughts with his mind, held out his begging bowl. "If you have anything to spare, my sister, please put it in my bowl."
>
> Cultivating faith in her mind, she poured (some rice-water) into his bowl. Then a fly fell in. She began to take it out when one of her fingers fell off into the rice-water. She reflected, "Although the noble one, out of respect for my feelings, hasn't thrown (this rice-water) away, he won't partake of it."
>
> Then the venerable Mahākāśyapa, understanding her thoughts with his mind, right before her eyes, sat down against the base of a wall and began to eat.
>
> She reflected, "Although the noble one, out of respect for my feelings, has partaken of this, he won't think of this food as a proper meal."
>
> Then the venerable Mahākāśyapa, understanding her thoughts, said this to that woman who was dependent on the city for alms: "Sister, I am happy! I can pass the whole day and night on the food (that you have given me.)"
>
> She became very excited, "The Noble Mahākāśyapa has accepted alms from me!" Then, while cultivating faith in her mind for the venerable Mahākāśyapa, she died and was reborn among the gods in the heaven known as Tusita. ("Contented")[29]

The above is from "The Story of a Woman Dependent on a City for Alms." The host of this story is a leprous beggar woman and the guest is the venerable Mahākāśyapa. In an ordinary sense, the host is the one with power and privileges. The conditionality of hospitality is dependent on the power and privileges of the host. Hospitality is always conditioned by the host and host countries. "No hospitality, in the classic sense, without sovereignty of oneself over one's home, but since there is also no hospitality without finitude, sovereignty can only be exercised by filtering, choosing, and thus by excluding and doing violence."[30] The host chooses, selects, invites, and welcomes the guest. The host filters and controls the guest. They exercise power to grant rights of the guest, asylum, immigrants, and the other. Hospitality, in an ordinary sense, is temporary and exclusive. It is dependent on the favors of the host. It is never unconditional, but always conditional on the relationship with the guest. However, it is always unconditional in the eyes of the host. The host believes that whatever is provided is unconditional and requires no return. Even if the host expects the cheaper labor of the guest and lures the guest to make sacrifices, the host believes cheaper labor and sacrifices are voluntarily provided because of their unconditional generosity. Depending on the exclusivity/generosity of the host, the space of the guest is granted and limited. Their rights are never granted permanently but can be given under the conditions of the host.

The power movement of ordinary hospitality is from the host to the guest. The host remains in absolute power to exclude or include the guest, whereas the guest remains in absolute submission to receive any benefits from the host. The binary paradigm between the host and the guest equates with the native/alien binary divide. These two binary paradigms are parallel to each other. As the native/alien binary divide protects natives' rights and benefits and makes aliens thieves and free riders, the host/guest binary divide protects the host's rights and benefits and makes the guest a dangerous unwelcome foreigner. The host/guest binary divide pictures the images of the host as the generous and unconditional provider, whereas it produces the images of the guest as the lazy and dangerous stranger. The natives control the rights and benefits of the aliens just as the host controls the rights and benefits of the guest in the name of the generosity of the host. The guest stands in between violence and the generosity of the host.

The relationship between the host and the guest is hierarchical. It is strictly limited and exclusive. The host controls the guest and the position of the guest. The relationship starts with the host and ends with the host. The host, and the host alone, is in charge of the relationship. The guest is the passive subject of the relationship. The host can exist without the presence of the guest. The host is completely independent. However, the guest cannot exist without the grace of the host. It is not a mutual, but a dependent relationship for the guest. The host and the guest do not share power. They do not share privileges. The power and privileges belong to the host. Obedience and submission are the duty for the guest to perform.

However, "The Story of a Woman Dependent on a City for Alms" offers a different paradigm of the host and the guest. The concept of hospitality starts from the woman who is poor, sick, powerless, marginalized, and oppressed. However, she is not the guest who needs to receive hospitality. She is the host who offers hospitality with humility. The poor, sick, marginalized, and oppressed offers hospitality to the other, the venerable Mahākāśyapa. The hospitality is shown not among the powerful but among the powerless and the vulnerable. The woman dependent on a city for alms can offer hospitality, rice-water, and food that makes God live day and night. The food that she provides for the divine, the guest, is not power and privileges. What she offers is her life that nourishes the divine and the divine mission to fulfill. Her hospitality takes her life to be the host. What makes hospitality radical in this story is offering the life of the poor, the sick, the powerless, and the marginalized.

The paradigm of God as a guest and the host as powerless breaks the ordinary concept of hospitality. It changes the order of hospitality movements. It is neither from the host to the guest nor from the guest to the host. It is both. It is mutual. As the venerable Mahākāśyapa understands her thoughts, this divine makes an initial movement to start the relationship. Without her thoughts, the venerable Mahākāśyapa would not or could not make the movement. At the same time, without the venerable Mahākāśyapa's movement, the leprous beggar woman could not make her move either. By the request from the venerable Mahākāśyapa, she is able to show her hospitality. This relationship starts with the request from the guest and the hospitable thoughts from the host. It does not start by the invitation from the host alone, but by mutual care from both of them. From their mutual understandings and needs, their relationship forms. It is a reciprocal movement that they create and in which they respond to each other. This movement shows a radical shift from ordinary hospitality to radical mutual hospitality that both the host and the guest embrace and act on.

The paradigm of God as a guest and the host as powerless requires mutual collaborative power and benefits to each other. As the guest fulfills the divine mission, the host receives the gift, reborn as a god. The relationship between the host and the guest is reciprocal in the act of radical mutual hospitality. The relationship starts with the divine and human relationship but ends with the divine and divine relationship. The result of the radical mutual hospitality is equality of relationships and power. It brings inclusive and horizontal relationships over finite hierarchical relationships. The host does not control the guest, and the guest differentiates the host. Both the host and the guest are in charge of the relationship. The guest is not the passive subject of the relationship, and the host is not the independent subject completely removed from the guest. The host cannot exist without the presence of the guest in this relationship. The host is completely dependent on the guest. At the same time, the guest cannot exist without the host. It is a codependent and interdependent relationship for the host and the guest. The host and the guest share power and privileges together in the process. They become cohosts and coguests in the end. Obedience and submission are not the duty for the guest to perform. Instead, mutuality and collaborative work are performed by both of them.

Even though it is not easy to practice radical mutual hospitality, practicing this hospitality is not uncommon for Asian immigrant groups. Preparing and sharing abundant excessive food for and with others is the most powerful but a very common, ordinary Asian hospitality practice. Many of them show hospitality around food in their daily life under the hardship of their immigrant contexts. Their hospitality is unthinkable without food. It often includes not only food but also excessive material supports and gifts. Providing abundant extra food for others has been a very important act of hospitality in terms of building relationships in various Asian traditions. When Asian and Asian immigrant groups think about guests, they always provide more food than they need. They do not prepare the food only for themselves and the guests. They *feel and think* that it is necessary for them to provide more than enough food so they can share the food with the people who they do not know but expect to come, such as unexpected guests, guests' families, neighbors, beggars, strangers, and even ancestors' spirits. They expect to see the familiar faces and at the same time are ready to welcome the unknowns. Hospitality in food is deeply rooted in their religious beliefs.

> The *anuvaka* (verse) begins by further elaborating the discipline of anna with the injunction that a guest should never be turned away from the door. And the seer continues with the insistence that a seeker ought to obtain a plenty of food somehow or the other, so that no guest ever needs to return un-sated from door: "Do not turn away from anyone who comes seeking your hospitality. This is the inviolable discipline for the one who knows. Therefore, obtain a great abundance of anna (food), exert all your efforts to ensure such abundance; and welcome the guests with the announcement that the food is ready."[31]

> From food, surely, are they born; all creatures that live on earth. On food alone, once born, they live; and into food in the end they pass.

For food is the foremost of beings, so it's called "all herbs."From food beings come into being; by food, once born, they grow."It is eaten and it eats brings." Therefore it is called "food."[32]

In many Asian religious traditions, including Buddhism, Hinduism, Islam, and Christianity, food is not just material to feed their bodies. It is not simply something to eat. Rather, food is part of the body. It is part of the self. It is part of the soul. "Food is the grounding of the observable world, and it exists of its nature as transactional, what living creatures consume, and what they become."[33] Keeping food and sharing food is their responsibility to show respect for human beings and spiritual beings. It includes their responsibility for life-nurturing memberships with soil, water, air, wind, animals, plants, insects, people, spirits, and God.[34] The act of keeping and sharing food is the act of building relationships with other members of the earth and the heaven. As they feed their guests, they start to build relationship with their guests, others. As they build the relationship with others, they build the relationship with God. Around food, they build communal life and practice spiritual maturity. Therefore, the act of food preparation is by no means trivial. As they prepare food, they prepare their heart to meet God. In this religious belief, God is their guest to feed because food is part of the divine and the divine gifts.

I am food! I eat him who eats the food! I have conquered the whole universe! I am like the light in the firmament![35]

(10) He gives a gift of food that results in his being free from the cravings of hunger. (11) He gives a gift of drink that results in his being free from thirst everywhere in all his lives (yet to come).[36]

Food is symbolized as the ground of God. It gives life to human existence and the existence of other beings. It starts the relationships and connections with others as the foundation of a relationship to grow. God creates food as a gift to human beings and to the earth. As God/gods become food, God/gods feed the hungry. As God/gods feed the hungry, God/gods liberate them from hunger. God relates to food in a way that feeds and liberates people. As people of faith feed the hungry, they feed God and participate in God's liberation. When they prepare food, they prepare their hearts to encounter the unknown guests who are God/gods. Cooking food and preparing food is the act of waiting for God to come in their houses. Sharing food is sharing the body of the divine together. In this sense, the concept of sharing food and drink in Buddhist and Hinduist traditions closely connects with the concept of communion in Christian traditions.

While they were eating, Jesus took a loaf of bread, and after blessing
it he broke it, gave it to the disciples, and said, "Take, eat; this is my
body." 27 Then he took a cup, and after giving thanks he gave it to
them, saying, "Drink from it, all of you; 28 for this is my blood of the
covenant, which is poured out for many for the forgiveness of sins.
29 I tell you, I will never again drink of this fruit of the vine until
that day when I drink it new with you in my Father's kingdom."[37]

For I received from the Lord what I also handed on to you, that the
Lord Jesus on the night when he was betrayed took a loaf of bread,
24 and when he had given thanks, he broke it and said, "This is my
body that is for you. Do this in remembrance of me." 25 In the same
way he took the cup also, after supper, saying, "This cup is the new
covenant in my blood. Do this, as often as you drink it, in remembrance of me." 26 For as often as you eat this bread and drink the
cup, you proclaim the Lord's death until he comes.[38]

Jesus is the center of this communion. Jesus offers his body and blood to
build the new covenant, the new relationship for and with the people. The
bread symbolizes the broken body of Christ, and the drink symbolizes the
blood of Christ. The act of eating becomes the act of remembrance of Jesus
that "join(s) in a *re-membering* of a world."[39] The act of remembrance of
Jesus requires the act of building a new relationship with the world and
transforms the lives of eaters from the death of hunger to the life of sharing. As food on the table is transformed into the body of the divine, it feeds
the hungry, the poor, the marginalized, the powerless, and the oppressed
to have a life-giving transformation. Jesus becomes food. As Jesus becomes
food, the eaters of the table are fed by God physically and spiritually and
invited to offer this food to others. The invitation to offer this food to
others extends beyond the space of this table. This communion table is
expected to be communal. It is a communal eating table beyond bodily
needs, including bodily needs. As people "consume Jesus as their food and
drink,"[40] they create unbounded communal space. In other words, as people share food at this table, they share their communal responsibility to
feed and nurture others.

When people share this communal responsibility to feed and nurture
others at this communion table, the binary divide of guest and host is naturally transformed. Jesus starts his role as the host at this table, but by inviting others as the cohosts, he becomes the cohost with them. Jesus refuses
to stay as the host. He invites others to take his role in the act of remembrance of him. As he offers himself at the table as food, he asks others to
offer themselves to feed the others. There are no unwelcome guests and

permanent strangers at this table. They are the welcome "coguests" and generous "cohosts" at the same time.[41] The act of sharing food is not a task for the host to do alone. As the eating happens repeatedly in the remembrance of him, the members of the table are extended and their role as the guests is transformed into cohosts. The binary paradigm of the host and the guest is broken at this table. It becomes not the host alone but the cohosts and their communal responsibility to provide hospitality together. The eaters are transformed from the guests to the cohosts and coguests as Jesus transforms himself from the host to the coguest and the cohost.

God becomes food in various religious traditions. Eating food is eating God. God offers Godself to be food to feed the hungry. In this sense, eating God means feeding others. As God offers God's self to share for the world as food, people are expected to offer their food to the communal table with and for others. Preparing and sharing abundant food in Asian and Asian immigrant groups is not just providing food. It is the act of transformation. It is the radical mutual hospitality that they exercise in their ordinary religious practices. As they prepare the food, they expect to heal their wounds of immigrant lives. As they offer the food, they expect to connect more tightly with others. As they share the food, they transform their role from the mere guests in a strange land to cohosts in a new home. As current U.S. society constructs "the intractable political problems that flow from understanding immigration as being akin to war and invasion,"[42] Asian immigrant groups experience hostility and fear in this war. However, despite fear and warlike circumstances, Asian immigrant groups try to overcome this fearful experience by practicing hospitality. Even though hospitality is not radical enough to change various binary paradigms directly, and even though it never meets the needs of others completely, it is still practiced because by practicing hospitality, they not only change their identity but also extend their relationship beyond their social binary relations.

Forgiveness and hospitality are the critical practices of transforming binary relations into postcolonial relationships. They are the first and most fundamental practices to cultivate postcolonial relationships. Whether justice, reconciliation, and equality are delivered or not, these practices can make Asian immigrant groups move toward and form postcolonial relationships. They lead Asian immigrant groups to hope for seeing justice, tasting reconciliation, and experiencing equality. Forgiveness and hospitality proactively performs seeing and seeking justice. These practices empower people to imagine the possibility of postcolonial relationships in creating connectedness intentionally. Forgiveness and hospitality provide people an opportunity to formulate different dimensions of postcolonial relationships. These practices also make people dream and implant the possibility of equality in their actual relationships. Delivering hospitality and acting on forgiveness are often performed by many Asian religious women and their leaders. As I described in my previous work *A Postcolonial Leadership: Asian Immigrant Christian Leadership and Its Challenges*, ordinary Asian immigrant women deliver radical hospitality through their religious communities. Even though they are not often seen as leaders in a traditional sense, by performing these practices, they become leaders. They are the ones who form postcolonial relationships in their daily spiritual practices. As they exercise forgiveness and hospitality, they learn how to assimilate, resist, adjust, challenge, and change binary constructions. These practices teach them to learn how to be authentic with themselves and others in front of God. Their faith and culture educate them on how to take communal responsibilities and hold individual autonomy without the expenses of others. As I claim that "not everyone is a leader, but everyone can be a leader," practicing forgiveness and hospitality is the most prominent leadership feature that trains everyone to become a leader. By practicing these, many extraordinary leaders learn consciously and unconsciously how to intentionally cultivate postcolonial relationships and transform binary paradigms into multidimensional relationalities.

When forgiveness and hospitality are intentionally trained and practiced, they will change the rules of the capitalist game. This noncalculative move changes the balance of capitalist expectations. It invites conditional and nonconditional mutuality. It is conditional because it requires the act of forgiveness and hospitality first. At the same time, it is unconditional because it does not expect a calculative return as forgiveness and hospitality are performed. They do not expect mutual exchanges necessarily. When forgiveness is truly performed as forgiveness, and hospitality is truly provided as extraordinary hospitality, they are perfectly, unqualifiedly, self-interested nonconditional acts. The acts of forgiveness and hospitality should be recognized as the acts of "ought to be" on the side of coleaders/cohosts, and they should be accepted as acts of grace on the side of participants/coguests. By practicing forgiveness and hospitality in this mutual manner, Asian immigrant groups form postcolonial relationships. Even though mutual advantages and benefits are not the goals of these relationships, they become the result of relationships because forgiveness and hospitality change the paradigms of capitalism and power of binary relations.

Postcolonial relationships are complicated, conflictive, and complex. They are born of complex dynamics between colonial oppression and resistance. They were formed in the past, reform in the present, and will transform in the future. They grow out of binary paradigms and challenge these paradigms out of survival. They can transform binary paradigms into authentic hybridized dialectical paradigms. One of the goals to form postcolonial relationships is cultivating difference as normality. Differences should not be seen as abnormal variations. They should be recognized as unlimited defined ranges of the infallible. Each existence has its own value and truth because of difference. Difference itself is the value of existence. However, without considering the reality of white colonial and postcolonial power, it does not reveal inner instability in binary paradigms that dismiss the dynamics of differences. Within binary divides, difference exists only in a binary sense. It is either white or black. It is either native or alien. It is one or the other. There is no variance. Difference is not difference but the irreconcilable discrepancy in binary paradigms. Being the third other is the result of this irreconcilable discrepancy in binary paradigms. It is the permanently invisible presence in binary structures. Cultivating difference as normality means cultivating difference as the standard and the norm of existence in equality. Difference is the recognition of primary and primordial forms of existence for any kind of beings. In this sense, being the third other needs to be recognized as a temporary given position and transformed as difference. Transforming binary paradigms to postcolonial paradigms is transforming one dominant belief to equally different values. It is transforming extra/ordinary relations into extraordinary power relationships. It transforms the position of being the third other to existence of a difference. Difference is often known as something extra. It is extra from the dominant existence. It is never recognized as the dominant existence itself. It is treated as an unnecessarily surplus existence. In consequence, difference is treated as extra powerless relations. However, when difference is recognized as the normal dominant form of existence, postcolonial relationships are spontaneously formed as nonbinary, nonhierarchical, dialogical, dialectic, multirelational, interrelational, transnational-relational, transworld relationships. These relationships are not extra relations but become extraordinary power relationships in imperfection.

Relationship is an essential part of human nature based on trust and love for and with others. To love and to be loved are the most basic human needs and wants. Relationships are consequential products of these needs and wants. People want to trust others and love them even when they fear and fail. Hate often comes after these relational failures and frustration. However, love is stronger than hate. Developing relationships is a process of seeking love. To connect and to be connected with themselves, others, and God are unstoppable human desires. Binary relations were formed and built based on hate. They are the ugly dysfunctional forms of relationship from which many Asian immigrant groups suffer. Analyzing failures and frustrations in binary relations and restoring justice and equality based on forgiveness and hospitality can transform these binary relationships into postcolonial relationships.

Through this transformation process, difference can be seen as the normality of existence in equality. Through this transformation process, people can reestablish their relationships with themselves, their communities, and their God/gods. Being the third other is institutionally, sociopolitically, and even psychologically conditioned in Asian immigrant contexts. However, by transforming binary paradigms into postcolonial paradigms, the third otherness can be transformed as common ground to love and live together.

Notes

INTRODUCTION

1. Choi Hee An, *A Postcolonial Leadership: Asian Immigrant Christian Leadership and Its Challenges* (New York: State University of New York Press, 2020), xiii–xiv.

2. Choi Hee An, *A Postcolonial Self: Korean Immigrant Theology and Church* (New York: State University of New York Press, 2015), 2.

3. Ibid., 2–3.

4. Kwok Pui-lan, *Postcolonial Imagination & Feminist Theology* (Louisville, KY: Westminster John Knox Press, 2005), 2.

CHAPTER 1

1. Hazel M. McFerson, "Asians and African Americans in Historical Perspective," in *Blacks and Asians: Crossings, Conflict and Commonality*, ed. Hazel M. McFerson (Durham: Carolina Academic Press, 2006), 28–29.

2. Ibid.

3. Ibid., 29.

4. George Yancey, *Who Is White?: Latinos, Asians, and the New Black/Nonblack Divide* (London: Lynne Rienner, 2003), 24; Susan Olzak, Suzanne Shanahan, and Elizabeth West, "School Desegregation, Interracial Exposure, and Antibusing Activity in Contemporary Urban America," *American Journal of Sociology* 100 (1994): 196–241; Michael Giles and Kaenan Hertz, "Racial Threat and Partisan Identification," *American Political Science Review* 88 (1994): 317–26; Marlee C. Taylor, "How White Attitudes Vary with the Racial Composition of Local Population: Numbers Count," *American Sociological Review* 63 (1998): 512–35.

5. Yancey, *Who Is White?*, 18; Charles C. Moskos and John S. Butler, *All That We Can Be* (New York: Basic Books, 1996); Stanley Lieberson, *A Piece of the Pie: Black and White Immigrants since 1880* (Berkeley: University of California Press, 1980); Andrew Hacker, *Two Nations: Black and White, Separate, Hostile, Unequal* (New York: Ballantine Books, 1992); Olzak, Shanahan, and West, "School Desegregation";

Giles and Hertz, "Racial Threat and Partisan Identification"; Taylor, "How White Attitudes Vary."

6. McFerson, "Asians and African Americans," 46–47.

7. Philip Kretsedemas, *Migrants and Race in the US: Territorial Racism and the Alien/Outside* (New York: Routledge, 2014), 42.

8. James H. Cone, *The Cross and the Lynching Tree* (New York: Orbis Books, 2011), Kindle location 317–21.

9. Ibid., 3569–80.

10. Lee H. Butler, Jr., *Liberating Our Dignity, Saving Our Souls: A New Theory of African American Identity Formation* (St. Louis: Chalice Press, 2006).

11. Ibid., 12.

12. Cornel West, *Race Matters* (Boston: Beacon Press, 2001), 14.

13. Ibid., 15.

14. Ibid.

15. Dale P. Andrews, *Practical Theology for Black Churches: Bridging Black Theology and African American Folk Religion* (Louisville, KY: Westminster John Knox Press, 2002), 68–82.

16. Cornel West, *Democracy Matters: Winning the Fight against Imperialism* (New York: Penguin Books, 2004), 27.

17. West, *Race Matters*, 19.

18. West, *Democracy Matters*, 27.

19. West, *Race Matters*, 107.

20. Butler, *Liberating Our Dignity*, 158–70.

21. Shannon Sullivan, *Good White People: The Problem with Middle-Class White Anti-Racism* (New York: State University of New York Press, 2014), 3.

22. Ibid., 3–4.

23. Ibid., 5.

24. Richard Swinburne, *Responsibility and Atonement* (New York: Oxford University Press, 1989), 14.

25. Sullivan, *Good White People*, 6.

26. Swinburne, *Responsibility and Atonement* 14.

27. Sullivan, *Good White People*, 59–84.

28. Ibid., 25.

29. Ibid., 30.

30. Ibid., 23–58.

31. Ibid.

32. Swinburne, *Responsibility and Atonement*, 10–12.

33. Samantha Vice, "How Do I Live in This Strange Place?" *Journal of Social Philosophy* 41, no. 3 (2010): 323–42, 324.

34. Shannon Sullivan, *Revealing White Privileges: The Unconscious Habits of Racial Privilege* (Bloomington: Indiana University Press, 2006), 4.

35. Vice, "How Do I Live," 323–42.

36. Ibid., 329.

37. Daniel Haggerty, "White Shame: Responsibility and Moral Emotions," *Philosophy Today* 53, no. 3 (2009): 2.

38. Ibid.

39. Ibid., 5.

40. Ibid., 6.

41. Ibid., 6–7.

42. Robin DiAngelo, "White Fragility," *International Journal of Critical Pedagogy* 3, no. 3 (2011): 54–70.

43. Ibid., 58–59.

44. Marzia Milazzo, "On White Ignorance, White Shame, and Other Pitfalls in Critical Philosophy of Race," *Journal of Applied Philosophy* 34, no. 4 (2017): 557–72, 560.

45. Ibid., 562.

46. Ibid., 569.

47. Refer to Juan F. Perea, "The Black/White Binary Paradigm of Race: The 'Normal Science' of American Racial Thought," *California Law Review* 85, no. 5 (1997): 1213–58; Katerina Deliovsky and Tamari Kitossa, "Beyond Black and White: When Going beyond May Take Us Out of Bounds," *Journal of Black Studies* 44, no. 2 (2013): 158–81; Kretsedemas, *Migrants and Race in the US*; Claire Jean Kim, "The Racial Triangulation of Asian Americans," *Politics and Society* 27, no. 1 (1999): 105–38.

48. Deliovsky and Kitossa, "Beyond Black and White," 163–64.

49. Perea, "Black/White Binary," 1219.

50. Kim, "Racial Triangulation," 106.

51. Deliovsky and Kitossa, "Beyond Black and White," 160.

52. Ibid.

53. Yancey, *Who Is White?*, 50.

54. Kim, "Racial Triangulation," 22; Jeannie Rhee, "In Black and White: Chinese in the Mississippi Delta," *Journal of Supreme Court History* 19, no. 1 (1994): 117–32, 120.

55. James Trosino, "American Wedding: Same Sex Marriage and the Miscegenation Analogy," 73 *Boston University Law Review* 93 (1993): 1–7.

56. Yancey, *Who Is White?*, 1–26.

57. Perea, "Black/White Binary," 1241–42.

58. Angela Harris, "Forward: The Jurisprudence of Reconstruction," *California Law Review* 82, no. 4 (1994): 741, 775, and n169; Perea, "Black/White Binary," 1214.

59. McFerson, "Asians and African Americans," 20.

60. Kenneth Prewitt, "Beyond Census 2000: As a Nation, We Are the World," *Carnegie Reporter* 1, no. 3 (2001).

61. Gary Y. Okihiro, "Is Yellow Black or White?" in *Blacks and Asians: Crossings, Conflict and Commonality*, ed. Hazel M. McFerson (Durham: Carolina Academic Press, 2006), 57.

62. Kretsedemas, *Migrants and Race in the US*, 1–12.

63. *Oxford English Dictionary* (Oxford: Oxford University Press, 2000), 1844, http://www.oed.com.ezproxy.bu.edu/view/Entry/125308?redirectedFrom=Nativism #eid.

64. Gabriele Pollini, "Socio-Territorial Belonging in a Changing Society," *International Review of Sociology* 13, no. 3 (2005): 493–96; Per Gustafson, "Mobility and

Territorial Belonging," *Environment and Behavior* 41, no. 4 (2009): 490–508; Kretsedemas, *Migrants and Race in the US*, 30.

65. Stuart Creighton Miller, *The Unwelcome Immigrant: The American Image of the Chinese, 1785–1882* (Berkeley: University of California Press, 1969), 159; Kim, "Racial Triangulation," 109.

66. John Higham, *Strangers in the Land: Patterns of American Nativism, 1860–1925* (New Brunswick, NJ: Rutgers University Press, 1955), Kindle location 30.

67. Ibid., 58.

68. Ibid., 32–35.

69. Ibid., 41–147.

70. Aristide R. Zolberg, *A Nation by Design: Immigration Policy in the Fashioning of America* (Cambridge, MA: Harvard University Press, 2006), Kindle location 103.

71. Robin Dale Jacobson, *The New Nativism: Proposition 187 and the Debate over Immigration* (Minneapolis: University of Minnesota Press, 2008), 190.

72. Ibid., 23.

73. Ibid., 23–24.

74. Ibid., 23.

75. Ibid., 109–34.

76. Zolberg, *Nation by Design*, 31.

77. Ibid., 126–28.

78. Ibid., 275.

79. Leo R. Chavez, "Immigration Reform and Nativism" in *Immigrants Out!: Nativism and the Anti-Immigrant Impulse in the United States*, ed. Juan F. Perea (New York: New University Press, 1997), 62.

80. Ibid.

81. Brian N. Fry, *Nativism and Immigration: Regulating the American Dream* (New York: LFB Scholarly Publishing, 2007), 5.

82. Ibid., 178.

83. George Anthony Peffer, *If They Don't Bring Their Women Here: Chinese Female Immigration before Exclusion* (Urbana: University of Illinois Press, 1999); Sucheng Chan, "The Exclusion of Chinese Women, 1870–1943," in *Entry Denied: Exclusion and Chinese Community in America, 1882–1943*, ed. Sucheng Chan (Philadelphia: Temple University Press, 1991); Catherine Lee, "'Where the Danger Lies': Race, Gender, and Chinese and Japanese Exclusion in the United States, 1870–1924," *Sociological Forum* 25, no. 2 (2010): 248–71, 248.

84. Lee, "Where the Danger Lies," 248–49.

85. Jennifer Gee, "House Wives, Men's Villages, and Sexual Respectability: Gender and the Interrogation of Asian Women at the Angel Island Immigration Station," in *Asian/Pacific Islander American Women: A Historical Anthology*, ed. Shirley Hune and Gail Nomura (New York: New York University Press, 2003), 90–105.

86. Lee, "Where the Danger Lies," 248–50.

87. Fry, *Nativism and Immigration*, 180.

88. Rhacel Salazar Parreñas, "Migrant Filipina Domestic Workers and the International Division of Reproductive Labor," *Gender and Society* 14, no. 4 (2000): 560–80, 562.

89. Zolberg, *Nation by Design*, 256.

90. Parreñas, "Migrant Filipina Domestic Workers," 564.

91. Martin Ruhs and Ha-Joon Chang, "The Ethics of Labor Immigration Policy," *International Organization* 58, no. 1 (2004): 69–102, 73.

92. Fry, *Nativism and Immigration*, 180.

93. Kretsedemas, *Migrants and Race in the US*, 37.

94. Clara Sue Kidwell, Homer Noley, and George E. "Tink" Tinker, *A Native American Theology* (Maryknoll, NY: Orbis Books, 2001), 129.

95. Ibid., 135.

96. Ibid.

97. Ibid., 138.

98. Ibid., 139.

99. Kretsedemas, *Migrants and Race in the US*, 44.

100. Ibid.

101. Ibid., 13.

102. Ibid., 11.

103. Gregory Korte and Alan Gomez, "Trump Ramps Up Rhetoric on Undocumented Immigrants: 'These Are Not People. These Are Animals,'" *USA Today*, May 16, 2018, https://www.usatoday.com/story/news/politics/2018/05/16/trump-immigrants-animals-mexico-democrats-sanctuary-cities/617252002/; Julie Hirschfeld Davis, "Trump Calls Some Unauthorized Immigrants 'Animals' in Rant," *The New York Times*, May 16, 2018, https://www.nytimes.com/2018/05/16/us/politics/trump-undocumented-immigrants-animals.html; "Herman Cain Proposes an Electrified Fence as Immigration Reform, Says He Was Joking," *Huffington Post*, October 18, 2011, https://www.huffingtonpost.com/2011/10/16/herman-cain-electrified-border-fence-immigration_n_1013872.html; Ediberto Román, *Those Damned Immigrants: Americas Hysteria over Undocumented Immigration* (New York: New York University Press, 2013).

104. Paige Schilt, "Queering Lord Clark: Diasporic Formations and Traveling Homophobia in Isaac Julien's The Darker Side of Black," in *Postcolonial, Queer: Theoretical Intersections*, ed. John C. Hawley (New York: State University of New York Press, 2001), 170.

105. Rosina Lippi-Green, *English with an Accent: Language, Ideology and Discrimination in the United States*, 2nd ed. (New York: Routledge, 2012). Kindle.

106. Toni Morrison, "On the Backs of Blacks," *Time*, December 2, 1993.

107. Linda S. Bosniak, "'Nativism' the Concept: Some Reflections," in *Immigrants Out!: Nativism and the Anti-Immigrant Impulse in the United States*, ed. Juan F. Perea (New York: New University Press, 1997), 281.

108. Deliovsky and Kitossa, "Beyond Black and White," 161–62.

109. Yancey, *Who Is White?*, 13

CHAPTER 2

1. *Oxford English Dictionary*, 1818, http://www.ocd.com.ezproxy.bu.edu/view/Entry/205691?redirectedFrom=triangulation#eid.

2. Donald Davidson, "The Emergence of Thought," in *Interpreting Davidson*, ed. P. Kotatko, P. Pagin, G. Segal (Stanford, CA: CSLI, 2001), 128; Kathrin Gluer,

"Triangulation," in *The Oxford Handbook of Philosophy of Language*, ed. Ernest Lepore and Barry C. Smith (Oxford: Oxford University Press, 2018), 9, http://www.oxfordhandbooks.com.ezproxy.bu.edu/view/10.1093/oxfordhb /9780199552238.001.0001/oxfordhb-9780199552238-e-039?print=pdf.

3. Donald Davidson, "Rational Animals," *Dialectica* 36, no. 4 (1982): 317–27, 327.

4. Ibid.

5. Gluer, "Triangulation," 3 of 16, http://www.oxfordhandbooks.com.ezproxy.bu .edu/view/10.1093/oxfordhb/9780199552238.001.0001/oxfordhb-9780199552238-e -039?print=pdf.

6. Ibid., 8 of 16, http://www.oxfordhandbooks.com.ezproxy.bu.edu/view/10.1093 /oxfordhb/9780199552238.001.0001/oxfordhb-9780199552238-e-039?print=pdf.

7. Kim, "Racial Triangulation," 107.

8. Ibid., 107–8.

9. Barbara Perry, *In the Name of Hate: Understanding Hate Crimes* (New York: Routledge, 2001), 68.

10. Ibid.

11. Kim, "Racial Triangulation," 106.

12. Jun Xu and Jenner C. Lee, "Asian Americans, Racial Relations, Triangulation: The Marginalized Model Minority: An Empirical Examination of the Racial Triangulation of Asian Americans," *Social Forces* 91, no. 4 (2013): 1363–97, 1363.

13. Ibid., 1373.

14. Ibid., 1363–97, 1384.

15. Min Hee Go, "It Depends on Who You Run against: Interracial Context and Asian American Candidates in US Election," *International Journal of Intercultural Relations* 65 (2018): 61–72, 64.

16. Adrian Cruz, "On the Job: White Employers, Workers of Color, and Racial Triangulation Theory," *Sociology Compass* 10, no. 10 (2016): 918–27, 918.

17. Eric Sorensen, "Asian Groups Attack MSNBC Headline Referring to Kwan—News Website Site Apologizes for Controversial Wording," *The Seattle Times*, March 3, 1998, http://community.seattletimes.nwsource.com/archive/?date= 19980303&slug=2737594.

18. Al Kamen, "The Honeymoon Sinks in the East," *Washington Post*, May 25, 2001, A37, https://www.washingtonpost.com/archive/politics/2001/05/25/the-honey moon-sinks-in-the-east/418c0685-f64e-4c62-8eef-44c2d17f514d/?noredirect=on& utm_term=.d0f2895c9d9e.

19. Sorensen, "Asian Groups Attack," http://community.seattletimes.nwsource .com/archive/?date=19980303&slug=2737594.

20. Frank H. Wu, *Yellow* (New York: Basic Books, 2002), 21.

21. Ibid.

22. Michael Schaller, Janette Thomas Greenwood, Andrew Kirk, Sarah J. Purcell, Aaron Sheehan-Dean, Christina Snyder, eds. *American Horizons: U.S. History in a Global Context*, Vol. II, *Since 1865*, 3rd ed. (New York: Oxford University Press, 2018), 624.

23. Robert S. Change, "Toward an Asian American Legal Scholarship: Critical Race Theory, Post-Structuralism, and Narrative Space," 81 *Calif. L. Rev.* (1993): 1241–323, 1298.

24. Lynn Thiesmeyer, "The Discourse of Official Violence: Anti-Japanese North American Discourse and the American Internment Camps," *Discourse & Society* 6, no. 3 (1995): 319–52, 325, https://www-jstor-org.ezproxy.bu.edu/stable/pdf/42887989 .pdf?refreqid=excelsior%3A29ffd8d5136e38dea540b3a559d6bb14.

25. Ibid., 320.

26. Ibid., 341–42.

27. Change, "Asian American Legal Scholarship," 1397.

28. Anti-Asian Violence: Oversight Hearing before the Subcommittee on Civil and Constitutional Rights of the Committee on the Judiciary, House of Representatives, One Hundredth Congress, first session, Nov. 10, 1987, 4, http://www.heinonline.org .ezproxy.bu.edu/HOL/Page?collection=congrec&handle=hein.cbhear/cbhearings4323 &id=5.

29. Ibid.

30. Change, "Asian American Legal Scholarship," 1255; Paul Crane and Alfred Larson, "The Chinese Massacre," *Annals of Wyoming* 12 (1940): 47–49, 47.

31. Ibid., 1252; Sucheng Chan, *Asian Americans: An Interpretive History* (Boston: Twayne, 1991), note 23 at 178; *U.S. Commission on Civil Rights, Civil Rights Issues Facing Asian Americans in the 1990* 1, no. 4 (1992): note 7 at 25–26 (hereinafter Civil Rights Report).

32. Ibid., 1254; Civil Rights Report, note 7 at 29.

33. Larry Yu, "Anti-Asian Violence in Black and White," *International Examiner* 17 (2010): 7.

34. Jennifer Lee, "Cultural Brokers: Race-Based Hiring in Inner-City Neighborhoods," *American Behavioral Scientist* 41, no. 7 (1998): 927–37.

35. Dae Young Kim and L. Janelle Dance, "Korean-Black Relations: Contemporary Challenges, Scholarly Explanations, and Future Prospects," in McFerson, *Blacks and Asian*, 160–61.

36. Pyong Gap Min, *Caught in the Middle: Korean Communities in New York and Los Angeles* (Berkeley: University of California Press, 1996).

37. Kim and Dance, "Korean-Black Relations, 159; Lee, "Cultural Brokers," 927–37.

38. Ibid., 163.

39. Ibid., 157.

40. Ibid., 160–61.

41. Lauren Aratani, "'Coughing While Asian': Living in Fear as Racism Feeds Off Coronavirus Panic," *The Guardian*, March 24, 2020, https://www.theguardian .com/world/2020/mar/24/coronavirus-us-asian-americans-racism.

42. Pilar Melendez, "Stabbing of Asian American 2-Year-Old and Her Family Was a Virus-Fueled Hate Crime: Feds," *Daily Beast Newsletters*, March 31, 2020, https://www.thedailybeast.com/stabbing-of-asian-american-2-year-old-and-her -family-was-a-coronavirus-fueled-hate-crime-feds-say.

43. Aratani, "Coughing While Asian."

44. Russell Jeung, "Incidents of Coronavirus Discrimination: March 26–April 2020," *Stop AAPI Hate Weekly Report*, April 3, 2020, Asian Pacific Policy & Planning Council, http://www.asianpacificpolicyandplanningcouncil.org/wp-content/uploads /Stop_AAPI_Hate_Weekly_Report_4_3_20.pdf.

45. Sabrina Travernise and Richard A. Oppel, Jr., "Spit on, Yelled at, Attacked: Chinese Americans Fear for Their Safety," *The New York Times*, March 24, 2020, https://www.nytimes.com/2020/03/23/us/chinese-coronavirus-racist-attacks.html ?referringSource=articleShare.

46. Jeung, "Incidents of Coronavirus Discrimination."

47. Rose Adams, "Asian-American Marchers Take to Brooklyn Streets after 89-Year-Old Woman Was Set on Fire," *AMNY Newsletter*, August 5, 2020, https://www.amny.com/news/asian-american-marchers-take-to-brooklyn-streets-after-89 -year-old-woman-was-set-on-fire/.

48. Kimmy Yam, "There Were 3,800 Anti-Asian Racist Incidents, Mostly against Women, in Past Year," *NBC News*, March 16, 2021, https://www.nbcnews.com /news/asian-america/there-were-3-800-anti-asian-racist-incidents-mostly-against -n1261257

49. Allison Aubrey, "COD Hospital Data Point to Racial Disparity in COVID Cases," *The Coronavirus Crisis*, April 8, 2020, https://www.npr.org/sections /coronavirus-live-updates/2020/04/08/830030932/cdc-hospital-data-point-to-racial -disparity-in-covid-19-cases; Tamara Keith et al., "Coronavirus Updates: New York Toll, Racial Disparity in Data," *All Things Considered*, National Public Radio, April 8, 2020, https://www.npr.org/2020/04/08/830205876/coronavirus-updates-new-york-toll -racial-disparity-in-data; Colin Dwyer, "New York City's Latinx Residents Hit Hard-est by Coronavirus Death," *The Coronavirus Crisis*, National Public Radio, April 8, 2020, https://www.npr.org/2020/04/08/829726964/new-york-citys-latinx-residents-hit -hardest-by-coronavirus-deaths; Kenya Evelyn, "'It's Racial Justice Issues': Black Americans Are Dying in Greater Numbers from COVID-19," *The Guardian*, April 8, 2020, https://www.theguardian.com/world/2020/apr/08/its-a-racial-justice-issue-black -americans-are-dying-in-greater-numbers-from-covid-19.

50. Aubrey, "COD Hospital Data"; Keith et al., "Coronavirus Updates"; Dwyer, "Latinx Residents Hit Hardest"; Evelyn, "It's Racial Justice Issues."

51. Wu, *Yellow*, 21.

52. 261 F. Supp. 3d 99 - Dist. Court, D. Massachusetts, 2017, https://scholar .google.com/scholar_case?case=5729884561067103908&q=Students+for+Fair +Admissions+v.+Harvard&hl=en&as_sdt=6,31&as_vis=1.

53. See Thomas J. Espenshade, Alexandria Walton Radford, and Chang Young Chung, *No Longer Separated, Not Yet Equal: Race and Class in Elite College Admission and Campus Life* (Princeton, NJ: Princeton University Press, 2009).

54. *The Jacksonville Free Press*, Feb. 24–Mar. 2, 19, no. 5 (2005): 2, https:// search-proquest-com.ezproxy.bu.edu/docview/365195504?accountid=9676&rfr_id= info%3Axri%2Fsid%3Aprimo.

55. Ibid.

56. Ibid.

57. Espenshade, Radford, and Chung, *No Longer Separated*, 346.

58. Wu, *Yellow*, 141.

59. Jerry Kang, "Negative Action against Asian Americans: The Internal Instabil-ity of Dworkin's Defense of Affirmative Action," *Harvard Civil Rights–Civil Liberties Law Review* 31 (1996): 1–47, 16.

60. Wu, *Yellow*, 141.

61. A. Liu, "Affirmative Action and Negative Action: How Jian Li's Case Can Benefit Asian Americans," *Michigan Journal of Race & Law* 13 (2007–2008): 391–431, 391; Kang, "Negative Action against Asian Americans," 1–47, 3; Michele S. Moses, Daryl J. Maeda & Christina H. Paguyo, "Racial Politics, Resentment, and Affirmative Action: Asian Americans as "Model" College Applicants," *The Journal Of Higher Education* 90, 20 (2018): 1–26, 5, https://doi/pdf/10.1080/00221546.2018.1441110.

62. Thomas J. Espenshade and Chang Young Chung, "The Opportunity Cost of Admission Preferences at Elite Universities," *Social Science Quarterly* 86, 2 (2005): 293–305, 293.

63. Ibid., 298; Moses, Maeda, and Paguyo, "Racial Politics, Resentment, and Affirmative Action: Asian Americans as "Model" College Applicants," 6–7.

64. Espenshade, Radford, and Chung, *No Longer Separated, not yet Equal: Race and Class in Elite College Admission and Campus Life*, 346.

65. Ibid.

66. Wu, *Yellow*, 139–140.

67. Kang, "Negative Action against Asian Americans," 5.

68. Arthur Sakamoto and Yu Xie, "The Socioeconomic Attainments of Asian Americans," in *Asian Americans: Contemporary Trends and Issues*, ed. Pyong Gap Min (Thousand Oaks, CA: Pine Forge Press, 2006), 55; Y. Xie and K. Goyette, *A Demographic Portrait of Asian Americans* (New York: Russell Sage Foundation, 2004).

69. Ibid., 63.

70. Jane Hyun, "Leadership Principles for Capitalizing on Culturally Diverse Teams: The Bamboo Ceiling Revisited," *Leader to Leader* 2012, no. 64 (2012): 14–9, 16.

71. "Glass Ceiling for Asian Americans Is 3.7x Times Harder to Crack: Ascend Foundation Publishes New Research on Silicon Valley Leadership Diversity; Offers Executive Parity Index Tool to Measure the Effect of Race and Gender," *PR Newswire*, May 6, 2015, http://www.prnewswire.com/news-releases/glass-ceiling-for-asian-americans-is-37x-times-harder-to-crack-300078066.html.

72. Anthony Ramirez, "America's Super Minority," *Fortune*, November 24, 1986, 148; Wu, *Yellow*, 41.

73. Daniel A. Bell, "The Triumph of Asian Americans: America's Greatest Success Story," *New Republic*, July 15, 1985; Wu, *Yellow*, 41.

74. Peter I. Rose, *Tempest-Tost: Race, Immigration, and the Dilemmas of Diversity* (New York: Oxford University Press, 1997), 4; Wu, *Yellow*, 41.

75. Zhen Zeng, "The Myth of the Glass Ceiling: Evidence from a Stock-Flow Analysis of Authority Attainment," *Social Science Research* 40 (2011): 312–25.

76. Kurtis Takamine, "Asian-Pacific Americans and the Glass Ceiling: How Far Have They Advanced?" *Diversity Factor* 9, no. 2 (2001): 28–34.

77. Lippi-Green, *English with an Accent*, 300.

78. Taunya Lovell Banks, "Both Edges of the Margin: Blacks and Asians in Mississippi Masala, Barriers to Coalition Building," in McFerson, *Blacks and Asian*, 322.

79. Elaine H. Kim, "At Least You're Not Black: Asian Americans in U.S. Race Relations," in McFerson, *Blacks and Asian*, 207.

80. Ibid., 208.

81. Banks, "Both Edges of the Margin," 322.

82. Kim, "At Least You're Not Black," 208–9.

83. Ibid.

84. See Lippi-Green, *English with an Accent*.

85. Hyung Chol Yoo, Gilbert C. Gee, and David Takeuchi, "Discrimination and Health among Asian American Immigrants: Disentangling Racial from Language Discrimination," *Social Science and Medicine* 68 (2009): 726–32.

86. J. M. Jones, *Prejudice and Racism*, 2nd ed. (New York: McGraw-Hill, 1997); H. F. Myers, T. T. Lewis, and T. Parker-Dominguez, "Stress, Coping, and Minority Health: Biopsychosocial Perspective on Ethnic Health Disparities," in *Handbook of Racial and Ethnic Minority Psychology*, ed. Guillermo Bernal, Joseph E. Trimble, A. Kathleen Burlew, and Frederick T. Leong (Thousand Oaks, CA: SAGE, 2003), 377–400.

87. Yoo, Gee, and Takeuchi, "Discrimination and Health," 726.

88. Gail Shuck, "Racializing the Nonnative English Speaker," *Journal of Language, Identity and Education* 5, no. 4 (2006): 259–76, 260; Lippi-Green, *English with an Accent*.

89. Ibid.

90. Ibid.

CHAPTER 3

1. Robert Redfield, Ralph Linton, and Melville J. Herskovits, "Memorandum for the Study of Acculturation," *American Anthropologist* 38, no. 1 (1936): 149–52, 149; Milton M. Gordon, *Assimilation in American Life: The Roles of Race, Religion, and National Origins* (New York: Oxford University Press, 1964), 61.

2. Robert E. Park and Ernest W. Burgess, *Introduction to the Science of Sociology* (Chicago: University of Chicago Press, 1921), 735.

3. Henry Pratt Fairchild, ed., *Dictionary of Sociology* (New York: Philosophical Library, 1944), 276–77; Gordon, *Assimilation in American Life*, 64.

4. John F. Cuber, *Sociology: A Synopsis of Principles*, 3rd ed. (New York: Appleton Century-Croft, 1955), 609; Gordon, *Assimilation in American Life*, 66.

5. Arnold M. Rose, *Sociology: The Study of Human Relations* (New York: Alfred A. Knopf, 1956), 557–58; Gordon, *Assimilation in American Life*, 66.

6. Robert Ezra Park, "Our Racial Frontier on the Pacific," in Park, *Race and Culture* (Glenocoe, IL: Free Press, 1950), 150.

7. Robert Ezra Park, "The Concept of Social Distance as Applied to the Study of Racial Attitudes and Racial Relations," *Journal of Applied Sociology* 8 (1924): 339–44.

8. Ibid., 343.

9. Ibid.

10. Emory S. Bogardus, "A Race-Relations Cycle," *American Journal of Sociology* 35, no. 4 (1930): 612–17.

11. Ibid., 615.

12. Ibid., 616.

13. Catherine M. Petrissans, "Assimilation," in *Encyclopedia of Diversity and Social Justice*, ed. Sherwood Thompson (New York: Rowman & Littlefield, 2015), 76–78.

14. Michael W. Foley and Dean R. Hoge, *Religion and the New Immigrants: How Faith Communities Form Our Newest Citizens* (New York: Oxford University Press, 2007), 25.

15. Jacques Derrida, *The Ear of the Other: Otobiography, Transference, Translation* (Lincoln: University of Nebraska Press, 1985), 10.

16. Fumitaka Matsuoka, *The Color of Faith: Building Community in a Multiracial Society* (Cleveland, OH: United Church Press, 1998), 36.

17. Refer to Charmaine L. Wijeyesinghe and Bailey W. Jackson, III, eds., *New Perspectives on Racial Identity Development: A Theoretical and Practical Anthology* (New York: New York University Press, 2001).

18. Kretsedemas, *Migrants and Race in the US*, 42.

19. Bailey W. Jackson III, "Black Identity Development," in Wijeyesinghe and Jackson, *Racial Identity Development*, 8–31; Jean Kim, "Asian American Identity Development Theory," in Wijeyesinghe and Jackson, *Racial Identity Development*, 67–90; Maurianne Adams, "Core Processes of Racial Identity Development," in Wijeyesinghe and Jackson, *Racial Identity Development*, 209–42.

20. Arnold Shankman, *Ambivalent Friends: African-Americans View the Immigrant* (Westport, CT: Greenwood Press, 1982).

21. Gary Y Okihiro, "Is Yellow Black or White? Revisited," in McFerson, *Blacks and Asians*, 55.

22. Ibid., 56.

23. Ibid.

24. Quintard Taylor, "Black and Asian in a White City, 1870–1942," in McFerson, *Blacks and Asians*, 107.

25. Okihiro, "Is Yellow Black or White?" 56.

26. Carina A. del Rosario, "Asian, African Americans Form Coalition for Peace," *International Examiner*, May 1994, 1, https://search-proquest-com.ezproxy.bu.edu /docview/368015956?accountid=9676&rfr_id=info%3Axri%2Fsid%3Aprimo.

27. McFerson, "Asians and African Americans," 20–21.

28. Ibid., 21.

29. Jared Sexton, "Proprieties of Coalition: Blacks, Asians, and the Politics of Policing," *Critical Sociology* 36, no. 1 (2010): 87–108.

30. Talmadge Anderson, "Comparative Experience Factors among Black, Asian and Hispanic Americans: Coalition or Conflicts?" *Journal of Black Studies* 23, no. 1 (1992): 27–38, 33.

31. Phil Tom and Trey Hammond, "Congregation-Based Community Organizing: Building Vibrant Congregations. Building Just Communities," 2, prepared by the General Assembly Mission Council (GAMC)'s Small Church and Community Ministry Office in partnership with the GAMC's Presbyterian Hunger Program (PHP), https://www.presbyterianmission.org/wp-content/uploads/pact-cbco.pdf.

32. Heidi Swarts, "Drawing New Symbolic Boundaries over Old Social Boundaries: Forging Social Movement Unity in Congregation-Based Community Organizing," *Sociological Perspectives* 54, no. 3 (2011): 453–77, 453.

33. Saul D. Alinksky, *Rules for Radicals: A Pragmatic Primer for Realistic Radicals* (New York: Vintage, 1971), 7.

34. Dennis Jacobson, *Doing Justice: Congregations and Community Organizing* (Minneapolis: Fortress Press, 2017), 36.

35. Ibid., 35–36.

36. Richard L. Wood, "Religion, Faith-Based Community Organizing, and the Struggle for Justice," in *Cambridge Handbook of the Sociology of Religion*, ed. Michele Dillon (Cambridge: Cambridge University Press, 2003), 392.

37. Ibid.

38. See Alexis Salvatierra and Peter Heltzel, *Faith-Rooted Organizing Mobilizing the Church in Service to the World* (Downers Grove, IL: InterVarsity, 2014).

39. Swarts, "Drawing New Symbolic Boundaries," 459.

40. Alisia G. T. T. Tran and Richard M. Lee, "Brief Report: You Speak English Well! Asian Americans' Reactions to an Exceptionalizing Stereotype," *Journal of Counseling Psychology* 61, no. 3 (2014): 484–90, 487.

41. Jacob Lesniewski and Marc Doussard, "Crossing Boundaries, Building Power: Chicago Organizers Embrace Race, Ideology, and Coalition," *Social Service Review* 91, no. 4 (2017): 585–620, 589.

42. Ibid.

43. Mark Warren, *Dry Bones Rattling: Community Building to Revitalize American Democracy* (Princeton, NJ: Princeton University Press, 2001), 91–112.

44. Kim Geron, Enrique de la Cruz, Leland T. Saito, and Jaideep Singh, "Asian Pacific Americans' Social Movements and Interest Groups," *Political Science and Politics* 34, no. 3 (2001): 619–24, 619, https://www.jstor.org/stable/1353549.

45. Don Nakanishi, ed., *Asian American Leadership: A Reference Guide* (Santa Barbara, CA: Mission Bell Media, 2015), 14.

46. Ibid., 26.

47. Ibid.

48. Geron et al., "Asian Pacific Americans' Social Movements," 620.

49. Randy Shaw, *The Activist's Handbook: Winning Social Change in the 21st Century*, 2nd ed. (Berkeley: University of California Press, 2013), 255.

50. Refer to Maria Mayan, Alina Tanasescu Turner, Lucenia Ortiz, and Jessica Moffatt, "Building a Multicultural Coalition: Promoting Participation in Civic Society among Ethnic Minority Communities," *Canadian Ethnic Studies* 45, nos. 1/2 (2013): 157–78.

51. Mike Miller, *Community Organizing: A Brief Introduction* (Cleveland: Euclid Avenue
Press, 2012), 2.

52. Jeffrey Stout, *Blessed Are the Organized: Grassroots Democracy in America* (Princeton, NJ: Princeton University Press, 2010), 18.

53. Charles Taylor, "The Politics of Recognition," in *Multiculturalism: Examining the Politics of Recognition*, ed. Amy Gutmann (Princeton, NJ: Princeton University Press, 1994), 25–26.

54. Heinz Kohut, *How Does Analysis Cure?* (New York: International University Press, 1984).

55. Katholiki Georglades, Michael H. Boyle, and Kelly A. Fife, "Emotional and Behavioral Problems among Adolescent Students: The Role of Immigrant, Racial/Ethnic Congruence, and Belongingness in Schools," *Journal of Youth and Adolescence* 42, no. 9 (2013): 1473–92, 1475.

56. Richard M. Lee and Steve B. Robbins, "Measuring Belongingness: The Social Connectedness and the Social Assurance Scales," *Journal of Counseling Psychology* 42, no. 2 (1995): 232–41, 233.

57. Ibid., 232.

58. Georglades, Boyle, and Fife, "Emotional and Behavioral Problems," 1474; M. McPherson, L. Smith-Lovin, and J. M. Cook, "Birds of a Feather: Homophily in Social Networks," *Annual Review of Sociology*, 27 (2001): 415–44.

59. Ibid., 1475.

60. Kyoung Ok Seol and Richard M. Lee, "Effects of Religious Socialization and Religious Identity on Psychosocial Functioning in Korean American Adolescents from Immigrant Families," *Journal of Family Psychology* 26, no. 3 (2012): 371–80, 371.

61. K. Anthony Appiah, "Identity, Authenticity, Survival: Multicultural Societies and Social Reproduction," in Gutmann, *Multiculturalism*, 154.

62. Kenneth Hoover, James Marcia, and Kristen Parris, *The Power of Identity: Politics in a New Key* (Chatham, NJ: Chatham House, 1997), 62.

63. Taylor, "Politics of Recognition," 33.

64. Ibid., 43.

CHAPTER 4

1. Young Lee Hertig, *The Tao of Asian American Belonging: A Yinist Spirituality* (New York: Orbis Books, 2019), Kindle location 2009.

2. Hazel M. McFerson, "Asians and African Americans in Historical Perspective," in *Blacks and Asians: Crossings, Conflict and Commonality*, ed. Hazel M. McFerson (Durham, NC: Carolina Academic Press, 2006), 21.

3. Choi Hee An, *A Postcolonial Self: Korean Immigrant Theology and Church* (New York: State University of New York Press, 2015).

4. Andrew Sung Park, *From Hurt to Healing: A Theology of the Wounded* (Nashville: Abingdon Press, 2004), 39–40.

5. Ibid., 35.

6. Choi, *Postcolonial Self*.

7. Bryant S. Thompson and M. Audrey Korsgaard, "Relational Identification and Forgiveness: Facilitating Relationship Resilience," *Journal of Business and Psychology* 34, no. 2 (2019): 153–67.

8. Park, *From Hurt to Healing*, 89.

9. Everett L. Worthington, Jr. and Steven J. Sandage, *Forgiveness and Spirituality in Psychotherapy: A Relational Approach* (Washington, DC: American Psychological Association, 2016), 204–21.

10. Ibid., 189.

11. Ibid.

12. Thich Nhat Hanh, *The Heart of the Buddha's Teaching: Transforming Suffering into Peace, Joy, & Liberation: The Four Noble Truths, The Noble Eightfold Path, and Other Basic Buddhist Teachings* (New York: Harmony, 2015), Kindle location 3072.

13. Reinhold Niebuhr, *Irony of American History* (New York: Charles Scribner's Sons, 1952), 63.

14. Luke 17:3–4, NRSV.

15. Alan Hunter, "Forgiveness: Hindu and Western Perspectives," *Journal of Hindu-Christian Studies* 20, no. 11 (2007): 35–42, 37; *Mahabharata* Book 3 (Vana Parva), Section 29.

16. Akanksha Tripathi and Etienne Mullet, "Conceptualizations of Forgiveness and Forgivingness among Hindus," *International Journal for the Psychology of Religion* 20 (2010): 255–66, 258.

17. Hanh, *Heart of the Buddha's Teaching*, 3072.

18. Choi, *Postcolonial Self.*

19. Judith Viorst, *Necessary Losses: The Loves, Illusions, Dependencies, and Impossible Expectations That All of Us Have to Give Up in Order to Grow* (New York: Free Press, 1986), 277.

20. Tripathi and Mullet, "Conceptualizations of Forgiveness and Forgivingness," 255; Worthington and Sandage, *Forgiveness and Reconciliation.*

21. Thompson and Korsgaard, "Relational Identification and Forgiveness."

22. A. Aron, E. N. Aron, and D. Smollan, "Inclusion of Other in the Self Scale and the Structure of Interpersonal Closeness," *Journal of Social and Psychological Psychology* 63 (1992): 596–612.

23. Worthington and Sandage, *Forgiveness and Spirituality in Psychotherapy*, 217.

24. Thompson and Korsgaard, "Relational Identification and Forgiveness," 156.

25. George Herbert Mead, *Mind, Self, and Society* (Chicago: University of Chicago Press, 1934).

26. K. Anthony Appiah, "Identity, Authenticity, Survival: Multicultural Societies and Social Reproduction," in *Multiculturalism: Examining the Politics of Recognition*, ed. Amy Gutmann (Princeton, NJ: Princeton University Press, 1994), 153.

27. Mike Miller, *Community Organizing: A Brief Introduction* (Cleveland: Euclid Avenue Press, 2012), 2.

28. Andy Rotman, "Buddhism and Hospitality: Expecting the Unexpected and Acting Virtuously," in *Hosting the Stranger: Between Religions*, ed. Ricard Kearney and James Taylor (New York: Continuum, 2011), 121.

29. Ibid., 120.

30. Jacques Derrida, *Of Hospitality: Anne Dufourmantelle Invites Jacques Derrida to Respond*, trans. Rachel Bowlby (Stanford, CA: Stanford University Press, 2000), 55.

31. Frank Clooney, "Food, The Guest and the Taittiriya Upanishad: Hospitality in the Hindu Traditions," in Kearney and Taylor, *Hosting the Strange*, 143.

32. Ibid., 140.

33. Ibid.

34. Norman Wirzba, *Food and Faith: A Theology of Eating* (Cambridge: Cambridge University Press, 2011), 144.

35. Clooney, "Hospitality in the Hindu Traditions," 142.

36. Rotman, "Buddhism and Hospitality," 119.

37. Matthew 26:26–29, NRSV.

38. 1 Corinthians 11:23–26, NRSV.

39. Wirzba, *Food and Faith*, 149.

40. Ibid., 148.

41. Choi, *Postcolonial Self*, 115–52.

42. Paul Gilroy, *Postcolonial Melancholia* (New York: Columbia University Press, 2005), Kindle location 94.

Selected Bibliography

Alinksky, Saul D. *Rules for Radicals: A Pragmatic Primer for Realistic Radicals*. New York: Vintage, 1971.

Anderson, Talmadge. "Comparative Experience Factors among Black, Asian and Hispanic Americans: Coalition or Conflicts?" *Journal of Black Studies* 23, no. 1 (1992): 27–38.

Andrews, Dale P. *Practical Theology for Black Churches: Bridging Black Theology and African American Folk Religion*. Louisville, KY: Westminster John Knox Press, 2002.

Aron, A., E. N. Aron, and D. Smollan. "Inclusion of Other in the Self Scale and the Structure of Interpersonal Closeness." *Journal of Social and Psychological Psychology* 63 (1992): 596–612.

Bernal, Guillermo, Joseph E. Trimble, A. Kathleen Burlew, and Frederick T. Leong, eds. *Handbook of Racial and Ethnic Minority Psychology*. Thousand Oaks, CA: SAGE, 2003.

Bogardus, Emory S. "A Race-Relations Cycle." *American Journal of Sociology* 35, no. 4 (1930): 612–17.

Butler, Lee H., Jr. *Liberating Our Dignity, Saving Our Souls: A New Theory of African American Identity Formation*. St. Louis: Chalice Press, 2006.

Chan, Sucheng. *Asian Americans: An Interpretive History*. Boston: Twayne, 1991.

———. ed. *Entry Denied: Exclusion and Chinese Community in America, 1882–1943*. Philadelphia: Temple University Press, 1991.

Choi, Hee An. *A Postcolonial Self: Korean Immigrant Theology and Church*. New York: State University of New York Press, 2015.

Cone, James H. *The Cross and the Lynching Tree*. New York: Orbis Books, 2011. Kindle.

Cruz, Adrian. "On the Job: White Employers, Workers of Color, and Racial Triangulation Theory." *Sociology Compass* 10, no. 10 (2016): 918–27.

Cuber, John F. *Sociology: A Synopsis of Principles*. 3rd ed. New York: Appleton Century-Croft, 1955.

Deliovsky, Katerina, and Tamari Kitossa. "Beyond Black and White: When Going beyond May Take Us Out of Bounds." *Journal of Black Studies* 44, no. 2 (2013): 158–81.

Derrida, Jacques. *Of Hospitality: Anne Dufourmantelle Invites Jacques Derrida to Respond*. Translated by Rachel Bowlby. Stanford, CA: Stanford University Press, 2000.

DiAngelo, Robin. "White Fragility." *International Journal of Critical Pedagogy* 3, no. 3 (2011): 54–70.

Dillon, Michele, ed. *Cambridge Handbook of the Sociology of Religion*. Cambridge: Cambridge University Press, 2003.

Espenshade, Thomas J., Alexandria Walton Radford, and Chang Young Chung. *No Longer Separated, Not Yet Equal: Race and Class in Elite College Admission and Campus Life*. Princeton, NJ: Princeton University Press, 2009.

———. "The Opportunity Cost of Admission Preferences at Elite Universities." *Social Science Quarterly* 86, no. 2 (2005): 293–305.

Fairchild, Henry Pratt, ed. *Dictionary of Sociology*. New York: Philosophical Library, 1944.

Foley, Michael W., and Dean R. Hoge. *Religion and the New Immigrants: How Faith Communities Form Our Newest Citizens*. New York: Oxford University Press, 2007.

Fry, Brian N. *Nativism and Immigration: Regulating the American Dream*. New York: LFB Scholarly Publishing, 2007.

Georglades, Katholiki, Michael H. Boyle, and Kelly A. Fife. "Emotional and Behavioral Problems among Adolescent Students: The Role of Immigrant, Racial/Ethnic Congruence, and Belongingness in Schools." *Journal of Youth and Adolescence* 42, no. 9 (2013): 1473–92.

Giles, Michael, and Kaenan Hertz. "Racial Threat and Partisan Identification." *American Political Science Review* 88 (1994): 317–26.

Gilroy, Paul. *Postcolonial Melancholia*. New York: Columbia University Press, 2005. Kindle.

Go, Min Hee. "It Depends on Who You Run against: Interracial Context and Asian American Candidates in US Elections." *International Journal of Intercultural Relations* 65 (2018): 61–72.

Gordon, Milton M. *Assimilation in American Life: The Roles of Race, Religion, and National Origins*. New York: Oxford University Press, 1964.

Gustafson, Per. "Mobility and Territorial Belonging." *Environment and Behavior* 41, no. 4 (2009): 490–508.

Gutmann, Amy, ed. *Multiculturalism: Examining the Politics of Recognition*. Princeton, NJ: Princeton University Press, 1994.

Hacker, Andrew. *Two Nations: Black and White, Separate, Hostile, Unequal*. New York: Ballantine Books, 1992.

Haggerty, Daniel. "White Shame: Responsibility and Moral Emotions." *Philosophy Today* 53, no. 3 (2009): 304–16.

Hanh, Thich Nhat. *The Heart of the Buddha's Teaching: Transforming Suffering into Peace, Joy, & Liberation: The Four Noble Truths, the Noble Eightfold Path, and Other Basic Buddhist Teachings*. New York: Harmony, 2015. Kindle.

Hawley, John C., ed. *Postcolonial, Queer: Theoretical Intersections*. New York: State University of New York Press, 2001.

Hertig, Young Lee. *The Tao of Asian American Belonging: A Yinist Spirituality*. New York: Orbis Books, 2019. Kindle.

Higham, John. *Strangers in the Land: Patterns of American Nativism, 1860–1925*. New Brunswick, NJ: Rutgers University Press, 1955.

Hune, Shirley, and Gail Nomura, eds. *Asian/Pacific Islander American Women: A Historical Anthology*. New York: New York University Press, 2003.

Hunter, Alan. "Forgiveness: Hindu and Western Perspectives." *Journal of Hindu-Christian Studies* 20, no. 11 (2007): 35–42.

Hyun, Jane. "Leadership Principles for Capitalizing on Culturally Diverse Teams: The Bamboo Ceiling Revisited." *Leader to Leader* 2012, no. 64 (2012): 14–19.

Jacobson, Dennis. *Doing Justice: Congregations and Community Organizing*. Minneapolis: Fortress Press, 2017.

Jacobson, Robin Dale. *The New Nativism: Proposition 187 and the Debate over Immigration*. Minneapolis: University of Minnesota Press, 2008.

Jones, J. M. *Prejudice and Racism*. 2nd ed. New York: McGraw-Hill, 1997.

Kang, Jerry. "Negative Action against Asian Americans: The Internal Instability of Dworkin's Defense of Affirmative Action." *Harvard Civil Rights–Civil Liberties Law Review* 31 (1996): 1–47.

Kearney, Richard, and James Taylor, eds. *Hosting the Stranger: Between Religions*. New York: Continuum, 2011.

Kidwell, Clara Sue, Homer Noley, and George E. "Tink" Tinker. *A Native American Theology*. Maryknoll, NY: Orbis Books, 2001.

Kim, Claire Jean. "The Racial Triangulation of Asian Americans." *Politics and Society* 27, no. 1 (1999): 105–38.

Kim, Geron, Enrique de la Cruz, Leland T. Saito, and Jaideep Singh. "Asian Pacific Americans' Social Movements and Interest Groups." *Political Science and Politics* 34, no. 3 (2001): 619–24.

Kohut, Heinz. *How Does Analysis Cure?* New York: International University Press, 1984.

Kretsedemas, Philip. *Migrants and Race in the US: Territorial Racism and the Alien/Outside*. New York: Routledge, 2014.

Lee, Jennifer. "Cultural Brokers: Race-Based Hiring in Inner-City Neighborhoods." *American Behavioral Scientist* 41, no. 7 (1998): 927–37.

Lee, Richard M., and Steve B. Robbins. "Measuring Belongingness: The Social Connectedness and the Social Assurance Scales." *Journal of Counseling Psychology* 42, no. 2 (1995): 232–41.

Lepore, Ernest, and Barry C. Smith, eds. *The Oxford Handbook of Philosophy of Language*. Oxford: Oxford University Press, 2018.

Lesniewski, Jacob, and Marc Doussard. "Crossing Boundaries, Building Power: Chicago Organizers Embrace Race, Ideology, and Coalition." *Social Service Review* 91, no. 4 (2017): 585–620.

Lieberson, Stanley. *A Piece of the Pie: Black and White Immigrants since 1880*. Berkeley: University of California Press, 1980.

Lippi-Green, Rosina. *English with an Accent: Language, Ideology and Discrimination in the United States*. 2nd ed. New York: Routledge, 2012. Kindle.

Liu, A. "Affirmative Action and Negative Action: How Jian Li's Case Can Benefit Asian Americans." *Michigan Journal of Race & Law* 13 (2007–2008): 391–431.

Matsuoka, Fumitaka. *The Color of Faith: Building Community in a Multiracial Society*. Cleveland: United Church Press, 1998.

Mayan, Maria, Alina Tanasescu Turner, Lucenia Ortiz, and Jessica Moffatt. "Building a Multicultural Coalition: Promoting Participation in Civic Society among Ethnic Minority Communities." *Canadian Ethnic Studies* 45, nos. 1/2 (2013): 157–78.

McFerson, Hazel M., ed. *Blacks and Asian: Crossings, Conflict and Commonality*. Durham, NC: Carolina Academic Press, 2006.

Mead, George Herbert. *Mind, Self, and Society*. Chicago: University of Chicago Press, 1934.

Milazzo, Marzia. "On White Ignorance, White Shame, and Other Pitfalls in Critical Philosophy of Race." *Journal of Applied Philosophy* 34, no. 4 (2017): 557–72.

Miller, Mike. *Community Organizing: A Brief Introduction*. Cleveland: Euclid Avenue Press, 2012.

Miller, Stuart Creighton. *The Unwelcome Immigrant: The American Image of the Chinese, 1785–1882*. Berkeley: University of California Press, 1969.

Min, Pyong Gap, ed. *Asian Americans: Contemporary Trends and Issues*. Thousand Oaks, CA: Pine Forge Press, 2006.

———. *Caught in the Middle: Korean Communities in New York and Los Angeles*. Berkeley: University of California Press, 1996.

Moses, Michele S., Daryl J. Maeda, and Christina H. Paguyo. "Racial Politics, Resentment, and Affirmative Action: Asian Americans as 'Model' College Applicants." *Journal of Higher Education* 90, no. 20 (2018): 1–26.

Moskos, Charles C., and John S. Butler. *All That We Can Be*. New York: Basic Books, 1996.

Nakanishi, Don, ed. *Asian American Leadership: A Reference Guide*. Santa Barbara, CA: Mission Bell Media, 2015.

Niebuhr, Reinhold. *Irony of American History*. New York: Charles Scribner's Sons, 1952.

Olzak, Susan, Suzanne Shanahan, and Elizabeth West. "School Desegregation, Interracial Exposure, and Antibusing Activity in Contemporary Urban America." *American Journal of Sociology* 100 (1994): 196–241.

Park, Andrew Sung. *From Hurt to Healing: A Theology of the Wounded*. Nashville: Abingdon Press, 2004.

Park, Andrew Sung, and Susan L. Nelson, eds. *The Other Side of Sin: Woundedness from the Perspective of the Sinned-Against*. New York: State University of New York Press, 2001.

Park, Robert Ezra. "The Concept of Social Distance as Applied to the Study of Racial Attitudes and Racial Relations." *Journal of Applied Sociology* 8 (1924): 339–44.

———. *Race and Culture*. Glenocoe, IL: Free Press, 1950.

Park, Robert Ezra, and Ernest W. Burgess. *Introduction to the Science of Sociology*. Chicago: University of Chicago Press, 1921.

Parreñas, Rhacel Salazar. "Migrant Filipina Domestic Workers and the International Division of Reproductive Labor." *Gender and Society* 14, no. 4 (2000): 560–80.

Peffer, George Anthony. *If They Don't Bring Their Women Here: Chinese Female Immigration before Exclusion*. Urbana: University of Illinois Press, 1999.

Perea, Juan F. "The Black/White Binary Paradigm of Race: The 'Normal Science' of American Racial Thought." *California Law Review* 85, no. 5 (1997): 1213–58.

———, ed. *Immigrants Out! Nativism and the Anti-Immigrant Impulse in the United States*. New York: New University Press, 1997.

Perry, Barbara. *In the Name of Hate: Understanding Hate Crimes*. New York: Routledge, 2001.

Pollini, Gabriele. "Socio-Territorial Belonging in a Changing Society." *International Review of Sociology* 13, no. 3 (2005): 493–96.

Redfield, Robert, Ralph Linton, and Melville J. Herskovits. "Memorandum for the Study of Acculturation." *American Anthropologist* 38, no. 1 (1936): 149–52.

Rhee, Jeannie. "In Black and White: Chinese in the Mississippi Delta." *Journal of Supreme Court History* 19, no. 1 (1994): 117–32.

Román, Ediberto. *Those Damned Immigrants: America's Hysteria over Undocumented Immigration*. New York: New York University Press, 2013.

Rose, Arnold M. *Sociology: The Study of Human Relations*. New York: Alfred A. Knopf, 1956.

Rose, Peter I. *Tempest-Tost: Race, Immigration, and the Dilemmas of Diversity*. New York: Oxford University Press, 1997.

Ruhs, Martin, and Ha-Joon Chang. "The Ethics of Labor Immigration Policy." *International Organization* 58, no. 1 (2004): 69–102.

Salvatierra, Alexis, and Peter Heltzel. *Faith-Rooted Organizing Mobilizing the Church in Service to the World*. Downers Grove, IL: InterVarsity Press, 2014.

Schaller, Michael, Janette Thomas Greenwood, Andrew Kirk, Sarah J. Purcell, Aaron Sheehan-Dean, and Christina Snyder, eds. *American Horizons: U.S. History in a Global Context*. Vol. 2, *Since 1865*. 3rd ed. New York: Oxford University Press, 2018.

Seol, Kyoung Ok, and Richard M. Lee. "Effects of Religious Socialization and Religious Identity on Psychosocial Functioning in Korean American Adolescents from Immigrant Families." *Journal of Family Psychology* 26, no. 3 (2012): 371–80.

Sexton, Jared. "Proprieties of Coalition: Blacks, Asians, and the Politics of Policing." *Critical Sociology* 36, no. 1 (2010): 87–108.

Shankman, Arnold. *Ambivalent Friends: African-Americans View the Immigrant*. Westport, CT: Greenwood Press, 1982.

Shaw, Randy. *The Activist's Handbook: Winning Social Change in the 21st Century*. 2nd ed. Berkeley: University of California Press, 2013.

Shuck, Gail. "Racializing the Nonnative English Speaker." *Journal of Language, Identity and Education* 5, no. 4 (2006): 259–76.

Stout, Jeffrey. *Blessed Are the Organized: Grassroots Democracy in America*. Princeton, NJ: Princeton University Press, 2010.

Sullivan, Shannon. *Good White People: The Problem with Middle-Class White Anti-Racism*. New York: State University of New York Press, 2014.

———. *Revealing White Privileges: The Unconscious Habits of Racial Privilege*. Bloomington: Indiana University Press, 2006.

Swarts, Heidi. "Drawing New Symbolic Boundaries over Old Social Boundaries: Forging Social Movement Unity in Congregation-Based Community Organizing." *Sociological Perspectives* 54, no. 3 (2011): 453–77.

Swinburne, Richard. *Responsibility and Atonement*. New York: Oxford University Press, 1989.

Takamine, Kurtis. "Asian-Pacific Americans and the Glass Ceiling: How Far Have They Advanced?" *Diversity Factor* 9, no. 2 (2001): 28–34.

Taylor, Marlee C. "How White Attitudes Vary with the Racial Composition of Local Population: Numbers Count." *American Sociological Review* 63 (1998): 512–35.

Thiesmeyer, Lynn. "The Discourse of Official Violence: Anti-Japanese North American Discourse and the American Internment Camps." *Discourse & Society* 6, no. 3 (1995): 319–52.

Thompson, Bryant S., and M. Audrey Korsgaard. "Relational Identification and Forgiveness: Facilitating Relationship Resilience." *Journal of Business and Psychology* 34, no. 2 (2019): 153–67.

Thompson, Sherwood, ed. *Encyclopedia of Diversity and Social Justice*. New York: Rowman & Littlefield, 2015.

Tran, Alisia G. T. T., and Richard M. Lee. "Brief Report: You Speak English Well! Asian Americans' Reactions to an Exceptionalizing Stereotype." *Journal of Counseling Psychology* 61, no. 3 (2014): 484–90.

Tripathi, Akanksha, and Etienne Mullet. "Conceptualizations of Forgiveness and Forgivingness among Hindus." *International Journal for the Psychology of Religion* 20 (2010): 255–66.

Trosino, James. "American Wedding: Same-Sex Marriage and the Miscegenation Analogy." 73 *Boston University Law Review* 93 (1993): 1–7.

Vice, Samantha. "How Do I Live in This Strange Place?" *Journal of Social Philosophy* 41, no. 3 (2010): 323–42.

Viorst, Judith. *Necessary Losses: The Loves, Illusions, Dependencies, and Impossible Expectations That All of Us Have to Give Up in Order to Grow*. New York: Free Press, 1986.

Warren, Mark. *Dry Bones Rattling: Community Building to Revitalize American Democracy*. Princeton, NJ: Princeton University Press, 2001.

West, Cornel. *Democracy Matters: Winning the Fight against Imperialism*. New York: Penguin Books, 2004.

———. *Race Matters*. Boston: Beacon Press, 2001.

Wijeyesinghe, Charmaine L., and Bailey W. Jackson, III, eds. *New Perspectives on Racial Identity Development: A Theoretical and Practical Anthology*. New York: New York University Press, 2001.

Wirzba, Norman. *Food and Faith: A Theology of Eating*. Cambridge: Cambridge University Press, 2011.

Worthington, Everett L., Jr., and Steven J. Sandage. *Forgiveness and Spirituality in Psychotherapy: A Relational Approach*. Washington, DC: American Psychological Association, 2016.

Wu, Frank H. *Yellow*. New York: Basic Books, 2002.

Xie, Yu, and Kimberly A. Goyette. *A Demographic Portrait of Asian Americans*. New York: Russell Sage Foundation, 2004.

Xu, Jun, and Jenner C. Lee. "Asian Americans, Racial Relations, Triangulation: The Marginalized Model Minority: An Empirical Examination of the Racial Triangulation of Asian Americans." *Social Forces* 91, no. 4 (2013): 1363–97.

Yancey, George. *Who Is White? Latinos, Asians, and the New Black/Nonblack Divide*. London: Lynne Rienner, 2003.

Yoo, Hyung Chol, Gilbert C. Gee, and David Takeuchi. "Discrimination and Health among Asian American Immigrants: Disentangling Racial from Language Discrimination." *Social Science and Medicine* 68 (2009): 726–32.

Zeng, Zhen. "The Myth of Glass Ceiling: Evidence from a Stock-Flow Analysis of Authority Attainment." *Social Science Research* 40 (2011): 312–25.

Zolberg, Aristide R. *A Nation by Design: Immigration Policy in the Fashioning of America*. Cambridge, MA: Harvard University Press, 2006.

Index

Go, Min Hee, 64
God, 18, 21–23, 114–115, 137–138,
    141–142, 144, 146–151
  God as a guest, 144
  Guest as a god, 142
Gordon, Milton M., 103, 105–106
Guest, 11, 90, 99, 135, 142–148

Haggerty, Daniel, 23–25, 27
Hanh, Thich Nhat, 138
Hate crime, 75, 77
Hertig, Young Lee, 132
Higham, John, 36–37
Hoge, Dean R., 106
Homophyly, 126
Hospitality, 136, 141–145, 148–150
Host, 142–145, 147–148
  host/guest, 3, 5, 8, 98, 143
  host society, 102, 105–106
Hybridized dialectical paradigms, 150

Ickes, W., 124
Immigration Act of 1924, 41
  Immigration and Nationality Act of
    1965, 51
  Immigration Act of 1965, 83
Imperfect other, 99, 107
In-betweenness, 4, 52, 54, 90, 92–93,
    120
In re Ah Yup, 68
Integration, 109
Interpenetration, 101–102
Intersubjective truth, 58–59, 65

Jacobson, Robin Dale, 37–38
Japanese, 69–70, 91–92, 102–1034,
    111–112
  anti-Japanese, 41, 69–70, 72, 74, 92
  Japanese immigrants, 69–70, 72, 92
Jesus, 147–148

Kim, Claire Jean, 30, 61, 63
Kim, Dae Young, 73
Kim, Elaine H., 92
King, Martin Luther, Jr., 113
Kitossa, Tamari, 29–30

Kohut, Heinz, 122, 125
Koreans, 40, 72, 91–92
  anti-Korean, 70, 72, 74
  Korean immigrants, 72–74, 92,
    120–121, 125–126
Korsgaard, M. Audrey, 136, 140
Kretsedemas, Philip, 48–50
Kwan, Michelle, 66–67, 70

Language discrimination, 94–95
Latinx, 1–4, 31–33, 50–54, 60, 64–65,
    78, 81–83, 90, 93–94, 103–104,
    113–116, 131
Lee, Jennifer C., 63–64, 73
Lee, Richard M., 125
Lesniewksi, Jacob, 116
Loving v. Virgina (1967), 30

Mahākāśyapa, 143–144
Manicheanism, 29
Marangoni, C., 124
Marginalization, 54, 87–88, 98, 119,
    125, 127, 141–142
Market mentality, 14–15
McCarran-Walter Act, 69
McFerson, Hazel M., 132
McPherson et al., 125
Mexicans, 103–104
Milazzo, Marzia, 23, 27–28
Min, Pyong Gap, 73
Minority/nonminority, 4, 79–80, 86–88,
    98, 138–139, 141
Miscegenation, 30
Mississippi Delta, 30, 60
Model minority, 60, 64, 81, 84–87
Mongolian, 10, 37, 68
Moral sanctimoniousness, 16–18
  morally good, 17, 20–22, 24, 78
Motherland, 40, 44–45, 51, 69, 88–93,
    96–97, 113, 116, 119, 122–124,
    126, 128, 134, 141

Native American, 12, 35–36, 45–48,
    90–91, 93, 103, 114
Natives, 3–4, 35–45, 51–54, 65, 74–75,
    78–79, 91, 95–96, 99, 121–122, 143